# The
# Script of Life
# in Modern Society

# The
# Script of Life
# in Modern Society

DISCARD

## Entry into Adulthood in a Changing World

## Marlis Buchmann

The University of Chicago Press
Chicago and London

Marlis Buchmann is privatdocent and lecturer in sociology at the University of Zurich.

The University of Chicago Press, Chicago 60637
The University of Chicago Press, Ltd., London
© 1989 by The University of Chicago
All rights reserved. Published 1989
Printed in the United States of America

98 97 96 95 94 93 92 91 90 89   54321

*Library of Congress Cataloging in Publication Data*

Buchmann, Marlis.
    The script of life in modern society : entry into adulthood in a changing world / Marlis Buchmann.
        p.      cm.
    Bibliography: p.
    Includes index.
    ISBN 0-226-07835-3
    1. Adulthood—United States.   2. Life cycle, Human—Social aspects—United States.   3. High school graduates—United States—Psychology.   I. Title.
HQ799.97.U5B83   1989
305.2'4—dc19                                                    88-23928
                                                                      CIP

∞ The paper used in this publication meets the minimum requirements of the American National Standard for Information Sciences—Permanence of Paper for Printed Library Materials, ANSI Z39.48-1984.

To Jürg

# Contents

Acknowledgments                                                          xi
Introduction                                                              1

**Part 1  Societal Provision of Life Scripts and Casts**
1  The Life Course in Modern Society: Social Construction and
   Individual Organization                                              15
    The Institutionalization of the Life Course      17
    Rationalization of the Economy and Polity         18
    The Ideology of Individualism                     22
    State Regulation of the Life Course               24
    Cultural Representation of the Life Course and of Life Stages:
        Validated Social Identities   29
    Social Structure and Action Strategies: An Outline of
        Bourdieu's Theory of Practice  31
    The Individual's Life Course: Actual Sequences of
        Positions and Roles           38
    Biographical Orientations and Strategies          39

2  Contemporary Societal Transformations and the Changing
   Nature of the Life Course                                           43
    Contradictory Effects of Education as a Credentialing System  46
    The Changing Structure of Occupational Careers    48
    Diversification of Family Life                     52
    Rationalization of Lifetime: The Impact of New
        Information Technologies       55
    Changing Cultural Representations of Life Stages: From
        Stability to Flexibility?     59

Social Dynamics between Rationalization and Individualization:
Destandardization of the Life Course? 67
The Dialectics between Choice and Constraint of
Individual Action 70
Destandardization of the Life Course and Biographical
Perspectives and Strategies 76

3 Changing Passages to Adulthood 79
The Social Construction of Youth 79
The Increasing Obsolescence of Youth as a Well-Defined
Status Passage 83

**Part 2 From the 1960s to the 1980s: Differing Life Conditions
and Life Experiences in the Transition to Adulthood**
4 The Sociohistorical Context of the High School Classes of 1960
and 1980 91
Historical Time and the Aging Process 91
The Impact of Historical Differences on the 1960
and 1980 Cohorts 93

5 Biographical Orientations and the Passage to Adulthood in a
Changing Society 100
Continuity and Change in Status Expectations and
Anticipated Timing of Life Events 101
Shifting Patterns in the Transition to Adulthood 110

6 The Increasing Prominence of Education in Everyday Life 117
Changing Composition of Credentials and New Forms of
Educational Tracking 117
Access to Higher Education: Who Profits from
the Educational Expansion? 121

7 Occupational Choices: Somethings Old and Somethings New 130
Male and Female Labor-Force Participation Patterns 131
Devaluation of Educational Credentials 135
Labor Market Value of Credentials and Social Value
of Degree Holders 141
Titles and Jobs: Growing Dependency of Occupational
Positions on Educational Credentials 144

Occupational Status Attainment: Direct versus
  Indirect Status Inheritance 147

8 The Growing Diversity of the Private Life Course 153
  The Timing of Marriage 153
  Timetables for Parenthood 159

9 Outcomes of Biographical Projects: Social Dependency of
Matches and Mismatches 170
  Outcomes of High School Educational Plans 171
  Outcomes of High School Occupational Plans 175

Conclusions 181

  Appendix 191
  Notes 197
  References 221
  Index 241

# Acknowledgments

In the course of work on this book, from its inception to its completion, I have benefited from the help, support, and encouragement of many; accordingly, there are many to thank. My first set of thanks goes to the Department of Sociology at the University of Zurich, and especially to its director Hans-Joachim Hoffmann-Nowotny, who has generously supported my work throughout the years I have been a member of his research and teaching staff.

Special thanks are extended to the Swiss National Science Foundation (Schweizerischer Nationalfonds) and the Committee for the Promotion of Young Academics at the University of Zurich (Kommission zur Förderung des akademischen Nachwuchses der Universität Zurich). Their grants largely supported my study and greatly facilitated my efforts to produce this book. These grants allowed me to be a visiting scholar at the Centre de sociologie de l'éducation et de la culture, Ecoles des Hautes Etudes en Science Sociales in Paris, where I benefited from discussions with Pierre Bourdieu. They also supported my stays as a visiting scholar at Stanford University, where John W. Meyer provided useful and timely guidance, and at the University of California at Berkeley, where Neil J. Smelser generously provided research facilities. These stays gave me the opportunity to discuss the issues raised in this work with many colleagues, each of whom offered new ideas and helpful comments. This work has profited much not only from the specific ideas stimulated by these discussions but also from inspiring "firsthand" experiences with different intellectual styles. These experiences made me more aware both of subtle cultural differences in scientific approaches and of their implicit (and unacknowledged) assumptions—including those embedded in my own style.

At the initial stage of this study, Monique de Saint-Martin, François

Bonvin, and Jean-Pierre Faguer offered me many animating ideas. For this, and for their friendship and intellectual support, I am very grateful. For careful comments and valuable criticisms on an earlier draft I would like to thank Annette Lareau, Yasemin Soysal, Chikako Usui, Deirdre Boden, Maria Charles, Frank Dobbin, Michèle Lamont, and Amy Wharton. In many discussions, each provided not only intellectual inspiration but also the kind of friendly support that greatly encouraged my work. Michael Hout gave me a hand in finding the data and Antonio Bettinaglio and Martin Schulz helped me solve computer problems. A special thanks is reserved for John Clausen, who not only showed a great interest in the progress of my study but also made very helpful and effective suggestions along the way. Troy Duster also deserves much thanks. His gentle support and kind generosity helped me keep up my spirits. I owe a special debt to Kathy Mooney for the careful editorial assistance she provided. This book has greatly benefited from her sensitive and incisive way of coping with my texts. I am also much indebted to Michael Böhler. His extensive comments on an early version of the manuscript prompted substantial improvements in this book. I could not have had a more careful or perceptive reader of my manuscript, who subtly encouraged my work along the way. My profound gratitude also goes to Beverly Allen for her wonderful friendship, excellent advise, and effective help. With her gentle warmth and splendid generosity she welcomed me over and over again in her home and made me feel at home on the other side of the Atlantic. Finally, thanks most of all to Jürg Kuoni. Sharing his life with mine, he let me partake in his boundless generosity and subtle humor that stimulates everything else. To give public voice to my private gratitude and appreciation he has known for a long time, I dedicate this book to him.

# Introduction

Contemporary Western societies are undergoing rapid and profound social and cultural transformations. Some aspects of these sweeping changes directly affect individuals' daily lives. Educational, occupational, and family careers no longer seem to follow stable, continuous, and highly predictable courses. This book explores the ways in which contemporary social changes alter the nature of the life course. It examines how, within this larger process, the passage to adulthood is reshaped with regard to its role transitions, status changes, and subjective meaning. The web of relations between larger social changes and the restructuring of entry into adulthood is assessed empirically by comparing two cohorts of white American high school graduates, one experiencing this transition period in the early 1960s, the other at the beginning of the 1980s.

The transition to adulthood is a strategic point at which to investigate shifts in the social structuring and the individual organization of the life course. It is a threshold—a period of new beginnings in several different life areas. Choices made at this stage in an individual's life are likely to have far-reaching consequences. The transition from school to work, for example, marks a pivotal point in the life conditions and life experiences of young people. Similarly, the decision to marry or to have children sets new demands with regard to the coordination and integration of careers and may have strong repercussions on an individual's future life prospects.

This book's primary analytic focus is on the following question: What shifts occur in the life course expectations and life course statuses between the members of the 1960 cohort of white American high school graduates and those of 1980? A second major question is: Which social groups "transmit" shifts in life course expectations as well as in role sequences and configurations? Specifically, who are the "trendsetters" and who are

1

the "latecomers" in this process? And lastly, what changes have occurred in the patterns that govern the determination of life course–related expectations and statuses?

The answers to these questions are formulated from an analysis that rests on three crucial assumptions: (1) Neither discrete life stages nor specific transitions can be understood apart from the life course as a whole; (2) social changes in the larger society provide the appropriate frame of reference for assessing the significance of changes in the patterns associated with particular life stages and in the life course as a whole; and (3) understanding how society organizes individual life courses and how people direct and give meaning to their own biographies requires an approach that integrates a macrosociological perspective with an actor-oriented one. Each of these assumptions is discussed separately below.

The ways in which entry into adulthood has been (and continues to be) transformed may tell us a great deal about the changing nature of the life course in contemporary society. Yet we are able to arrive at a meaningful interpretation of the altering features of the passage to adulthood only if we first understand the structural and cultural features of the *entire* life course. Neither a single life stage nor a transition period can be validly analyzed in isolation. It is an understanding of the logic of the social construction of the complete life course in a given society which provides the analytical framework for apprehending particular aspects of single life stages. Thus, I examine how the social and cultural features of the life course in modern United States society structure the life stage youth and the transition to adulthood, especially in relation to the specific historical periods covered by the empirical data.

It is particularly important that a life stage be understood in the wider context of the life course when the analysis focuses on a life stage and a transition period in a changing society. Shifts in the shaping of the life course and in single life stages are related to the social and cultural developments in the larger society. Throughout this book, I try to show the linkages between the structural and cultural changes in the organization of society and in its various institutional domains on one side and the reshaping of the life course with regard to its different career lines and symbolic meaning systems on the other. Understanding how and to what extent contemporary societal transformations affect the principles of the social construction of the life course provides a basis for integrating diverse empirical data on life course– and life stage–related changes. This, in turn, makes it possible to predict the direction in which the (transformed) life course patterns may be heading.

This theoretical approach is meant to offer a comprehensive framework within which a wide variety of life course–related problems and questions can be empirically analyzed. The argument applies what might be called an "inward" perspective, analyzing a "smaller" system from the perspective of "larger" ones: I begin with broad social and cultural changes, link them to the nature of the social construction of the life course, and then assess their joint impact on a single life stage. This type of analytic approach implies a particular relationship between theory and data. Two aspects of this relationship are of special interest in explaining the status of the theory and the function of the empirical analysis in this book.

First, the conceptual framework is necessarily much broader than the empirical analysis. Put differently, the theory "overshoots" the empirical investigation presented here. The data do not provide comprehensive answers to all of the theoretical claims. To the extent that the existing data do support the hypotheses tested here, however, the utility of the comprehensive framework is enhanced. It is in this sense that the present empirical investigation may be regarded as an initial test of the theory. One of the aims of this book is to make an empirically grounded contribution to the theoretical discussion in the sociology of the life course.

Second, within this conceptual framework, the choice regarding which particular life stage or transition period to analyze is of strategic importance. I consider entry into adulthood an especially fruitful area for probing the utility and validity of some of the major claims of the theory. This transition period, because it typically involves changing access to various life spheres, shedding old roles and assuming new ones, and making (sometimes extensive) adjustments in biographical trajectories, provides a rich opportunity to assess the ways in which the social structuring of the individual life course is changing. This study thus is well suited for testing some of the claims proposed in the comprehensive framework, while at the same time it is a substantial empirical analysis of the changing transition patterns to adulthood. In this sense, the book contributes to the sociology of youth and the transition to adulthood.

Focusing on how society constructs, organizes, and defines the lives of individuals as they progress in time and space constitutes a macrosociological approach to the study of the life course and life stages. Because such a perspective deals only with the larger structural and cultural settings of the individual life, it cannot fully capture the ways in which individuals enact their lives and give meaning to them. To understand how individuals perceive, evaluate, and carry out their lives, and to grasp the ways in which they cope with the opportunities and constraints imposed by the structural and cultural settings of the larger society, requires the inclusion of a concept of the individual as an *actor*. Thus, I advocate the use of a theory that links structure and action. From this point of view, life course outcomes are conceived of as the dynamic interplay between the characteristics of the broader social and cultural contexts and the specificities of the individual's action orientations and strategies.

This approach bypasses the long-standing dichotomy that has shaped much of the existing theory on the life course—on one side are the objectivist tendencies in sociological research on educational and occupational careers, on the family cycle, and on social mobility; on the other side, there are the subjectivist tendencies in the life history research. By developing a conceptual framework that focuses on the relation of social structure to individual choice in the life course, I hope to avoid the pitfalls of analyzing "actions without actors." A major aim of this book is to assess how the interplay between social and cultural transformations in contemporary society has affected individuals' outlooks on life, their plans for the future, and their strategies for action. More specifically, I examine how institutional transformations in the educational, occupational, and family domains have molded expectations about the transition to adulthood and the broader life plans of young people as they are about to finish high school.

### The Empirical Data

This book is based on a study of the experiences in the transition to adulthood of two cohorts of white American high school graduates: the classes of 1960 and of 1980. This design permits us to compare entry into adulthood in the United States in the early 1960s with entry at the beginning of the 1980s. The data are drawn from two sources: The 1960 cohort is drawn from the Project TALENT, and the 1980 cohort from the High School and Beyond sample.[1]

Project TALENT is a longitudinal study of American youth. A probability sample designed to be representative of all United States high school students in grades nine through twelve was selected. The students were surveyed for the first time in 1960, with periodic follow-up surveys one, five, and eleven years following the expected year of graduation from high school. The "Public Use File" of Project TALENT contains data for a subsample ($N = 4,000$) of the original sample ($N = 400,000+$) of students in grades nine through twelve. This subsample is composed of 1,000 men and women from each of the high school classes of 1960–1963, all of whom had responded to the eleven-year follow-up survey. From this sub-sample (which was designed to be *self-weighted*), I selected for the present study 877 white high school students of both sexes who were seniors in 1960.[2] The students were surveyed in that year and resurveyed in 1961, 1965, and 1971. In this subsample, the response rate in the one-year fol-low-up was 71.7 percent; in the five-year follow-up, 51.7 percent. Because of the initial selection criteria for the subsample, there is by definition no sample attrition in the eleven-year follow-up. The poor response rate in the five-year follow-up survey can be partly bypassed because the eleven-year follow-up provides all the necessary retrospective information on the chronology of the respondents' positions and roles (e.g., educational and occupational status, marital status, parent status). This enables us to recon-struct for a given year the life course–related data for those students who did not participate in the intermediate follow-up surveys. This procedure ensures that the conclusions to be drawn from the data are meaningful. It is also justified on the grounds that the subsample made available by the "Public Use File" of Project TALENT is self-weighted, that is, each member of the subsample is selected with probability proportional to the number of individuals in the population he or she represents. (More infor-mation on this issue is provided in the Appendix.)

The High School and Beyond study provides a nationally representative probability sample of American high school sophomores and seniors in 1980. Over 30,000 sophomores and about 28,000 seniors participated in the base-year survey. High School and Beyond was designed as a longitu-dinal study with periodic resurveys. Follow-up surveys of subsamples of students surveyed in the base year were conducted in 1982 and again in 1984. For the present study, the data are taken from the stratified sample of 11,500 male and female high school seniors of the class of 1980 who were selected for the follow-ups. In order to ensure comparability with the Project TALENT study, I randomly selected 877 cases of white high school seniors of both sexes, all of whom had responded to the 1982 and 1984 follow-ups. This procedure is also justified on the grounds that the High School and Beyond's follow-up response rates are very high (e.g., 94 per-cent in the 1982 survey). It guarantees, for example, that the comparison of significance tests between the Project TALENT and the High School and Beyond cohort will not be affected by the initial differences in the sample sizes. Careful checking of possible differences between the se-lected subsample and the full sample of High School and Beyond in the distributions of relevant background variables (sex, socioeconomic status, educational attainment) shows that the subsample is not biased in any particular direction. (A more complete description of the two studies, the samples, and the methodological issues is presented in greater detail in the Appendix.)

Throughout this book, these subsamples are referred to as cohorts. A cohort is a numerically defined aggregate of individuals of a given population who experience a specific event (e.g., birth, completion of [compulsory] schooling, marriage) at a given time, usually in a given calendar year.[3] The two-cohort design and the imposed time frame used here bring with them both opportunities and limitations. On the positive side, cohort analysis recognizes explicitly that individual orientations and actions must be viewed in their sociohistorical context. It can thus be used as a powerful empirical tool for relating global social change to alterations in life trajectories (cf. Ryder, 1965; Mayer, 1981; Müller, 1978, 1983). More specifically, it is a useful strategy for capturing the ways and degrees to which social and historical conditions critically affect the transition to adulthood.

The comparison of succeeding cohorts makes it theoretically possible to evaluate the impact of (continuous) structural and/or cultural change and of (discontinuous) historical events on the life courses of the members of a given cohort. And using data from different cohorts, each of which has been followed up at least once, makes it possible to address the question of change in the structuring of the life course. Finally, because transition phenomena need to be conceptualized longitudinally, cohort analysis is appropriate. A *time-lag* design (see Power, 1983) is the most fruitful methodological approach for analyzing transition phenomena.[4] Different samples (cohorts) are tested at the same social age (e.g., completion of schooling, marriage) and/or at the same chronological age at several points in time. The suitability of a time-lag design for my research problem strongly favored the combination of data from Project TALENT and the High School and Beyond study. This study thus uses an intercohort model with longitudinal data for each cohort. The particular structure of each of the two data sets (e.g., time span covered and timing of successive survey waves) enables us to compare the two cohorts over the first four years after high school graduation. (See Appendix for a detailed description of this issue.)

The effectiveness of a cohort approach is highly dependent on the selection of appropriate cohorts. This is certainly true in the present study. The Project TALENT and the High School and Beyond studies are among the few comprehensive longitudinal studies of the transition to adulthood that include cohorts that also meet the criteria of a time-lag design. In selecting the cohort of 1960 high school graduates, I chose a group whose vast majority was born in 1942; among the members of the second cohort, the graduates of the high school class of 1980, the vast majority were born in 1962. Each group grew up in a period of significant social and cultural developments that might be expected to affect the cohort members' transition to adulthood.

The selection of the earlier time period was based on results from studies of historical changes in the transition to adulthood (cf. Hogan, 1978, 1980, 1981; Modell et al., 1976; Winsborough, 1979) which show that, for cohorts of men born in the 1940s or in the early 1950s, events in this life passage have become more uniform, more rapid, and more age-graded (i.e., more standardized) than they were for cohorts born in the 1910s, 1920s, and 1930s. Since I argue in this book that the trend toward accelerated timing and increasingly standardized passages to adulthood has slowed down or even come to a halt since the late 1960s, it makes sense to compare a cohort that moved into adulthood in what appears to have been the apex of the standardization of the life course with one that is presently experiencing this transition.

The selection of the later time period was guided by two considerations. The analysis of *contemporary* conditions surrounding the transition to adulthood in the United States is of major interest in this study. Additionally, my argument assumes that the social and cultural conditions that the members of the high school class of 1980 experience in their passage to adulthood are most likely to be typical ones for young generations in the next few years. With regard to the economy, for example, there is consensus that full employment, characteristic of the postwar period until the early 1970s, is unlikely to be restored in the near future (cf. Beck, 1985).

Overall, the structural and cultural developments that have occurred over the last two decades in the educational system (the mass expansion of tertiary schooling), in the occupational structure (the transformation of employment structures and occupational careers induced by new technologies), and in the family system (the pluralization of living arrangements) make the assumption of shifts in the transition patterns between the 1960s and the 1980s a highly plausible one. Against this background, the cohort match used here is a reasonable one.[5]

The selection of these two cohorts does have drawbacks, however. Conceptually, my research problem includes all youths—not just high school graduates. However, since over 70 percent of youths of all races graduated from high school in 1960 and in 1980 (see Appendix), it seems legitimate to conceive of this pathway as the normal educational career trajectory—a more or less uniform early part of the life course. Therefore, I believe these cohorts of high school graduates form a legitimate sample for my research. Strictly speaking, the empirical findings are valid only for high school graduates. I do occasionally generalize the results to all youths, on the grounds that the 70 percent of high school graduates are more likely to be trendsetters for shifts in juvenile attitudes and behaviors regarding the transition to adulthood than the 30 percent of high school dropouts. Nevertheless, it is a shortcoming of this study that high school dropouts (especially those who leave school legally at age sixteen) cannot be observed, thus excluding those pathways in the transition to adulthood that are based on very low educational attainment.

A second limitation is that the research design permits comparisons of the two cohorts only over the first four years after high school graduation. This is an admittedly brief segment of the life course—but it is not a random time span. First, it begins at high school graduation, a significant and objective turning point in the life course of young people. At this time, most young people are making major decisions about their future careers. As I shall argue in this book, it is especially at such objectively defined career steps and transitions that individuals are likely to deliberately call attention to their future and thus to devise "life plans." Differences between the members of the two cohorts in the expectations and plans regarding the timing of various life events and status attainments may reveal changing intentions regarding transitions and thus signal shifts in the social modalities of becoming an adult in American society. Moreover, for those youths who do not attend a four-year college (the majority even in the early 1980s; see Chapter 6), the first few years after high school graduation are spent "converting" their socially ascribed attributes and individually achieved assets into attainments and achievements in public life. In this respect, this short period of the life course exerts a considerable influence on life outcomes. Lastly, the multidimensionality of entry into adulthood results in a highly intense period of role transitions and status changes, compared with other phases and stages in the life course. Some of these changes, at least, are accomplished by a considerable proportion of a cohort in the first four years after high school graduation.

All studies based on secondary data inevitably encounter one or more discrepancies between the *ideal* research design and corresponding data on one side and the *real* possibilities offered by existing data, on the other. Typically, the new research problem's data requirements cannot be met fully using available secondary sources. The crucial issue in secondary analysis is whether the use of available data is likely to prove worthwhile, despite the constraints in sample design and data collection. For the reasons already noted, and others discussed below, I believe that the data used in this study are well-suited to provide answers to the research questions posed.

The high comparability of Project TALENT and the High School and Beyond studies with regard to sampling design, topics covered, and questions asked make them especially suitable for the present research problem. For example, careful checking of the questions asked in both studies shows that a large proportion of the variables relevant to my research problem are either identical or highly similar in the two studies, although each study was undertaken independently of the other. Perhaps more importantly, the two data sets make a good match substantively. For some issues in the study of the transition to adulthood, the combination of Project TALENT data with that from the study High School and Beyond offers greater resources and options than other secondary data on youths.

In addition to these essential advantages, the combination of these two data sets helps overcome shortcomings that have plagued other studies of the transition to adulthood. As in many other areas of sociological research, women are frequently "invisible" (Oakley, 1974) in studies of the life course. Longitudinal studies of the transition to adulthood often have excluded female youths. Reviewing literature on the sociology of youth, Ostner (1986) points out that until the 1970s, *youth* sociology was mainly *boys* sociology. The two data sets used here allow investigation of both men's and women's transition expectations and behaviors, thus potentially contributing to new theoretical insights into the situation of youth in contemporary society.

Juvenile transition and status expectations and their influence on subsequent behaviors are another important aspect of this study. The interplay between "subjective" and "objective" factors—between plans and their outcomes—has been consistently neglected in the literature on the life course, including those studies that have focused on the transition to adulthood (cf. Hogan & Astone, 1986). This is due partly to the absence of suitable longitudinal data on expectations, preferences, and behaviors and partly to the lack of appropriate theory. The two data sets chosen for this study partly overcome this gap in the literature.

Much of the research on the life course and its transitions has also paid insufficient attention to subgroup variations in early life transitions. This omission is particularly glaring in comparative research. Cohort analysis recognizes that the particular social and cultural contexts that characterize a historical period vary in their effects across subgroups of the cohort. A major focus here, therefore, is the comparison of gender-based and class-based variations in transition expectations and behaviors between the 1960 and the 1980 high school graduates. Potential shifts in subgroup differences are related to both the sociohistorical context in which the members of the two cohorts experienced their formative years and to the social and economic conditions they face as they make the transition to adulthood.

## The Organization of the Book

This book is composed of two parts: Part one presents the theoretical framework, part two the cohort comparison of white American graduates of the high school classes of 1960 and of 1980 as they move into adulthood.

The organization of part one is guided by the three major theoretical assumptions outlined in this introduction. The conceptual framework proposed in Chapter 1 relates the structural and cultural developments in modern society to the social construction and individual organization of the life course. To capture, at the macrosociological level, the logic of the social construction of the life course, the first chapter elaborates the notion of the institutionalization of the life course as the key mechanism for organizing and regulating the individual's lifetime and his or her progression in social space. To more fully capture the ways in which individuals themselves plan and organize their lives within this framework of social constraints, the chapter also includes a concept of individual actors' structural realities. Drawing mainly on Pierre Bourdieu's work, the discussion elaborates the notion of strategies of action that are associated with an actor's structural position(s) and which define his or her access to and control of social and economic resources.

Chapter 2 uses this dual-level conceptual framework to examine the interplay between social change and changing life course patterns. I argue that, over the last two decades, structural and cultural changes in the areas of education, occupation, and the family have provoked a partial transformation of the life course regime. Specifically, as a result of the dynamics between standardization and individualization, life course patterns have become more flexible, more discontinuous, and increasingly diversified. The various social mechanisms through which these effects are produced are related to the accelerated pace of rationalization and individualization that characterize advanced industrial societies.

This general hypothesis is specified in Chapter 3 for the life stage youth and the transition to adulthood. I argue that the recent rapid integration of youth into the process of societal individualization and parallel structural and cultural changes in the educational, occupational, and family systems have gradually transformed the transition to adulthood. What was once a standardized period involving various rapid role and status changes is now an increasingly extended, diversified, and highly individualized in-between period.

Part two uses this conception of the changes in the transition to adulthood to structure the cohort comparison. Chapter 4 presents some background information on the social and cultural context of the larger society during the decades in which the two cohorts grew up; basic characteristics of their family milieus are also sketched. The patterns of entry into adulthood are investigated in Chapter 5, beginning with transition expectations and life plans at high school graduation, followed by a comparison of overall transition patterns to adulthood four years after high school graduation. This approach provides insight into potential changes in the structuring of the life course. These shifts are then analyzed in detail with regard to educational careers (Chapter 6), occupational trajectories (Chapter 7), and family life (Chapter 8). The empirical investigation ends (Chapter 9) with an analysis of subgroup variations in the relationship between life course expectations at high school graduation and their behavioral outcomes four years later.

## Part One

# Societal Provision of
# Life Scripts and Casts

# 1 The Life Course in Modern Society: Social Construction and Individual Organization

There are many different angles from which to examine the individual life course. From a sociological point of view, it is of primary interest to assess how living in organized social groups—societies—shapes the ways in which human life unfolds and becomes imbued with meaning. It is the main purpose of this chapter to explore how these processes and mechanisms work within *modern* society. I develop a conceptual framework that permits us to capture the logic of the social and cultural construction of the life course in modern society and to link it to individuals' modes of addressing and coping with life's opportunities and constraints. I begin with some analytic distinctions that underlie the conceptual structure used throughout this book.

The individual's life can be described as a progression in social time and space. Here I analyze that progression across two dimensions. The first designates the *scope* of analysis: Individuals' lives are examined from the macrosociological perspective of the social system and from the microsociological perspective of the actor. The second dimension refers to the *level* of analysis—the analytical distinction between structural and cultural analysis. The structural perspective focuses on problems of social action and exchange in the life course; the cultural perspective centers on the symbolic structuring of life. From the macrosociological perspective, the crucial question is how society constructs, organizes, and defines the life course. From the point of view of the actor, the issue of interest is how individuals perceive, evaluate, and carry out their lives. These four aspects of the analysis, the macro and micro perspectives and the structural and cultural levels, represent four distinct ways to study the life course (see Table 1.1).

From the macrosociological structural perspective, individual life is conceived of as the *institutionalization of the life course*. This concept designates a formal set of rules which organize the individual's lifetime progression within social space. These rules define the legitimate partici-

15

Table 1.1
Analytical Distinctions and Concepts in the Study of the Life Course

| Level of Analysis | Scope of Analysis | |
|---|---|---|
| | Macrosociological | Microsociological |
| Structural | Institutionalization of the life course as a set of rules; institutionalized status/role configurations | The life course as an actual sequence of status/role configurations |
| Cultural | Collective representations and ideologies of the biography | Individual representations of the biography; biographical perspectives and strategies |

pation in and transitions between different social institutions (e.g., education, occupation). In this respect, the life course represents a sequence of *institutionalized status/role configurations* (i.e., a sequential order of positions and roles). The *collective representations of the biography* (e.g., social definition of childhood and its properties) frame the analysis of the life course from the macrosociological cultural perspective. These representations provide organized images that legitimate structural features of both the life course and separate life stages (e.g., confinement of children to school).

At the level of the individual actor, the life course can be conceived of as the *actual sequence of positions and roles*. Whereas the institutionalized status/role configurations represent the normative linkages between social positions at a given time or across time, the sequence of positions and roles from the actor's point of view refers to his or her actual progression in social time and space. The conscious and practical appropriations of an individual's time constitute *biographical perspectives and strategies*. These include the individual's expectations, aspirations, and action orientations toward different spheres of life. On a more comprehensive level, they designate the individual's life designs and life plans.

The institutionalized life course and the culture's view of the biography define the frame of reference within which individual actors construct their biographical perspectives and strategies. Rather than being "a continuous flux of undifferentiated time and experience" (Mayer & Müller, 1986, p. 12), the life course is structured; it is given distinct, recognizable phases with meanings understood and acknowledged by society at large as well as by the individual actor.

An elaboration of these distinct aspects of the life course in the succeeding sections of this chapter will provide a sufficiently detailed theoretical background to identify and assess the link between structure and action.

## The Institutionalization of the Life Course

From the macrosociological perspective, the question of central interest is how society organizes and defines individual life courses. This section identifies four characteristics of the institutionalization of the life course.

First, the individual's progression in social time and space is governed by a set of formal rules. They order life as a sequence of life stages and regulate the transitions between them. Access to different institutional domains of society in terms of positions and roles is officially regulated (Levy, 1977; Kohli, 1983, 1985a; Mayer & Müller, 1986; Meyer, 1986b); the transitions between organizationally and functionally differentiated institutional domains are similarly subject to formal regulation. These formal rules define access to positions and roles with respect to time of life, regulate their sequences, and ascribe the associated rights and obligations. As a result, individuals come to be classified in terms of both legitimate participation in and transitions between institutional spheres.

Second, the state is increasingly involved in defining and enforcing the rules pertaining to the social structuring of the life course (Mayer & Müller, 1986). The mode of the social organization of life thus follows the logic of state intervention. The state's right to regulate different dimensions of the life course is based on formal law (Mayer & Müller, 1986). By ordering the individual life according to universal, rational principles of law, the state produces a formalized, standardized, and bureaucratized life course. The more the state regulates individuals' progression through organizationally and functionally differentiated institutional domains, the more the life course assumes a bureaucratic structure.

Third, state regulation of the life course transforms aspects of life into institutionally defined life events and institutionally arranged life stages. As such, they represent institutionalized sequences of status/role configurations (Levy, 1977). These normatively prescribed sequences of positions and roles constitute trajectories or "careers" through which individual actors progress during their lifetime. Thus, state regulation turns these aspects of life into "public" life events and "public" life stages from which the noninstitutionalized elements (i.e., the "private" life course) are isolated. The life course "regime" is thus characterized by a dual structure consisting of the public and the private life course.

Finally, a peculiar dynamic exists between individualization and standardization of the life course: Life comes to be less constrained by traditions and customs and thus more susceptible to individualized action orientations, but it has to be fitted into the standardized and bureaucratized life patterns defined by state rules (Beck, 1983; Beck-Gernsheim, 1982, 1983). Individuals *can* make life course–related choices, but they also *must* make them in correspondence with the requirements of the standardized life course.

Assuming a structural affinity between the logic of life course organization and the principles of societal organization helps explain why these distinct features of the life course exist in modern society. The institutionalization of the life course may be regarded as a concomitant of the rationalized and individualized society. The next two sections examine these two organizing principles of modern society: rationalization at the level of social action and exchange and the ideology of individualism at the level of the cultural meaning system.[1]

### Rationalization of the Economy and the Polity

Conceiving of the development of Western society as a continuous process of rationalization requires, first, a definition of this concept. In Max Weber's ([1922] 1968) theory, rationality designates a specific type of action orientation. Weber constructed a typology of action orientations based on the degree of awareness and reflection (i.e., the degree of rationality) the action requires on the part of the individual. Increasing rationality designates a greater likelihood that actions will be susceptible to intellectual insight. Weber distinguishes the following types of action orientations: the emotional/affective, the traditional, the value-rational (*wertrational*), and the rational (*zweckrational*). The first type, which is governed by "blind affects," is not at all accessible to reflection; and the second requires only a minimal awareness and reflection on the individual's part. The traditional action orientation is grounded in unquestioned adherence to customs, conventions, and habits. A higher degree of rationality is involved in the value-rational action orientation. Weber defined it as dominated by a belief in the absolute validity of claims and precepts to which ends are subordinated. The rational action orientation involves the highest level of awareness and reflection. Both ends and means are susceptible to the individual's intellectual insight.[2]

Methodologically, Weber conceives of the rational and all other types of action orientation as *ideal types*. These are empirically grounded and, hence, historically based concepts depicting essential features of social reality (cf. Adatto & Cole, 1981). Ideal types are useful as guidelines for analyzing social reality; they provide a sort of benchmark from which deviations may be apprehended and explained. Accordingly, Weber employs ideal types to analyze the ways and degrees to which the rational action orientation is institutionalized in the structure of modern Western society. In his account, societal development in the West emerges—as far as the principle of social organization is concerned—as the continuous rationalization of society. This process entails, above all, the rationalization of the economic and the political spheres. The former corresponds to the establishment of the market, the latter to the emergence of the nation state and citizenship.

Economic action and exchange can be regarded as rational if it is purposive, in the sense that means and ends are calculated, and if it is not restricted to the service of particular needs, but rather is "open" to fulfill any end pursued using the most efficient means (cf. Lenhardt, 1984, p. 117; Döbert, 1985, pp. 523–524; Collins, 1986, p. 22). The rationalization of the economic sphere presupposes production factors and economic exchange relations that are not restricted by traditional norms defining and regulating economic transactions. This involves, on one hand, the establishment of market freedom in the exchange of labor, land, commodities, and capital and, on the other hand, the emergence of a universalistic accounting system. With respect to the latter, the monetarization of the economy constitutes the universalistic principle of economic action and exchange. As Meyer et al. (1981, pp. 15–16) note, "Money provides the means by which commensurability can be established and local (traditional) social exchange can be reconstructed as rational exchange." With respect to the former, the rationalized economy requires individuals who can exchange and dispose of their property according to the logic of economic calculation. The social construction of the individual as the primary unit of economic action and exchange was facilitated by the institutionalization of individual rights and obligations in the political sphere.

The rationalization of the political sphere, that is, of authority relations in modern society, is based on formal law, which represents a universalistic, standardized principle for regulating social relations. According to Weber ([1922] 1968), authority based on formal law constitutes the most rational form of domination because it is rooted in a belief in the binding nature of purposively constructed order. The implementation of authority relations in formal law gives rise to a reflective level of justification which replaces the ontological form of legitimation that characterized premodern society (Habermas, 1979).

The legal authority of the state evolved through the establishment of citizen rights and obligations (Thomas & Meyer, 1984). As a result of the secular increase in societal membership rights and obligations, the individual increasingly enters into direct relationships with the state and thus is freed from obligations to other social collectivities.[3] The notion of citizenship also involves a recognition of the fundamental equality of human beings (Marshall, 1964; Bendix, 1964; Thomas & Meyer, 1984). The attribution of rights and the imposition of obligations on the basis of equality among individuals reflects a universal, standardized, and rationalized principle regulating social relations. The institutionalization of citizenship thus provides a structure for integrating the individual into society.

In Marshall's (1964) description of the expanding institution of citizenship since the eighteenth century, the attribution of civil rights to the individual[4] is followed in the nineteenth century by the institutionalization of political rights and obligations which encompass "the right to participate in the exercise of political power, as a member of a body invested with political authority or as an elector of the members of such a body" (p. 78). During the twentieth century, the process of the individual's integration into society on a universalistic, standardized, and rationalized basis has progressed rapidly;[5] especially with regard to social rights,[6] which guarantee the right to a minimum of economic welfare and security (p. 105).

Although modern political and economic institutions are based on the same principle for organizing social action and exchange, they differ in some fundamental respects. In the economic structure, individuals are officially located in highly differentiated positions, whereas they formally occupy equal positions in the political structure.[7] The social organization of modern society thus is based on principles in dialectical tension.

Social stratification in modern society is rooted in the unequal distribution of individual actors in the economic system. Higher positions in the social hierarchy are legitimized on the basis of the individual's contribution to society. By contrast, political institutions in modern society place all individuals in formally equal positions; in this sense, these institutions facilitate a structure of universalistic integration. An individual's position in the political system is not assessed according to his or her actions and personal achievements; rather it is attributed on the basis of fundamental human rights.

It makes sense to think of the integrating political structure as a counterpart to the differentiating economic system. The former provides a partial legitimation for the structure of social inequality. Marshall (1964, p. 77) regards citizenship in modern society as "the architect of legitimate social inequality." Rationalization of the political and economic spheres thus places the individual simultaneously in a highly integrated and in a highly differentiated social structure, both of which are predicated on the individual as the relevant unit of action, that is, on the individualization of membership in society.

The expansion of individual membership in modern society has been characterized by various social theorists as a process of gradual release (*Freisetzung*) in which the individual's linkages to traditional social collectivities (e.g., extended family, local community, status group) have tended to weaken.[8] Societal individualization is a twofold process: It loosens traditional constraints on the individual's freedom of action. At the same time, it raises the problem of how to ensure the individual's adherence to rules governing state and society. Hobsbawm and Ranger (1985, p. 265) note that the modern system "raised unprecedented problems of how to maintain or even establish the obedience, loyalty, and cooperation of its subjects or members."[9]

Thus, the rationalization of the economy and the polity and the accompanying individualization of society requires a new order of social subordination. The new kind of direct social control over the individual's worldview and behavior evolves on two levels. It is linked—on the level of action and exchange—to the expansion of the state authority, and it is related—on the level of culture—to the ideology of individualism.

In order to secure the individual's integration into the rationalized economy and polity, ever more aspects of social life come to be incorporated into the state's jurisdiction: Previously private relationships are more and more subject to state regulation. A particularly dramatic example of this process is the continuous expansion of the welfare state's social security programs (benefits covering unemployment, disability, old age, health, etc.) (Flora & Heidenheimer, 1981).[10] This "politization of society" (see Thomas & Meyer, 1984; Templeton, 1979) increases the number of rights that an individual may claim on a universalistic, standardized basis, while at the same time it restricts the individual's freedom to organize many aspects of social life.

From the system's perspective, the state penetrates society and so assumes responsibility for it. The shift from the family as the main socializing agent (i.e., privately organized socialization) to a state-controlled system of education illustrates this process (Boli-Bennett & Meyer, 1978; Somerville, 1982; Lenhardt, 1984, 1985; Mayer & Müller, 1986). Similarly, family relations are continuously subjected to state intervention, with the result that family concerns are gradually subsumed under the logic of rationality and regarded more as public than as private matters (cf. Sachse,

1986). State expansion into society also includes systematic intervention in the economy. The state's penetration of the economic sphere occurs at two different levels: It regulates problems resulting from private economic activities that cannot be handled by private enterprise, and it provides economic incentives, especially for the development of knowledge and technology (cf. Bell, 1973).

Expanding state regulation of social life follows a specific pattern induced by the instruments of action and the organizational means available to the state: State activities are based on formal law and performed within an organizational framework characterized by bureaucratic rules (Weber, [1922] 1968; Habermas, 1983; Lenhardt, 1985). Impersonal objectivity is the essential characteristic of bureaucratically organized social relations. The expanding bureaucratic organization of social life forces individual action and exchange into a formalized and impersonal structure. As Weber ([1922] 1968, p. 1116) put it, individual action is controlled "from without." The bureaucratic structure sets the imperatives for individual action, systematically undermining opportunities for the expression of individual autonomy.

Some scholars (cf. Habermas, 1979) couple the growing bureaucratization of society with the gradual expropriation of individual action autonomy (*Handlungsautonomie*). The modern bureaucratic system is seen as impeding the articulation of autonomous subjectivity. This is explained as the result of the contradiction inherent in the development of modern society: Although societal rationalization is a prerequisite for individual freedom, it simultaneously restricts individual autonomy because of the bureaucratic organization of social relations.

Certainly, bureaucratic social relations—given their impersonal objectivity—restrain the expression of subjectivity, but modern society's collective cultural representations depict the individual as an autonomous and purposive actor. And, in fact, the modern system rests in part on the idea of the individual as an autonomous entity capable of acting on his or her own behalf and responsible for his or her actions. The ideology of individualism provides the cultural resources upon which the individual can draw to organize his or her action and to express his or her subjectivity. Since this cultural meaning system represents an essential characteristic of the modern system, its main features are outlined below.

### The Ideology of Individualism

A dominant cultural account—understood as "stock" in the sense of a collective memory—provides an organized and relatively integrated image of society and its essential properties. It encompasses, according to Meyer et al. (1981), a "theory" of the relationship between society and the individual. It is a collective representation of social reality which never fully corresponds to that reality.

In order to understand the dynamics between structure and culture within society, it is essential to recognize that both spheres—social organization and the cultural system—possess a relative autonomy, permitting each to develop according to its own inner logic. Nevertheless, there is a correspondence between the principle of social organization and the structure of social representation because collective worldviews provide a general legitimating framework for the entire social structure. In fact, the degree of correspondence can be used as an analytical frame of reference for evaluating the impact of structure and culture, respectively, on social development.[11]

The rationalization of both state and society is built on a unified cultural base (Thomas & Meyer, 1984) that emphasizes the individual as the basic social unit[12] and defines his or her "nature," that is, identifies the essential qualities and properties of the human being.[13] One such fundamental property is the equality of all individuals. This general notion is put in more concrete forms in, for instance, the ideology of political equality, which in turn is partially institutionalized in citizenship. Moreover, it finds expression in the ideology of economic justice based on the principle of advancement through merit. Second, the ideology of individualism incorporates a theory of personality. Individuals are conceived of as having a range of needs, motives, capacities, and competencies;[14] as being capable of engaging in purposive action, of making suitable choices, and of feeling responsible for their actions. Ultimately, it is the individual who takes the initiative, makes choices, and justifies them.[15] In this sense, "personhood is a resource actors can use to further whatever goals they may have" (Kohli & Meyer, 1986, p. 149).

In a society partially dependent on individual action, producing, controlling, and ensuring appropriate behavior on the part of the individual is potentially problematic. The ideology of individualism thus incorporates a conception of individual development as a gradual unfolding of the potential to engage in purposive, responsible action. As Meyer (1986a, p. 217) notes, "The individual is to know, to understand, to explain, to choose, and ultimately to become an effective person capable of making suitable choices and engaging in proper action." This task is achieved through appropriate socialization, which becomes institutionalized in the educational system.[16]

Thus, the concept of socialization and theories of equality and of personality are collective social representations and definitions that (partially) organize the subjective experience of the individual; they are not, as it is sometimes assumed by social scientists, private views, that is, products of individuals' attempts to give meaning to their own experiences (cf. Meyer, 1986a).

## State Regulation of the Life Course

The essential principles of societal organization outlined above suggest why the life course in modern society assumes the characteristics described in the first section of this chapter: As soon as the individual ceases to be primarily a member of a collectivity and enters the market as an economic actor and the political sphere as a citizen, his or her life course is no longer prescribed by corporate groups such as the family and local communities. Rather, the life course takes the form of individualized progressions in social time and space.[17] The institutionalization of the life course represents a social mechanism for organizing and regulating the individual's lifetime, integrating the requirements of the rationalized society with the demands of the ideology of the individual as the sole legitimate actor. The standardization and individualization of the life course thus corresponds to the rationalization of society.[18]

The structural and cultural features of the life course as a social institution are mediated by two sets of rules with which the state regulates the individual's life: The first group orders the individual's life on the basis of chronological age (i.e., chronology of life); the second governs status allocation and status linkages, especially through educational credentials and professional titles. These rules define exchange relations between subsequent positions and roles within and between institutional fields.

The codification of life according to chronological age (i.e., age-grading) represents one of the most visible aspects of the standardized and bureaucratized life course (Elder, 1975; Smelser & Halpern, 1978; Smelser, 1980a; Buchmann, 1983; Kohli, 1983, 1985a, 1985b, 1986; Mayer & Müller, 1986; Meyer, 1986b).[19] All institutions in modern society are at least partially age-organized (Riley, 1976, 1987; Riley et al., 1972; Neugarten & Hagestad, 1976). The organization of the *educational system*, for instance, is to a great extent age-graded.[20] The use of chronological age as an organizing principle is clear also in the *occupational system*, where the prospects of promotion are subject to seniority rules and the transition to *retirement* is based on chronological age. The same principle applies to the definition of political rights and obligations, social security laws, and the penal law.

The tendency to classify individuals and to assign them to positions and roles according to chronological age transforms chronological age into *social* age (Neugarten & Hagestad, 1976).[21] Age classifications emerge as social constructions that serve as a basis for both role differentiation (i.e., prescription of tasks and age-appropriate behaviors) and social stratification (i.e., distribution of highly valued resources, such as material goods, power, and prestige).

Unlike in traditional society, where a single age-grade system cross-cuts all major social institutions (cf. Neugarten & Hagestad, 1976), age-grading in modern society is a multidimensional social classification system. Age-based assignments of positions and roles occur in different institutional fields and are not fully synchronized. Differentiated age-grading in relation to particular institutional fields engenders not only a multiplicity of time schedules, but also induces the probability of asynchronies regarding role entry and exit. Giving up one role does not necessarily coincide with the allocation of another. And access to highly valued goods may vary according to the institutional field, giving rise to status inconsistencies (Lenski, 1954). Against this background, the individual's life course may be described as a sequential ordering of status/role configurations greatly regulated by formal age ascription.

In the development of modern society, the number of life stages has increased and they have become more clearly defined and set apart in relation to chronological age.[22] Sociohistorical studies have documented the "invention" of distinct life stages, such as childhood (Ariès, 1962, 1983; Somerville, 1982), youth (Demos & Demos, 1969; Kett, 1971; Keniston, 1971; Gillis, 1974; Platt, 1969), adulthood (Smelser, 1980a, 1980b), and "third age" (Graebner, 1980; Lenoir, 1979; Conrad & Kondratowitz, 1983). Since formal age criteria grant access to different social institutions (e.g., school, labor market, retirement), a life stage may be distinguished by the number and composition of institutional fields in which an individual participates.

Legal definitions related to chronological age seem to function as baselines for various age typifications and age norms. For example, when an individual becomes legally eligible for Social Security benefits, he or she is soon thought of as "old" (Neugarten & Hagestad, 1976). Analytically, we can distinguish age criteria for role assignment and status allocation according to their degree of institutionalization (see Figure 1.1). We find the highest degree of institutionalization in legally defined ascription of roles and statuses. Age criteria based on informal consensus represent those aspects of the age-regulated life course with the lowest degree of institutionalization. The social relevance of such "age-appropriate" timing

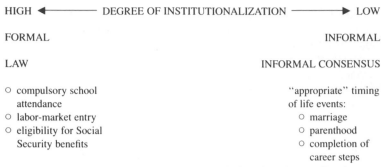

Figure 1.1  Degree of institutionalization of age criteria for role and status allocation.

of life events may be deduced from the regularities found in the scheduling of marriage, steps in the work career, and so forth. They may be further inferred from the extent to which individuals are aware of such appropriate life scheduling. Hareven (1986) compared perceptions regarding the timing of life transitions of cohorts born between 1900 and 1909 with the perceptions of cohorts born either between 1910 and 1919 or 1920 and 1929. She found that the awareness of life events and life transitions in relation to chronological age is much stronger among the members of the younger cohorts. Members of the oldest cohort perceived their lives as a continuous whole, whereas members of the younger cohorts, especially the youngest, were aware of age-related stages and discontinuities in their life courses. These perceptual differences highlight contemporary society's tendency to define life course transitions more strictly by age criteria and to give less weight to factors such as economic needs or familial obligations (Hareven, 1986).

The officially regulated stages, transitions, and events of the (public) life course influence the sequences of positions and roles in the noninstitutionalized (private) spheres of life. The timing of events and transitions in the latter spheres can be understood as the result of the practical acknowledgment of the objective requirements that the state-regulated "pace" of life imposes on the individual's scope of action.[23] Thus, the temporal structuring of major life events induced by formal age rules results in "social timetables" (cf. Neugarten, 1968; Neugarten & Hagestad, 1976; Elder, 1975; Clausen, 1972, 1981, 1986) that define temporal expectations about a wide range of noninstitutionalized life transitions. Some of these expectations are sharply defined, while others outline a band of years within which specific life events and life transitions should occur.

For example, the growing state-defined organization of the life course in the development of modern society has been paralleled by increasing regularities in the timing of family life events. These regularities are partly attributable to the steady increase in the average life expectancy, which relegates death to higher ages (von Imhof, 1981, 1985). As most people are likely to reach old age, family life becomes more predictable, thus contributing to regular family life cycles. Sociohistoric studies of the last hundred years (Demos & Boocock, 1978; Uhlenberg, 1974; Modell et al., 1976, 1978; Hareven, 1977; Kohli, 1978; Rosenmayr, 1978; for overviews see Elder, 1978; and Hagestad & Neugarten, 1985) have shown that there has not only been a drop in the average age at marriage for both men and women, but the dispersal in the marriage age also has rapidly decreased. The same tendencies can be observed with regard to the mother's age at first childbearing. Furthermore, the number of years during which childbearing takes place has declined. It is only over the past twenty years that this standardization of the family cycle has slowed, giving way to more dispersed patterns of family life events and a greater variety of living arrangements.[24]

In a critical review of the noninstitutionalized age-related sequencing of positions and roles over the life course, that is, of the "timing-of-life-events" model, Marini (1984a, 1984b) argues that many expectations regarding the "proper" scheduling of life events are not globally valid but, instead, are subculturally defined. Moreover, she doubts whether "social timetables" really assume the status of norms. She categorizes them as empirical regularities, which are—at the aggregate level—the result of educational, occupational, and family requirements that structure the timing of individual behavior.

These criticisms do not invalidate the theoretical assumption that the state, by legally defining age groups, regulates life stage entries and exits and transforms life into a distinct sequence of stages. The state thus contributes to the differentiation and to the segmentation of the life course.

The social organization of the life course is also based on the codification of exchange relations among educational status, occupational position, and retirement status. The establishment of such codified rules is predicated on the rationalized and standardized *formation* and *deployment* of labor power.[25] This includes the establishment of rationalized procedures of recruitment and promotion (i.e., the growing importance of meritocratic principles for hiring and advancement) which presupposes the professionalization of the occupational structure. In such a structure, state-approved professional qualifications—institutionalized as educational credentials—regulate the supply of labor; the professionalization of occupational positions—the state-certified definition of work tasks included or excluded from an occupational role—structures the demand for labor.[26] This expanding state regulation of the labor market results in the decreasing significance of free contractual relations for organizing the supply of and demand for labor (Lenhardt, 1984, 1985).[27]

As the state regulates the relationship between the educational system and the occupational structure, "it defines the interface between institutionally specific segments of the life course in terms of [the] rules of access and [of] transitions" (Mayer & Müller, 1986, p. 22). State-approved educational certificates thus entitle their holders to particular occupational positions. They legitimize access to differential professional status. Accordingly, educational credentials designate the social recognition of cultural and professional competencies (Bourdieu & Boltanski, 1975; Bourdieu, 1978; Collins, 1979). They function as a classification system, sorting individuals into career tracks.

Moreover, the codified linkage between an educational certificate and a professional position persists through retirement. The individual's former occupational status partly determines his or her status as a pensioner. The amount of money earned during one's professional life entitles the worker to a corresponding pension, although the state guarantees a minimum income for all pensioners. In the latter respect, the state redistributes income over a lifetime, whereas in the former respect, the state safeguards ascribed and achieved economic and social status (Mayer & Müller, 1986).

Overall, state activities with regard to the life course assume integrating as well as differentiating functions. On one hand, they segment time into distinct sequences of life stages that sort and classify individuals into different positions and roles. On the other hand, they interlock the separate life stages and different institutional spheres. In defining linkages between different institutional spheres in terms of rules of access and of transition, the state orders and interlocks the individual's positions and roles in these spheres and thus furthers continuity over a person's life span. In other words, the state constructs the *public life course*. It regulates educational tracks, prescribes professional trajectories, and designates the age of retirement.

These integrating and differentiating processes have always been part of the state's responsibility for the life course. Although appropriate empirical material is not available, it makes sense to hypothesize that early state penetration of the life course placed greater emphasis on differentiating aspects, whereas later state regulations have stressed integrating functions. (This is especially true with regard to social security legislation.) It is clear that in the development of modern society, the state has assumed ever more responsibility for the life course, transforming the individual's life into a rationalized and standardized structure.

### Cultural Representation of the Life Course and of Life Stages: Validated Social Identities

The life course as a social institution has been described as a system of rules that sort and categorize individuals. Official categorization systems homogenize and formalize social meaning and social action (Bourdieu, 1986a).

One important effect of the codification of social phenomena is the reduction of the scope of possible meanings attributed to them, ultimately resulting in social consensus. Thus, the state-regulated aspects of life, that is, the codified elements, constitute the official, socially validated and recognized life course. These public life events are distinct from those of private life. Moreover, participation in the public life course is accompanied by the acquisition of institutionalized identities—public identities based on acknowledged and certified capacities—which are separated from the private notion of the "I," that is, the "private" self.[28]

The formal definition of age categories, for instance, involves the social construction of legitimate representations and legitimate practices granted to people of different ages. Age categories define the qualities, competencies, needs, and motives—as well as rights and obligations—thought to be appropriate to the members of a given age group.[29] They legitimize age-specific behavioral norms, which, in turn, structure the expectations of the members of specific age groups toward their own behavior as well as toward the behavior of other age groups.[30] In this respect, age status represents a set of socially defined and ascribed attributes, which, at the individual level, form the basis of a validated personal identity. The increasing differentiation of age groups in the development of modern society—the invention of childhood, youth, and the third age—give rise to an ever-finer definition of age status and associated identities. A growing number of needs, motives, competencies, and qualities are attributed to the members of each given age group.

The formalization of the life course on the basis of chronological age categories is linked to a specific social effect: All the qualities and properties contained in the public definition of a given age status are attributed to the respective members of an age group, irrespective of their properties, competencies, and/or capacities as particular persons.[31] Children, for instance, are conceived of as having a specific level of intelligence—quite independent of any individual child's particular intellectual capacities. The social importance of this conception is recognized in the fact that children of a given age are required to learn the same things in school at the same speed (cf. Boli-Bennett & Meyer, 1978; Boli-Bennett et al., 1985). At the other end of the life course, the formalization of the retirement age and the corresponding cultural representation of a pensioner also illustrate this effect. Individuals of a given (advanced) chronological age are socially certified as "unable to work" (or "unfit for work")—again, an assessment quite independent of their particular work capacities.

The same logic adheres to educational degrees and professional titles: The holders of given educational or professional certificates are endowed with specific, publically recognized attributes. As Boli-Bennett et al. (1985) point out, however, there is little factual evidence to support the idea that the socially attributed competencies and actual qualities of the particular individual do correspond. Educational certificates and professional titles nevertheless engender socially constructed differences between those who possess titles and those who do not. The former are endowed with all the qualities and competencies legally guaranteed by their title, although they might not possess these qualities or competencies as (private) persons. By contrast, the latter are deprived of all these properties, although, as private individuals, they might incorporate them (Bourdieu, 1978, 1982, 1984a). In this respect, educational certificates and professional titles are less indicative of socialization processes per se and more of the state-approved authority residing in these categories (Lenhardt, 1984; Meyer, 1977; Boli-Bennett et al., 1985).

Although there may be a discrepancy between the socially validated and the actual knowledge and competency of an individual, the effect of symbolic imposition should not be underestimated. As Bourdieu (1984a, p. 25) notes, "The official differences produced by academic classifications tend to produce (or reinforce) real differences by inducing in the classified individuals a collectively recognized and supported belief in the differences, thus producing behaviors that are intended to bring real being into line with official being." In addition, the more members of a given society believe in the constructed properties, competencies, rights, and duties of given educational certificates and professional status, the more these beliefs structure the real world and bring about real differences. The social efficiency of codification systems is thus the product of individuals' dispositions to perceive and to recognize the properties and requirements of given official categories (Bourdieu, 1977c).

The cultural representations residing in certified educational and occupational categories not only offer validated social identities with regard to attributed qualities and competencies, but they also structure progression through time. Occupational categories, especially, are associated with typical developmental patterns. Although the institutionalization of occupational tracks varies considerably, the occupational categories incorporate an average structure of professional opportunities with regard to the point of entry, the sequences of professional development and related transitions, mobility chances and their timing, and the culmination of a (successful) professional career (Lappe, 1985).

The life course–related concepts introduced so far refer primarily to *institutionalized* beliefs and rules. The social structure (i.e., the distribution of *actual* behavior and the *real* patterns of progression in life) has not been taken into consideration. To fully understand how individual actors located in different social positions organize and give meaning to their lives, we must link the societal mechanisms which impose order in life (i.e., the institutionalized life course regime and the accompanying cultural representations) to the structural situation (i.e., position in the stratification system) which shapes the individual's socialization experiences and defines his or her life chances. Bourdieu's theoretical approach is useful in making that connection.

### Social Structure and Action Strategies: An Outline of Bourdieu's Theory of Practice

One of the most fundamental problems in social theory is the relationship between social structure and action, between macrosocial structure and microsocial relations. Individual actions are not unique inventions, nor are they organized only in terms of situational experiences, as the subjectivist branch of social theory assumes.[32] Actions are not the sole product of the conscious actor interacting with his or her immediate experiences. But neither are they the outcome of the mechanical determination of action imposed by social structure without any contribution from the conscious actor. "Action without actors"—the implicit assumption of the objectivist branch of social theory—thus also provides an incomplete theoretical account of the relationship between social structure and action. To avoid either theoretical bias, a social theory must acknowledge the relative autonomy of individual action from social structure and recognize that societal development is not merely the result or the sum of individual actions. To put it another way: Since both the logic of action and the logic of the social system are partially autonomous, an analysis of the relationship between structure and action is fundamental to any explanation of the social dynamic as a whole.

Bourdieu's theory of "practice" (1977b, 1980b) addresses this fundamental problem. He views structure as a prefabricated social reality confronting the individual; he simultaneously sees each actor as endowed with consciousness, capacities, and competencies for action. The theory's main concern is to develop a conceptual framework able to overcome opposition from objectivists who champion structuralism and/or functionalism as well as subjectivists who champion symbolic interactionism, ethnomethodology, and phenomenology.

To avoid these two "false alternatives," Bourdieu directs his attention to the principles of classification upon which the production and, especially, the reproduction of the social order rest. In modern society, the main social function of classification is to coordinate the intergenerational reproduction of the material conditions of existence and to legitimate social inequalities. Bourdieu assumes that the modern social order is predicated on two different principles of classification: the habitus as an *implicit* system of categorization and the principle of codification as an *explicit* system. The former is an incorporated system of classification; the latter is an objectified one (institutionalized in the form of law[33]). The two systems overlap to the extent that the objectified categories are incorporated into the habitus; but, as a principle of categorization, the habitus encompasses much more than the formalized and objectified categories. Thus, the habitus can be regarded as the fundamental principle of classification in any society.[34]

For Bourdieu (1977b, 1980b, 1984a), the habitus provides the most basic link between social structure and action. It objectively coordinates the practices between individual actors. He describes the habitus as a generative principle of objectively classifiable practices *and* a system of classificatory judgments of these practices. Thus, the habitus has the capacity to produce practices that are objectively classifiable, and it has the capacity to differentiate and to appreciate the engendered practices. Bourdieu refers to this latter aspect as "le sens pratique" (1980b). The habitus may be regarded as an acquired system of dispositions, skills, knowledge, habits, worldviews, and representations.[35]

The habitus is not a randomly acquired system; rather, it is the internalization and incorporation of one's position in the social structure and of the history of one's positions, that is, the social trajectory. Thus, the habitus is a *structured* principle in the sense that it incorporates objective conditions of the individual's position in the social structure: The internalization of the material and cultural world in terms of the past and in terms of present living conditions and experiences results in the acquisition of a structured set of skills, habits, perceptions, and actions. To use Bourdieu's *jeu de mot*: The individual's positions are related to his or her dis-positions, the objective social di-visions to the actor's visions of him/herself and the surrounding world.

If the habitus is conceived of as the incorporation of one's entire past experience in the social world, it follows that there is a *structural affinity* between the schemes of perception, appreciation, and action orientation among those individuals who have experienced a similar history of social positions (social trajectory). Bourdieu (1980b) maintains that each system of individual dispositions represents a structural variant of the system of perception, appreciation, and action acquired through the same or similar objective conditions. Although the habitus is an individual property, it is not an individually, but a socially structured phenomenon, "a logic derived from a common set of material conditions of existence to regulate the practice of a set of individuals in common response to those conditions" (Garnham & Williams, 1980, p. 213). Thus, the habitus represents a group and, especially, a class phenomenon, since the material conditions of existence depend to a great extent on position in the class structure. Differences in the same class habitus—the structural variants—reside in the singularity of one's social trajectory. The variants of the class habitus are related homologically (Bourdieu, 1984a, p. 175) in the sense of diversity in homogeneity. It is this relationship that makes it possible to recognize and identify with actors who display the same practices.

These general properties of the habitus as a structured and structuring principle of action and judgment represent Bourdieu's main conceptual tool for linking structure and action. To understand exactly how the habitus provides this linkage requires a short discussion of Bourdieu's conception of social structure and practice.

The social structure—or the social formation—is conceived of "as a hierarchically organized series of fields within which human agents are engaged in specific struggles to maximize their control over the social resources specific to that field" (Garnham & Williams, 1980, p. 215). Individuals, social groups, and social classes are interested in ensuring and enhancing their positions in these fields and, through this, in the social structure as a whole: They struggle to reproduce their own social position. Bourdieu stresses that in all societies social groups, classes, or fractions of classes struggle to maximize their specific interests in order to ensure their reproduction.

When actors enter the struggle in different fields with this aim, each field constitutes, at any point in time, a hierarchy of positions determined by a specific distribution of the field's dominant resources. Bourdieu (1983, 1984a, 1984b) refers to these resources as *capital*. In the economic field, for instance, the hierarchy of positions is determined by the distribution of material resources—economic capital. The cultural field, composed of subfields such as art, literature, philosophy, and the educational system, is characterized by the distribution of cultural capital in the *incorporated* form (legitimate knowledge, expertise, skills, habits, tastes, etc.) and in the *objectified* form (educational certificates), constituting specific relations of domination and subordination (Bourdieu, 1980c).

What is at stake in different fields is a specific form of capital over which agents try to maximize their control.[36] The more individuals or social groups accumulate different kinds of capital, the higher becomes their position in the social structure. These individuals have more resources at their disposal to influence the social environment materially as well as symbolically. In this respect, different forms of capital constitute power bases, and the distribution of capital in a given field designates the power structure. Although each field is based on a specific kind of capital and has, therefore, its own specific, relatively autonomous logic, the hierarchical organization of all fields is structured by the social field of *class struggle*. In this struggle, individuals and social groups compete for the distribution of material resources. Each subordinate field, although endowed with its own structural logic, reproduces the logic inherent in the competition for economic capital.

Bourdieu (1984a) calls this structural affinity in the social organization of different fields the *homology of fields*: The power structure (in terms of relations of domination and subordination) ultimately is dependent on economic capital. Moreover, the homology of different fields is based on the convertibility of cultural and economic capital in both directions. The exchange rates between these two forms of capital differ according to the given state of competition for different forms of capital in each field and in the social field as a whole.

The social dynamics within different fields, conceived of as changes in the distribution of positions, result from the struggle between agents attempting to gain control over the highest amount of capital in its various forms. The modes of transformation depend, to a certain extent, on the *strategy of investment* actors develop in order to maintain or enhance their position. Bourdieu starts out from the assumption that all practices—regardless of the actors' conscious intent—are ultimately directed towards the reproduction of the social position. To attain this end, agents invest their resources in such a way as to maximize their material and symbolic profits. They adopt the strategies of investment likely to yield the greatest chances for reproducing or enhancing the amount of capital at their disposal.

These strategies of investment or lines of conduct represent structured and organized sequences of action. Each action is an integrated part of the larger activity of organizing one's life. Thus, the significance of a single act can be apprehended only in its relation to the overall strategy of action.[37] Similarly, the rationality of a single act is a function of a larger strategy of action, and the rationality of a line of conduct is related to the volume and to the structure of different kinds of capital at the agent's disposal. Strategies of investment are rational, then, insofar as they yield the highest possible return given one's assets and the field's distribution of positions and power.

At any given time, each agent enters the field of struggle with given endowments or assets (dispositions, competencies, skills, and habits, as well as material resources and educational certificates). The strategies an actor engages in or the investments he or she pursues are structured by the available incorporated and objectified resources. These shape the lines of conduct an agent is most likely to adopt. As such, they function as principles of inclusion and exclusion: Strategies of investment for which one's resources and competencies are not well suited tend to be excluded—they are perceived as unsuitable. Conversely, lines of conduct that allow the individual to make maximum use of his or her own resources and skills are valued highly. In Bourdieu's (1984a) terms, agents make "a virtue of necessity." In sum, individuals invest in what they know and have mastered, in areas with which they are familiar and feel at ease. They engage in activities for which their know-how, their skills, and their habits are best suited.

Although the skills and habits of agents located in different positions in the social structure are not suited for the same ends, all individual or group investments are guided by a desire to maximize their return. There are no actions without interests—though these interests are not all economic ones. There are, according to Bourdieu (1984d), as many forms of interests as there are fields of investment: Each system of exchange has its own logic, governed by the rationale of optimal calculability. Put differently, each system of exchange in a given field is based on a specific logic yielding particular profits.[38] In sum, there is a *universalistic* tendency to maximize one's profit with a given investment, but there are also *particularistic* strategies of investment that depend on the individual's own capacities and judgments about a strategy's likely success.

This description of Bourdieu's concept of social structure and action provides the necessary background for understanding how the habitus links social structure and action. Two aspects of this linkage are directly relevant here. First, as an individually internalized—but socially structured—set of dispositions, the habitus encompasses a disposition toward the future. Through the internalization of the trajectory of his or her social position, the actor assesses the objective possibilities that the past has offered and the opportunities the present position may allow in the future. The objective chances of one's trajectory are transformed, in subjective expectations regarding the future, into what Bourdieu (1975, 1978) has called the *probabilistic logic of practice*. Individuals thus aspire to those futures that have high objective chances of being fulfilled. There is a sense of one's position, a sense of what is appropriate and what is beyond discussion. A sense of one's place in the world implies a tacit acceptance of one's position; it is an acknowledgment of limits objectively imposed. Thus, present actions are conditioned by their anticipated outcomes as well as by past experiences (Garnham & Williams, 1980). Since the habitus is largely structured by class position and by one's previous trajectory in the class structure, the disposition towards the future (in the sense of the expected future) reflects the objective chances of the collective trajectory of the social group/class to which an individual belongs. The assessment of the future in terms of the collective destiny of one's social class results in actors in similar social positions devising comparable investment strategies. Subjective expectations of one's opportunities in the future structure the individual's lines of conduct; in this sense, the strategies of action individuals choose (or happen upon) are rational.

Second, needs, perceptions, competencies, and skills acquired through experiences in the social environment provide resources as well as constraints for specific lines of action. The individual's specific expertise, habits, and skills dispose him or her toward investing in strategies of action suited to these attributes; by contrast, the lines of conduct requiring competencies and skills one does not possess are likely to be excluded a priori.

Bourdieu's ideas are summarized in Figure 1.2. Specific lines of conduct are the result of the encounter of two structures, one objectified in the particular field(s) of action, the other incorporated in the habitus. At any given time, the structure of the field contains objective probabilities of successful action and the habitus contains subjective expectations about the outcome of action in terms of the likelihood of success. The higher the correspondence between these two structures, the greater the chances for the reproduction of the social structure.

The next sections apply Bourdieu's insights, first to actual sequences of

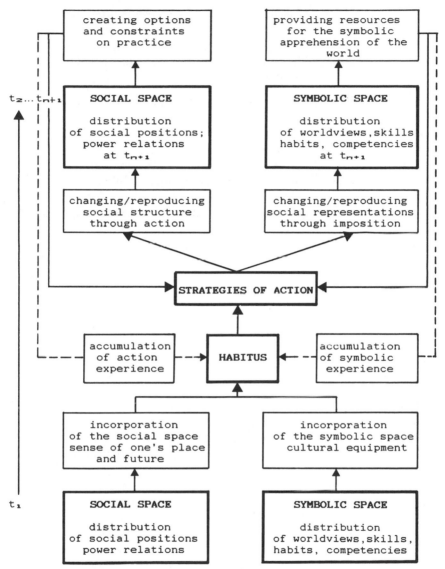

Figure 1.2. The dynamic relationship between structure and actor in Bourdieu's theory of practice.

positions and roles and then to individual biographical orientations and strategies.

### The Individual's Life Course: Actual Sequences of Positions and Roles

Discrepancies between societal norms and rules pertaining to the sequential order of status/role configurations and the individual's real linkages of positions may occur with regard to both the timing of life events (age norms and rules) and to the ranking of positions. Individual status/role configurations that depart from such societal expectations engender tensions that the actor is inclined to reduce by revising his or her action strategies.

Heintz (1972, pp. 127–139, 140–148) distinguishes three types of tensions related to particular components of the status/role configuration. One involves rank—the tension related to the struggle for upward mobility.

This refers to Bourdieu's concept of the individual's struggle to maximize his or her control over particular resources, eventually over economic capital. Linkages between positions in different social institutions that do not correspond to the institutionalized norms of equivalence (i.e., a non-equilibrated status configuration; for example, between a given educational certificate and a certain occupational status) engender action strategies aimed at realizing such norms. We may relate tensions resulting from such status configurations to Bourdieu's concept of different forms of capital for which exist, at a given time, specific rates of conversion, that is, "exchange rates" in the transformation of one form of capital into another. Actors thus try to achieve as high a "currency" as possible in the process of capital transformation. Incomplete status/role configurations refer to deviations in the number of roles and positions an individual is expected to hold at a given age/time.

This theoretical framework makes it possible to deduce a wide variety of hypotheses regarding the impact of particular types of linkages between institutionalized expectations and rules and actual configurations on individuals' biographical perspectives and strategies[39]. For example, dissimilar or time-lagging structural changes in different institutional spheres (e.g., in the educational or occupational system) may cause tensions and disturbances as transitions occur, thus affecting the likelihood of "choosing" strategies of getting "on-track" again or, on the contrary, investments aimed at pursuing alternative—"off-track"—careers.

Social group membership partly determines the likelihood and the degree of deviations from institutionalized status/role configurations. Since membership in such groups is related to the possession of particular resources and assets, it affects the action strategies: Resources, skills, habits, and so forth must be readily available in order to be successful.

Age stratification in society is a permanent force for creating discrepancies between institutionalized expectations and rules pertaining to the life course organization and individuals' actual configurations: Subsequent cohorts with unequal birthrates produce unequal life chances which "are partly unalterable 'givens' for the individuals and thus assume structural character" (Mayer, 1986, p. 169).

## Biographical Orientations and Strategies

Biographical orientations and strategies are formed on the basis of both the actual status/role configuration and the codified elements of the life course (i.e., the objective classifications), which constitute the officially recognized, public life trajectory. Age status, educational certificates, and professional titles function as "landmarks" for subjective biographical orientations and strategies.

At the individual level, members of a given age group or the holders of specific educational certificates or professional titles are recognized by the public as possessing certain qualities and competencies, and they are treated accordingly. The public signals, as well, that these individuals are entitled to specific expectations toward their own futures: Their claims to material profits and symbolic recognition are legitimated. The social validation of symbolic (identity) and material (income) claims, however, implies that the claimant must act toward him/herself as well as toward others according to the guaranteed attributes. As Bourdieu (1984a, p. 25) notes, "Individuals are called upon to really procure the attributes assigned to them by their status." Official classifications thus structure the individual's own expectations and aspirations as well as what others expect of him or her (Bourdieu, 1982). In this sense, the individual's social identity and his or her biographical perspectives are the more secure and stabilized the more they can be reinforced in publicly recognized categories. Conversely, the more the individual experiences insecurities with regard to his or her identity and biographical perspectives, the less his or her social position and corresponding attributes are officially recognized.

For example, educational certificates represent socially recognized opportunities of access to specific occupational positions and as such foster material as well as symbolic expectations and aspirations. The more closely regulated the relationship between the occupational category and the educational certificate, the clearer the individual's expectations about professional work, social prestige, and income. The transformation of educational certificates into occupational status on the labor market is not an automatic process. It has to be individually realized. It is at that point that the *real* social value of an educational certificate is established on the labor market.[40] Social attributes such as social class membership and gender play an important role in defining the "exchange rate" or the "rate of conversion:" The value of an educational certificate on the labor market is as high as the social value of its holder (Bourdieu, 1978). The chances for redeeming professional entitlements inherent in an educational certificate depend on the economic and social resources, that is, the economic and cultural assets, an individual can mobilize. They are all the more dependent on these attributes, the greater the divergence between the number of certified candidates and the number of corresponding occupational positions.

Similarly, the socially defined occupational trajectories constitute the frame of reference for the individual's professional biography. They define what is attainable and what is beyond reach in the course of a professional life. Individuals orient their plans and actions toward the steps and sequences of the professional trajectory, and they reorient themselves each time they complete a step. The more highly regulated professional trajectories are, the more these features may be anticipated and predicted. They present individuals with clear-cut alternatives from which to choose, using their past experiences and their present needs as guides. Overall, individuals judge their own professional accomplishments with regard to these socially standardized trajectories (Hartmut Wolf et al., 1985). In this way, socially constructed occupational development patterns shape the individual's expectations and aspirations—they offer a biographical identity.

In the case of less well structured occupational trajectories, there are only vague, informal ideas about the course of the professional life. Such trajectories contain a higher amount of contingency; they are less calculable and predictable. They do not permit a clear apprehension of occupational attainments nor do they allow for timing the professional life. Accordingly, the biographical identity structures associated with these occupational tracks are likely to be diffuse.

Moreover, the temporal structuring of the professional life in highly institutionalized trajectories establishes well-defined timetables that function as schedules for the timing of events in the individual life. In the case of highly sequenced, lifelong professional trajectories, especially, the biographical time perspective seems to be very long and the present is experienced as an outcome of the past that leads to the future. The linearity of the professional trajectory is reflected in the subjective experience of time.

By contrast, discontinuous trajectories are less suited to act as a framework within which the past, the present, and the future may be related in a linear way (Brose, 1982, 1984, 1985a). Such trajectories are likely to engender short time horizons and action orientations aimed toward the present.

Highly institutionalized trajectories equip individuals with stable expectations and aspirations toward their own future (Mayer & Müller, 1986; Meyer, 1986b). They represent secure frameworks and provide criteria for deciding what is (socially) within reach and what is unattainable. The status and trajectory of a child or a pensioner, for instance, is very well defined in terms of the granted attributes, competencies, skills, and needs. Thus, it may be hypothesized that the increasing institutionalization of the life course gives rise to the growing calculability and predictability of sequential steps in the course of life, structuring the individual's expectations, aspirations, and claims. Given a secure framework, in the sense of an externally induced reality to be taken into account, individuals tend to internalize and to respect the social limits encoded in the institutionalized trajectories. Two conclusions follow: First, the individual's identification with the objectively given trajectory tends to be high, since the clearly structured sequences of positions and roles provide a framework for constructing secure and stable representations of one's self, one's biography, and the social world. Second, highly institutionalized trajectories tend to be very well delineated from each other, producing a high structural affinity in the life courses of individuals endowed with similar social attributes, resources, skills, and competencies. This structural condition provides the background against which the individualized life course is inscribed in the "collective destiny" of one's social group (Bourdieu, 1975). As Bahrdt (1975, p. 25) notes, an individual's participation in the collective history of his or her social group is mediated by his or her own personal destiny; and, conversely, the collective destiny of the social group helps explain the steps and sequences of the individual's personal life. In sum, the social and biographical identity of the individual is highly embedded in the collective identity of the social groups to which he or she belongs.

The category of biographical perspectives, that is, the conscious and practical appropriation of one's past, present, and future, makes (social) sense only against the background of the institutionalized and individualized life course. Under these social conditions the life course is conceptualized as "a coherent career and is believed to be determined by individual decision, effort, and ability" (Lenhardt, 1985, p. 15).

"Life plans" or biographical perspectives are the outcome of two interrelated aspects. On one hand, individuals devise their plans against the background of socially defined trajectories. The steps and sequences of such careers—especially in professional life but also in private life—set the objective frame within which the construction of one's future takes place. On the other hand, individual biographical projects are structured by past experiences which help determine future development. Individuals compare the objective opportunities incorporated in an institutionalized trajectory[41] with their previous personal attainments.

It is especially at objectively defined career steps and transitions that individuals are likely to make such comparisons and thus call deliberate attention to "life plans" and "life designs." Such situations are socially induced triggers for a deliberate reflection on past experiences and future prospects so that individuals may restate biographical projects or reassure themselves of their plans, which function as a guideline for action (cf. Kohli, 1981b; Kohli & Robert, 1984; König & Schumm, 1985; Jürgen Wolf et al., 1985). Individuals thus act in a biographical perspective, that is, applying their biographical strategies at such "switchpoints" of the biographical trajectory.

The subjective construction of biographical projects against the background of objective opportunities and subjective experiences may be interpreted as the individual's choice among structurally given alternatives. Such a theoretical conception of biographical orientations and strategies allows for the integration of structural and subjective aspects in the study of the life course,[42] that is, for the linkage between structure and action.

# 2

## Contemporary Societal Transformations and the Changing Nature of the Life Course

The life course in modern society has been described in the preceding chapter as consisting of institutionalized (and hence well-structured) sequences of events, positions, and roles which shape the individual's progression in social time and space. It is in this sense that it is possible to speak of the standardization of the life course as the rationalization of life in modern society. The discovery of each new life stage is accompanied by the cultural definition of needs, competencies, tasks, and behaviors thought to be appropriate for individuals belonging to a given age group. Such officially recognized attributes constitute the basic elements of individual identity. Within this structural and cultural setting, individuals use their resources and assets to plan their actions, acknowledging the opportunities and constraints inherent in their social positions.

This conceptual framework permits us to examine now the linkages between institutional transformations and shifts in life course patterns in contemporary society. This chapter explores the ways in which social change in education, work, and the family over the last two decades has provoked modifications in the social structuring of the life course. Recent shifts in cultural imagery in the private sphere of life (specifically, love ideology) and in the public sphere (specifically, work ideology) are evaluated in order to gain insight into the process by which the symbolic contents of particular life stages (especially adulthood) are redefined. I show how these structural and cultural transformations in the life course may be related to the accelerated pace of rationalization and individualization that characterizes advanced industrial societies. My analysis would be incomplete, however, if I did not integrate this macrosociological approach with an actor-oriented perspective. The concluding sections of this chapter thus deal with the ways in which individuals organize and enact their lives within the changed social contexts.

Before examining these substantial topics, it is necessary to discuss in

43

more detail how I conceptualize the dynamic interplay between institutional transformations and changing life course patterns.

Alterations in the organization of the life course may be prompted by demographic, technological, economic, political, and cultural changes in society. Developments in different social institutions and transformations of the cultural meaning system lead to changes in the formal (i.e., legal) and informal (e.g., social timetables) structuring of the life course and in cultural representations of life stages. Asynchronous change in the economic, political, or family system, for example, induces "leads and lags" in the time- and status-related aspects of life course organization, thus fostering further change in the life course regime. In a similar way, demographic changes, such as differences in the size of successive cohorts, necessitate adaptations in different institutional spheres, which in turn give rise to further alterations in life course structuring. Such shifts in the structural and cultural setting of the life course affect the subjective construction of biographical perspectives and strategies. At the aggregate level, alterations in the ways in which individuals devise their plans and work out their progression in social time and space exert a collective force for social- and life course–related change.

People born in the same year (i.e., a birth cohort) share a unique slice of history. That is, they share a particular sequence of economic, political, and cultural events and phases in the societal development (Riley, 1982, 1986). This time- and context-specific social conditioning helps shape the ways in which members of a given cohort confront problems in their lives and give meaning to their own biographies. Based on the opportunities and constraints both of their social positions and of their historical times, cohort members develop distinct biographical orientations and strategies for managing the inequalities in education, occupations, and even marital opportunities that confront them. At the aggregate level, these responses constitute incentives for change in the institutionalized elements of the life course. Shifts in the size of successive cohorts, moreover, may provoke tensions between different age groups in society.[1] Members of differently sized age groups struggle over the redefinition of age-appropriate practices. The outcomes of these contests may ultimately affect the cultural representation of life stages (e.g., the redefinition of achievement norms among the elderly) and lead to new institutionalized rights and obligations for particular age groups (e.g., retirement age).

Not only do differences *between* cohorts influence the ways in which people respond to particular life course–related demands and problems, but specific constellations *within* cohorts (e.g., sex ratio, race and social

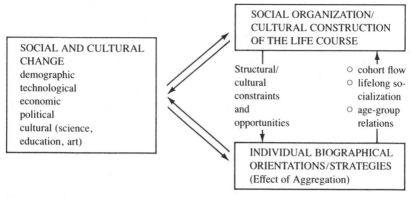

Figure 2.1. Dynamic interplay between social change and the social construction and individual organization of the life course.

class composition) may also give rise to altered biographical orientations and strategies. In addition, as individuals progress through social time and space, they continuously accumulate experiences: Socialization is lifelong. If these individual experiences—especially among members of successive cohorts—have some features in common, they may crystallize into a collective consciousness and lead to (collective) action on life course–related problems (e.g., social security legislation, voting age, educational policy). Figure 2.1 illustrates an analytical approach to the dynamic interplay between social change and alterations in social and individual life course organization. This approach is necessarily schematic. The actual relationship between changes at the macro- and microlevels of society are highly complex. Alterations in the way individuals progress through social time and space are not related directly to changes in institutionalized elements of the life course. Rather, they are outcomes of the aggregation of individual needs and interests, some form of organizational representation (e.g., pressure groups), and the balance of power between social groups favoring and opposing the intended changes. Changes in institutionalized elements, however, do not necessarily have an effect on individual life course organization. There may be great discrepancies between the institutionalized norms and the structural reality.

We turn now to an exploration of the influences recent social changes have exerted on the social construction and individual organization of the life course, looking first at trends in the development of higher education as an institutional domain.[2]

## Contradictory Effects of Education as a
## Credentialing System

Over the last twenty years, the system of higher education has expanded rapidly in highly developed industrial societies (Lutz, 1983; Lenhardt, 1984; Burris, 1983; Barnhouse-Walters, 1984; Oeuvrard, 1984). Others have analyzed this expansion in detail (see Bourdieu, 1985b; Boli-Bennett et al., 1985; Amos, 1985; Perrenoud, 1985; Tully & Wahler, 1985); here I stress two aspects. On one hand, the educational expansion is linked to the increasing professionalization of the occupational structure; on the other hand, it reflects changing educational investment behavior of individuals.

Increasing professionalization is predicated on state-sanctioned professional status, which, in turn, is tied to educational certificates. Access to a growing number of occupational positions is monitored through educational credentials (Collins, 1971, 1979). The individual's status allocation in the occupational structure is determined in great measure by the possession of educational degrees. With the growing professionalization of work—tantamount to state regulation of the labor market (Lenhardt, 1984, 1985)—schools and the labor market become closely linked: Professional success is more and more dependent on educational achievement.

Increasingly, market principles of status allocation have been replaced by bureaucratically defined rules regulating access to occupational positions (Lenhardt, 1985). As a consequence, individual chances of mobility are dependent less on performance and more on educational credentials. The expanding system of educational certificates does not, however, correspond perfectly with the growth of equivalent occupational positions. Thus, the coordination of the educational and occupational system becomes more problematic (Blossfeld, 1983). Bureaucratically determined status allocation persists sufficiently to produce structural tensions which have an impact on individual behavior.

The increasing dependence of occupational status on educational certificates causes individuals to make higher educational investments in order to enhance their chances for acquiring occupational status. A generalized increase in educational demands engenders what Bourdieu (1978) and Collins (1979) have called "the inflation of educational certificates." A structural concomitant of the overproduction of educational degrees is their continuous devaluation (Affichard, 1981); this produces even higher educational demands as individuals struggle to achieve as high an educational degree as possible (Amos, 1985; Perrenoud, 1985; Mertens, 1984). Individuals must intensify their educational investments and must do so under conditions of diminishing prospects for equivalent returns. In sum, aggravated competition for educational certificates and the accompanying inflation and gradual devaluation of educational titles in the labor market have become a structural constant in advanced industrial society (Collins, 1979). They are self-perpetuating processes engendering ever-new shifts in the relations between educational title and occupational status.

Barnhouse-Walters (1984) offers an alternative explanation for the expansion of the educational system. She points to the "warehousing function" of schools in periods in which the labor market is "tight" and assumes that school enrollments are at least partially a function of simultaneous—as opposed to future—work opportunities. Higher school retention rates are not only the result of the desire for more education but also a reaction to declining employment prospects. Her argument stresses the fact that schools compete *concurrently* with paid work. Accordingly, school enrollment rates should vary with changes in the occupational structure, employment patterns, and work opportunities. The results of her empirical analysis indicate short-term occupational effects on schooling in periods in which schooling is discretionary, that is, "when the choice between work and school is a real alternative" (p. 669).

Since school enrollments have historically risen over time, the argument that schools act as "warehouses" or as "waiting rooms" for otherwise unoccupied individuals does not contradict the credentials-inflation thesis. Rather, the warehousing function of schools raises the minimal standard of educational attainment over time, which, in turn, affects the certification requirements for specific occupational positions. These changes may again stimulate the demand for more education. Barnhouse-Walters's argument is thus an incisive explanation of *one* of the mechanisms through which the credentials inflation is produced.

This inflation and devaluation of educational titles necessarily produces groups of individuals who are "misplaced" in the social structure, or who are afraid of becoming misplaced. These mismatches between individuals endowed with certified qualities and their positions in the social structure represent imbalanced status configurations (see Chapter 1, "The Individual's Life Course: Actual Sequences of Positions and Roles"). They do not correspond to the socially defined norms of equivalence between educational title and occupational status. Alterations in these *actual* exchange relations in the labor market have a delayed impact on the educational system. Because of this lag, discrepancies arise with regard to the expectations, aspirations, and claims imparted by the educational system and the real value of educational degrees on the labor market: The gap between the *expected* and the *real* convertibility of educational titles into occupational roles widens considerably. Moreover, the discrepancy between expected and real exchange rates is greater the higher the devaluation of educational certificates. The degree of devaluation can be assessed as the indirect proportional increase in the number of holders of a given educational degree and the number of corresponding occupational positions.

From the individual's perspective, these shifting exchange relations affect the calculability and predictability of educational and occupational trajectories and, especially, the transitions between these two institutional spheres. They are less predictable the more the educational entitlements have been subject to devaluation during the time between entry into and exit from an educational track.[3] Overall, the structural tensions between educational title and occupational status contribute to an increasing individualization of career tracks. This is not only the result of less predictable trajectories, but also is due to the individualizing effects of increased competition for educational degrees (Beck, 1983; Hartmut Wolf et al., 1985) and to the longer stay in such situations as educational trajectories expand rapidly. In addition, individualizing effects are introduced by the increasingly ambivalent (social and individual) meaning of schooling, as the future payoffs of educational investments grow more insecure (Baethge, 1985). The increasing frictions between educational certificate and occupational status result in the increasing dissociation between institutionalized and actual status/role sequences, thus amounting to a partial destandardization of actual life courses.

## The Changing Structure of Occupational Careers

Within the occupational system, there are also indications of less stable career trajectories. Three structural factors that contribute to this destabilization in occupational status/role sequences are discussed below.

First, the number of workplaces has decreased since the beginning of the 1970s (Bonss & Heinze, 1984; Matthes, 1982; Offe, 1984). Unemployment due to structural (technological) change or to economic factors undermines the "lifelong" integration in the occupational system that has characterized male occupational careers since World War II (Müller, 1978). Thus, the individual's movement through the occupational system is gradually losing its highly standardized form. Male occupational careers are beginning to take on the "chaotic" forms of professional trajectories previously found exclusively in female professional tracks. Of course, the probability of unemployment due to structural or economic factors is highly dependent on an individual's occupational status (see Heinze et al., 1981), age (see Lenhardt, 1979; Baethge et al., 1980, 1983; Apel, 1984; Beckenbach, 1984; Hills & Reubens, 1983; Affichard & Amal, 1984; for studies of unemployment among older workers, see Bonss & Riedmüller, 1982; Brinkmann, 1982; Wacker, 1982), and sex (see Huet & Monnier, 1984). Men with high occupational status continue to be more likely to experience stable and standardized professional trajectories endowed with high calculability and predictability (Eichhorn et al., 1981).

Less stable occupational careers result not only from the greater likelihood of unemployment, but also from the introduction of certain new technologies. Technology that is based on microelectronics, in particular, seems to affect the temporal validity of professional qualifications and competencies (Buck, 1985; Brock & Vetter, 1984; Negt, 1984). Buck's analysis of the relationship between vocational qualifications and new technologies suggests an acceleration in the pace at which vocational qualifications are being socially devaluated. He argues that this accelerated obsolescence is due to the gradual automation of those elements of vocational work susceptible to standardization and formalization. Lappe (1985) observes that the more professional qualifications are geared to specific methods of production and/or to specific machines, the greater the likelihood that they will be susceptible to rationalization. Accordingly, individuals in professions with a disproportionate share of such elements risk the loss of their professional qualifications as well as unemployment.[4]

With the increase in automation, there has been a rise in the number of occupations that can no longer guarantee long-term (in the extreme, lifelong) occupational stability (i.e., job security provided by vocational qualifications; Lappe, 1985). Changes in the occupational structure no longer coincide with the exchange of generations in the labor market (Müller, 1983). The cycles of innovations have become much shorter, thus reducing the "half-life" of the validity of professional qualifications. Given accelerated obsolescence of professional expertise, the image of a profession providing a long-term perspective that incorporates high calculability and predictability tends to lose social significance (Projektgruppe Automation und Qualifikation, 1983; Brose, 1984). Although occupational mobility has always been an important aspect of work careers[5]—due both to upward mobility chances and to economic recessions—increasingly structural obsolescence of occupational qualifications introduces new elements both in the *social* construction of occupational careers and mobility paths and in the *individual* strategy for coping with work life.

The rapidly decreasing half-life of the usability of acquired expertise gives rise to short-term work perspectives and induces a relatively high degree of occupational insecurity and, accordingly, a relatively low degree of calculability and predictability. These tendencies are likely to affect the kind of social commitment individuals make toward their work[6] and the relevance individuals attribute to their work lives.[7] A further inducement to short-term work perspectives is that the social devaluation of professional competencies is not within the control of those professionals who hold these now-obsolete qualifications. Instead, it is dependent on external factors such as the global economic situation and international competition, as well as on management's decisions regarding further automation. In this respect, unstable occupational trajectories are beyond individual control; they are the result of structural discontinuities.

This new structural situation imposes a twofold constraint on the individual's scope of action with regard to work-related biographical orientations and strategies. Individuals with vocations in professions likely to become automated are forced to invest in further professional qualifications in order to preserve the marketability of their labor. This professional updating, however, occurs in a social situation that is characterized by great flux in employment. Individuals thus must renew their professional qualifications (to try to avoid their devaluation), and they must also overcome the constraints of specialization. They must acquire qualifications that open up as broad a range of employment opportunities as possible (Mertens & Kaiser, 1978). This furthers the tendency toward the individualization of the professional updating. An important manifestation of this process is the transfer of professional updating investments into leisure time (Negt, 1984; Brock & Vetter, 1984).

Overall, individuals are compelled to invest in further professional qualifications in a structural situation that offers few chances for corresponding returns: The convertibility of professional investments into occupational positions and, finally, into financial rewards is highly uncertain. The social demands on the individual induced by structural changes in the occupational sphere match those in the educational system: It is necessary to invest in educational certificates or further professional qualifications with uncertain prospects of gaining corresponding rewards.

One positive aspect of this process is that the repeated renewal of professional qualifications may foster a proliferation of work-related biographical alternatives, producing a greater flexibility of occupational trajectories and enhancing the individual's scope of action. Decisions about the acquisition of new professional qualifications and their combination and about the timing of investments in professional updating are becoming more dependent on individual action strategies. Innovative behavior (i.e., forward-looking mix of professional qualifications, right timing of investments), although risky, can result in good career advancement possibilities.

To discuss the effects of new technologies solely in terms of continuity versus discontinuity of professional trajectories would be overstating the case. This is only one aspect of the complex and profound transformations of the occupational system now occurring. Another probable impact of technology, on which most scholars agree,[8] is the increasing polarization of the structure of qualification and, as a consequence, of the labor market. What is likely to emerge is a smaller, highly qualified work force with stable work prospects alongside a larger, marginal work force that experiences more and more short-term employment and uncertain work prospects. Radical segregation of the labor market will further individualize and diversify work situations and occupational trajectories.

In addition to the decrease in the number of workplaces and the impact of new technologies, a third group of structural factors contributes to the partial destandardization and destabilization of professional trajectories. These factors are directly and indirectly related to the emergence, over the past twenty years, of "the new professions" (Bourdieu, 1978, 1984a). Although the growth of these new jobs affects only a small proportion of the occupational structure, it is a noteworthy phenomenon.[9]

Emerging professions, having not yet acquired social recognition, represent "zones of structural uncertainty" (Bourdieu, 1978). They are not yet linked to well-defined professional trajectories with specific rules of access, acknowledged levels of social prestige, and calculable income chances. Due to weakly institutionalized exchange relations between investments and rewards, the new professions give rise to biographical strategies with a short time perspective. Structural uncertainties engender in the individual open-ended visions of opportunities; flexibility is highly valued in order to preserve as many opportunities as possible. It follows that professional expectations, aspirations, and claims are structurally ill-defined because of the underdetermined relationship between the expected and the real chances associated with the professional trajectories of these occupations. As a result, an individual's strategies may reflect either over- or underestimation of structural chances.[10] With respect to the former, biographical strategies are based on anticipation of professional careers for which few chances objectively exist; the unrealistic aspirations soon conflict with the realities of the labor market. In the opposite case, structural opportunities are not perceived and, as a result, structural chances are not utilized. In both cases, the objective uncertainties of professional opportunities give rise to highly fluid biographical perspectives.

### Diversification of Family Life

Over the past twenty years, major demographic changes in family life have been observed in all highly developed industrial societies.[11] The following changes, especially, have been noted: decreasing rates of first marriage, increasing mean variation of age at first marriage, increasing divorce rates,[12] decreasing rates of remarriage, increasing divorce rates of remarriage, increasing dispersal of mother's age at first childbearing, increasing rates of single parents, declining birthrates, and reduced periods of childrearing and prolonged periods of the "empty nest." These changes indicate the increasing variety in contemporary living arrangements (Hoffmann-Nowotny, 1987, 1980a; Beck, 1985; Hareven, 1983; Held, 1986; Kohli, 1986; Lüscher, 1985; Meyer & Schulze, 1983). They affect not only actual family careers, in terms of status/role sequences, but also the meaning given to family life.

Although these global demographic shifts are signs of social change within the family, they are not distributed equally over the entire population. They are dependent on the family's social class background and the educational attainment of men and women. Deviations from the highly standardized and highly predictable family cycle occur not only at the lower end of the social hierarchy, but also at the upper end—the educated strata in urban settings. In this respect, the bourgeois or traditional family consisting of "a man and a woman (married to each other) as parents and their child/children" (Hoffmann-Nowotny, 1987, p. 4) is losing ground to diversified and pluralized family models.

These demographic changes are partially the result of rapid structural and cultural changes, which have further undermined the functional importance of the family.[13] As noted earlier (see Chapter 1, "Rationalization of the Economy and the Polity"), the state has rapidly taken over functions previously fulfilled by the family. Except for the early years of childhood, the formal, state-run educational system oversees socialization. Large areas of family interaction have become obsolete as the welfare state has taken over "protective and welfare functions" previously available only through the family. The decline of the family enterprise (Lenoir, 1985a) has helped weaken the constituent base of the family. Instead of the previously common collective production, family members today share only collective consumption (Hoffmann-Nowotny, 1987, p. 54).

The most important impact on the family, however, has been the widespread education of women, particularly the increase in the number of women with advanced education. In addition to working-class women, who have always joined the labor force for family-related economic reasons, women with middle- or upper-class background and higher educational degrees have been investing their educational capital in the labor market over the last twenty years.[14] An increasing proportion of these women continue to stay in the labor market after marriage and childbirth. In fact, the increase in women's employment rate is directly associated with the sharp decrease in the number of women who quit professional work after marriage and childbirth (Lefaucheur, 1982; Skolnick & Skolnick, 1983). Thus, the changed status of women has contributed significantly to both the decreasing stability of the family cycle and the growing interest in new family models. As individuals become less and less dependent on the family with regard to existential needs and interests, the structural and cultural "necessity" or "compulsion" for the traditional (bourgeois) family model steadily dissolves. The lack of structural and cultural support increases the individual scope of action for establishing "private relationships." The increasing variety and complexity of living arrangements today "can be regarded as an outcome of deliberate and individualized choices" (Hoffmann-Nowotny, 1987, p. 49).

In this sense, the reduced stability of family careers (evident in rapidly increasing divorce rates and decreasing rates of remarriage) partly reflects the diminishing dependence of women on the family (Swidler, 1980; Leupold, 1983; Boigeol et al , 1984; Held, 1986). As women enter the labor force on a longer-term and more uninterrupted basis, they become less economically dependent on marriage and the family as a lifelong institution. Thus, the terms of private relationships become open to negotiation between partners, and the vows exchanged at the time of marriage are no longer considered irrevocable. The economic independence of women and men eases the way to dissolve marriages in instances where these unions no longer fulfill mutual needs and interests. In sum, the changed status of women in society contributes to the increasing flexibility of family trajectories, which, at the same time, reflects the *gradual individualization of the female life course* (Beck-Gernsheim, 1982, 1983, 1986; Ley, 1984).[15] Decreasing female dependence on the family (i.e., on a man) as a result of greater financial independence holds, however, only for a minority of women—the well-educated. Thus, the declining stability of the traditional (bourgeois) family must also be nurtured by changes in men's roles. In fact, the "crisis of the family" is as much a product of the changes in masculine roles as it is the result of the changed status of women in society.

In the traditional masculine role model, men were expected to marry, to support a wife and children, and to sustain a long-term commitment to the family. According to Ehrenreich (1983), this ideology of men-as-breadwinners has deteriorated over the last twenty years. To postpone marriage and to avoid women who are likely to become financial dependents are more and more socially acceptable behaviors for men. Ehrenreich thus regards the decreasing willingness of men to be the only breadwinner for the family and to support a wife and children as the male "contribution" to the declining stability of the traditional family. Men's "flight from long-term commitment" to women (and thus from the long-term emotional responsibility toward women) is the male revolt against the core of the traditional masculine role.

This male revolt has structural causes. Ehrenreich identifies the dissolution of what she calls the principle of the family wage system as the major cause of the deterioration of the breadwinner ethic. According to this principle, which greatly structured the economic relations between the sexes in the middle of the twentieth century, the male wage should be high enough to support a family at the (socially defined) average living standard. This principle has never been fully realized, and it has lost ground rapidly over the last twenty years. Ehrenreich notes that in the United States, men's wages are often insufficient to support a family.

The decline of high-paid "men's jobs" has been accompanied, however, by the growth of low-paid "women's jobs." [16] The economic consequences of men's rejection of the breadwinner ideology fall squarely on women. Since most are locked into low-paid "women's jobs," they encounter financial difficulties if they divorce. [17] Society still denies most women the possibility of successfully fulfilling the role of the family breadwinner. Women in high-paid career jobs are an exception; ironically, they seldom have to support a family. Single mothers who raise and support children on their own are the fastest-growing group that falls below the poverty line in the United States (Ehrenreich, 1983). Newcomers to the welfare system include women who were middle class until they divorced and encountered difficulties in making a living on their own—a group Ehrenreich calls the "suburban nouvelles pauvres." Therefore, under conditions of a sex-segregated labor market, the male revolt against the breadwinner ideology results in the "feminization of poverty" (Pearce, 1978).

The declining stability of the traditional family thus may be regarded as the result of two opposing tendencies that affect women differently according to their social class background and their level of schooling: The higher the woman's social position and education is, the lower is her *willingness* to "put all her eggs in one basket" (i.e., the family); women with low social family backgrounds and low level of schooling, on the other hand, can no longer count on a man's lifelong willingness to support a family.

These tendencies indicate that, in the future, women either will prefer to rely on or will be forced to rely on their own resources more. In addition, with the growing "feminization of the sex ratio" among the elderly, it is "rational for women to expect to be single and to have to rely on their own resources for an extended period of their lives" (Held, 1986, p. 161).

The heightened interest in "new family models," including cohabitation and single parents; new types of exchange relations between partners, such as changes in the division of labor inside and outside the household; and new images and representations, in the social definition of love and sexuality for instance, accompany the changes described above, as well as those in the educational and occupational system. They affect family behavior and, especially, the female scope of action.

Lefaucheur (1982) explains the heightened interest of well-educated women in these "new family models." She interprets their willingness to stay in the labor market after marriage and childbearing as a biographical strategy to secure the inherited or expected social status of the family. The exploitation of female educational capital in the labor market instead of in the marriage market is a reaction to the expansion of the educational system, which was not followed by a comparable increase in the number of occupational positions requiring higher education (see the discussion in this chapter, "Contradictory Effects of Education as a Credentialing System"). The investment of female educational capital in the labor market makes it possible for the family to counter threatening downward mobility due to men's lowered chances of finding status-securing jobs. In this sense, the capital investment represents a strategy for reproducing the social position of the family, that is, a strategy of reclassification (Bourdieu, 1978). The success of this strategy, however, depends to a great extent on women's capacity to coordinate and synchronize their professional and family careers (Gerson, 1985; Hoffmann-Nowotny et al., 1984). The emergence of new family models and the corresponding representations may be regarded as factors that enable and facilitate this task. The rapid expansion of these new models also underscores the validity of this interpretation.

## Rationalization of Lifetime: The Impact of New Information Technologies

Current social change in different institutional fields is likely to affect the social construction of time. Its potential impact on the time structure of the life course is discussed below.[18]

The rationalization of time is an important aspect of the development of modern society. It is reflected, for instance, in the *chronology* of life. As a socially ruled sequence of events, positions, and roles based on the individual's chronological age, the life course objectifies time as a rational structure that also impinges upon the subjective perception of time.

Work life is directly linked to the rationalized economy and thus is subject to a "time economy" (i.e., the economical utilization of time). The private life course has been much less affected by the rational calculability of time. This distinction is becoming blurred. The practical application of new technologies—especially new information and communication technologies—contributes to a further rationalization of the (entire) life course that affects the subjective experience and use of time.

Most of the discussions by social scientists of the recent transformation induced by new technologies (especially those based on microelectronics) have focused on the effects of these technologies on the employment rate, on the structure of work qualifications, and on the mechanization of human communication. Less attention has been paid to the question of how the new technologies affect the objective and subjective structure of time. Hoffmann's (1982) study of the relationship between new information and communication technologies and the new economy of the lifetime is a notable exception. She argues that these new technologies represent not only an organizational but also a societal rationalization strategy. They are potentially able to reorganize lifetime as well as to restructure work.

In the service occupations, especially, the application of new information and communication technologies [19] bears the potential for restructuring work in a fundamental way by making the production of services less dependent on time and space (Staudt, 1984; Beck, 1985). The spatial and temporal decentralization of work is a very likely consequence. Furthermore, work tasks may be transferred into the individual's leisure time without losing their meaning as work. These implications are discussed below, since they are directly related to the question of the further rationalization of lifetime.

The decreasing dependence of work performance on time and space in the production of services represents a cost-saving strategy.[20] It is likely to result in the decentralization of work*places* and work *hours*. This division is further reflected in such terms as new homework, flextime, temporary work, job sharing, and annual work time contracts (Mertens & Kaiser, 1978; Heinze et al., 1984; Negt, 1984; Schmid, 1985). Although the reorganization of the time patterns of work is far from complete, it does indicate a social trend toward an increased flexibility in work time. These new temporal forms challenge, on one side, the model of lifelong (career-like) occupation and lifelong (uninterrupted) employment that has regulated the time structure of the occupational biography (Brose, 1982). On the other side, increased flexibility of working hours undermines the standard work day, which represents the core of the worker's existence (Berger, 1985).[21] Increased variation in individual working hours with regard to their location, duration, and distribution in time amounts to an individualization of the work day.[22] As a result, the relationship between work time and nonwork time is changing.

The application of new information and communication technologies decentralizes work with respect to time and space. It also affects the distribution of work tasks across individual workers. It facilitates the transfer of professional duties to "new housework" (Ostner & Wilms, 1982), so that work tasks previously defined as elements of professional work roles—and as such paid work—are now individually performed outside of official work time. Services previously offered by professional suppliers (e.g., certain services provided by banks and insurance companies) today are the province of "private" individuals. This shift from paid labor to private work[23] constitutes a major cost-saving strategy for private enterprise. It also affects the content of professional work roles and the relationship between the individual's work role and his or her leisure role. Its major impact, however, is on the reorganization of the relationship between work time and nonwork time. This influences both the social time structure and subjective experience with time and its use (Brose, 1982, 1984).

The individualization of working hours and the substitution of labor affect the social time structure by reducing the differences between the time structure that predominates in the professional world and the one that prevails in the private realm of life. Until recently, family and leisure time has been at least partially exempt from the continuous rationalization of time that has accompanied the development of modern society. Now, public and private time structures tend to merge, as the boundaries between professional and private life courses dissolve. This interpenetration of time structures leads to the reorganization of time in the entire life course. Specifically, the imperatives of calculability that govern the professional life penetrate the private sphere; social time patterns are restructured on the basis of the rational time logic characteristic of the professional life. This means that time that previously was more or less individually controlled and autonomously organized in private life is now slowly being subsumed into a common standard time applicable to the entire life course. Modern society is witnessing the gradual triumph of the imperatives of economical time utilization. It is against this background that the impact of the changing time structure on the subjective experience of time must be understood.

The gradual individualization of working hours makes the mediation between work and nonwork time—the synchronization between the public and private spheres of life—more dependent on individual action. Thus, the ways in which the individual manages his or her time and copes with time shortages (and overages) become increasingly important. Since the individual is more and more responsible for mediating the time overlap between the public and private course of life, he or she has to invest more in coordinating various lines of action. Competent coping skills with respect to the use of time become one of the most important resources for the organization of action. The appropriate timing of action, the "timing of life" (Hoffmann, 1982), is the concrete expression of the further rationalization of the life course: The individual's action orientation in public and private is subject to the logic of economical time use.

If the entire organization of life becomes subsumed under the rationale of economical time use; if the right timing of action is one of the most important resources in the individual's organization of the life course; and if the coordination, mediation, and synchronization of various lines of action are increasingly the responsibility of the individual actor and his or her competent use of time, the question arises whether the further rationalization of lifetime enhances or restricts the individual's sovereignty over time. Does it increase or diminish the amount of time at the actor's disposal?

There is no clear-cut answer to this question. On one side, the further rationalization of lifetime does increase time sovereignty, since the individual is now able, for instance, to structure work schedules according to his or her own interests and needs. On the other side, flexible working hours—individually chosen arrangements between work and nonwork time—put more pressure on the individual in terms of action coordination and synchronization dominated by the imperatives of the economical use of time. In Weberian terminology, the timing of life is induced "from without." The individual has little or no control over standards of time utilization. In this respect, the individual is not really in charge of the organization of time and, hence, does not have more time at his or her disposal. In sum, the further rationalization of lifetime—the subordination of the entire life course under the rationale of economical time use—is a double-edged process: As the synchronization of various lines of action grows more dependent on the individual actor, this same synchronization must be done according to predetermined standards of time use. Which side of this process will eventually predominate depends in some degree on the social characteristics (e.g., social class background, sex, age) of the affected actors.

Interestingly, to the extent that flexible work time structures are in place today, they are found particularly in women's workplaces and in jobs occupied predominantly by youths.[24] Women are used to coping with time competently (Ostner & Wilms, 1982), since many have to accommodate and integrate the demands of paid work and those of homework.

Thus, women's resistance to the new time regimen is frequently hypothesized to be low. The same argument applies to individuals newly entering the work force. Since they are unacquainted with the old time regimen, they (supposedly) are more easily socialized into the new time structure.

### Changing Cultural Representations of Life Stages: From Stability to Flexibility?

The culture's view of the life course and, especially, of life stages provides a general structure of meaning—an imagery, a language, or a set of symbols—within which people enact their lives (Swidler, 1986). Individuals use these symbols and images to model their own trajectories. I use this perspective to analyze the symbolic contents of specific life stages and to trace the changes these cultural patterns are undergoing. The discussion focuses on the cultural imagery of adulthood and its current redefinitions.[25]

At the structural level, adulthood is the stage at which the problem of integrating and balancing the requirements of the occupational world with those of family life must be confronted. The cultural models and images of adulthood thus have to provide solutions to problems surrounding the "themes of work and love" (Smelser & Erikson, 1980; Smelser, 1980b). In offering such answers, the cultural account pictures a certain relationship between the individual and society, between the self and the social world, or, in general, between structure and action. Shifts in the cultural image of adulthood thus always are indicative of changes in the relation between the individual and society.

### The Changing Love Ideology

Swidler (1980) provides a very useful approach for studying the culture's view of adulthood in the private realm of life. She assumes that in modern society the love ideology is one of the central anchors of adulthood, "integrating the issues of individual identity, moral choice, and social commitment" (p. 125). To assess the ways in which individual interests and societal demands are integrated in the symbolic structure of the love myth, Swidler distinguishes four relations, each linking the individual's life to a specific aspect of the social world: the relation of choice versus commitment, of rebellion versus attachment, of self-realization versus self-sacrifice, and, finally, of libidinal expression versus libidinal restraint. Whereas the dominant love myth in American culture, according to Swidler, resolves the tensions between the two competing sides of each relation by emphasizing *social* demands, the current shifts in the love ideology stress *individualistic* aspects of the relationship. The emphasis given to one over the other side of each of these four relationships highlights the direction toward which the love imagery, and, as a consequence, the social definition of the subject and its relation to society, is heading. Swidler's account of how these four relationships are structured by the dominant love ideology is summarized below to provide background for a discussion of contemporary changes.

First, the love imagery provides an answer to the question of (individual) choice and (social) commitment. It ensures individuality in the private sphere by permitting individuals to define their own identities by the free choice of a love and marriage partner. Long-term social commitment and social integration result from the cultural prescription that one should be faithful to one's choice; "the capacity to make a commitment and to stick to it is the measure of identity formation" (Swidler, 1980, p. 128). Individual fulfillment thus is achieved through committed choice. Swidler conceives of the second relationship—rebellion versus attachment—as the individual's simultaneous desires not to be constrained by society and to be integrated into society. The dominant love ideology's solution to this problem is to tolerate the individual's detachment from society in order to find his or her true attachment: Individual rebellion against society is regarded as the adherence to a cause which ultimately proves to be for the social benefit. In Weberian terms, such a rebellion corresponds to a value-rational action orientation.

In the dominant love ideology, the metaphor of selfless giving through which personal fulfillment is achieved provides an answer to the tension between self-realization and self-sacrifice—the third aspect of the relationship between individual freedom and social demands. Since the balance between satisfaction and sacrifice in a love relationship is grounded on the belief that "one realizes himself *through* self-sacrifice" (Swidler, 1980, p. 136), it does not involve the continued calculation of costs and returns.

The final aspect of the relationship between individual interests and social demands modeled by the love ideology concerns the tensions between sexual expression and restraint. The dominant answer to this problem strengthens commitment by conceiving of sexual exclusiveness as a "seal of emotional bondedness" (p. 141) and by symbolizing fidelity as a way through which "the integrity of the self is demonstrated by its capacity for unified devotion" (p. 139).

The current shifts in the symbolic meaning system of love place greater stress on the individual side of the four relationships. Instead of commitment to one's life choice, the ability to develop in love relationships and to experience personal growth—a process that may involve continuing choices—becomes the yardstick for successful identity formation (cf. Leupold, 1983). Lifelong attachment to a cause is replaced by the capacity for flexible adjustments to new demands and for exploring new experiences. Flexible instead of stable identities are likely to become the new standards of identity construction. Self-realization as a reflective process involving one's needs and interests, to which a love relationship contributes, is more highly valued than personal fulfillment through selfless giving to a love partner (with little consideration of changing personal needs and desires). Self-expression is conceived of as continued development and self-exploration and is set against the virtue of self-restriction. The emerging love ideology emphasizes continuing attention to one's needs and interests and their immediate gratification in a love relationship. The opening of the self to new experiences makes deferred gratification as a value increasingly obsolete.

In sum, the current reconstruction of the symbolic system of love abandons the conception of lifelong stability (accompanied by a life-cycle-encompassing concept of identity) as the ultimate value and dismisses permanent commitment and achievement in favor of ideas of lifelong personal development. Instead of the ideas of permanence, ultimate achievement, and commitment, the images of flexibility, choice, and self-exploration emerge. In this changed symbolic system, the individual is understood as an entity developing and growing throughout his or her lifetime. Thus, adult life in the private sphere is turned into a lifetime of choice instead of a period of stability reached by having made permanent achievements.

The transformations that the love myth and, as a consequence, the overall relationship between the individual and society seem to undergo suggest a gradual redefinition of the private sphere of life. The emerging image of the self and its relation to society incorporates a conception of love relationships as rational exchange: Love becomes a matter of negotiation, the terms of which must be constantly scrutinized and reestablished. Love is no longer defined primarily as a commitment to a choice made once and for all, but rather as a continuing transaction that involves bargaining for specific terms and evaluating costs and rewards. In this exchange of investments, it is the short-term balance, not the balance over a lifetime, that is the most important criterion of evaluation (Held, 1986). In this new imagery, love is increasingly evaluated on the basis of its contribution to the individual's development and his or her personal growth. Consequently, traditional identities based on the ability to make lifelong commitments and unlimited attachments are replaced by personalities capable of making choices over a lifetime.

These changes in the culture's view of private relationships can be traced in part to the transformations in the educational, occupational, and family systems discussed in detail earlier in this chapter. Increasing instability of lifelong professional and vocational work undermines long-term occupational commitment and attachment; accelerated rates of innovation in the work field demand from the individual high flexibility and adaptability to ever-changing circumstances; the decreasing (functional) importance of the traditional family, demographic changes in the family, and the growing economic independence of an increasing number of women contribute to the dissolution of the image of the family as a lifelong institution. Given these structural changes, the question arises, which social groups are most affected by the accompanying shifts in the cultural meaning system?

Since cultural changes to a certain extent reflect structural transformations, it follows that those social groups experiencing structural changes most directly would be most likely to embrace a new ideology that is bettersuited to their interests and thus is able to provide meaning to their lives. As Bourdieu (1978, 1984a) has argued, individuals and social groups most interested in the language of change, continuous development, and permanent self-exploration are those whose present situation (in terms of their social positions) and future condition (in terms of expected trajectories) are highly uncertain. In this sense, the structural uncertainties are translated into the appropriate ideology: The groups' unstable social positions and their fluctuating trajectories find expression in an ideology of uncommitment.

Individuals with highly uncertain positions and trajectories are those who are "misplaced" in the social structure. As discussed earlier in this chapter, the "deviant" allocation of individuals is mainly the result of the professionalization of the occupational structure engendering bureaucratically defined relationships between education and occupation. The closer these relationships are, the greater the structural risks of uncoordinated and unsynchronized developments in these spheres (Brater & Beck, 1982; Mertens, 1984) resulting in abnormal status allocations. The ideology of continuing change is most appealing to these mismatched individuals. It is clearly in their interests not to define their present situations as definite or final since these are positions for which the individuals are not prepared and to which they did not aspire. To interpret their actual situation as provisional, transient, and temporary permits them to escape the reality that their positions are not at all transient, but are instead fairly fixed, at least in terms of their statistical probability. Thus, the emergence of the ideology of life as a continuous development process which only ends with one's death can partially be interpreted as modern culture's response to contradictory developments in the social structure.

### The Changing Work Ideology

The love ideology represents only one part of the culture's view of adulthood. The symbolic structure of love in modern society has been conceived of as a system of meaning depicting the relationship between the individual and society from the perspective of the private realm of life. What kind of symbolic resources does the culture provide to shape the relationship between the individual and society in the public realm of life? As with the love image, action orientations in the public realm are not simply invented but are an integrated part of a larger frame of organizing one's life: The work ideology offers biographical meaning to the individual's work life. In this respect, it provides symbolic resources upon which individuals can draw to organize their own work lives. A comparison between the traditional work ideology in capitalist society and its current shifts illustrates the ways in which work helps to integrate individuals into society.

The development of capitalist society—especially in the European form of industrialization—was accompanied by a work ideology centering on skilled (i.e., craft) labor. For a long time, this ideology constituted the dominant cultural meaning system of work (Kern & Schumann, 1982). At the core of this ideology lies a professional ethos, one that defines the relationship of workers to their work. It depicts the worker as a person equipped with relatively broad professional knowledge and experience, capable of working cooperatively, responsibly, and independently, and adhering voluntarily to the standards of work. The social organization of work depended on this type of work orientation, but it simultaneously offered symbolic resources that allowed the demands of work to be understood as more than external constraints. Workers could view work demands as an opportunity to develop their own personalities, to enhance their professional qualifications and competencies, and to regard their commitment to work as a prerequisite for meaningful leisure time.

In this sense, the work ideology centering on skilled labor provides the means for integrating the individual's aspirations and expectations toward work and leisure with the social requirements and demands of work. In so doing, this work ideology is able to resolve the tensions between individual needs and interests and the social demands of work. It provides a sound basis for organizing one's work life and giving meaning to one's work biography. It succeeds in establishing a long-term balance between the social demands of the economy and the personal interests of the worker—a balance that ensures social commitment.

To summarize, the traditional work ideology shapes and frames the relationship between the individual and society in such a way that it accommodates individual interests and the social demands of work. This accommodation is possible because it is applicable to a wide variety of work. Such general applicability renders this cultural account a collective meaning system with widely accepted cultural commonalities able to function as a frame of reference within which individuals can organize their own work lives.

Since this imagery corresponds to a specific social organization of work—the one in the traditional sector of the economy (Brock & Vetter, 1984)—recent changes in the social structure of industrial production affect the ideology's capacity to structure the biographical meaning of work. Brock and Vetter argue that the changes in work tasks and work relationships brought about by the application of new technologies undermine the cultural meaning system so that it no longer successfully integrates the social demands of work with individuals' expectations toward work.

Brock and Vetter's conclusion is based on their study of technological innovation in the printing industry in West Germany. They analyzed how the introduction and application of computer-controlled typesetting technology changed the work tasks as well as the social interaction patterns and relationships among typesetters. They found that the traditional understanding of work engendered conflicts both on the objective and subjective side of work. The altered social organization of work produced new social demands requiring different work capacities and competencies. The individual expectations and aspirations toward work built upon the established work ideology were no longer met by the new objective work conditions.

The authors' description of the workers' modes of coping with the new situation provides first indications of what promise to become the new cultural images of work. It must be emphasized that the evidence does not yet indicate the birth of a new work ideology. Nevertheless, it is important to register these first signs of an altered language to encode (and to decode) the new work experience so that the general direction of change in the work ideology may be assessed.

Brock and Vetter found three typical patterns of coping with the new situation. The collectively shared conception of work had been replaced by more individualized approaches for interpreting the biographical significance of work. One approach attempts to implement the old work ideology in the changed environment. The other two emerging images seem to indicate new ways of giving meaning to work life and of integrating work into a biographical perspective. These are described below.

One group of workers coped with their altered conditions of work by centering their life projects around work. For them, professional success individually strived for constitutes the central meaning of the biographical experience of work. This "professional attachment" ideology stresses the importance of individual willingness and readiness to stay professionally up to date as a bulwark against professional downgrading. The rapid changes in work tasks and in work relationships loosen the individual's integration within a stable work process and thus further an understanding of work as an individual enterprise and as a continuous development for which the individual is responsible. Professional continuity—in the sense of the profession as a lifelong commitment—is interpreted as stagnation. Thus, the new social demands of work in terms of flexibility are conceived of as opportunities for individual choice and professional development, engendering a high readiness to invest in the professional sphere of life. The biographical significance of work is hypostatized; the traditional balance between professional life and private life—the balance between social demands and personal interests—is abandoned in favor of the greater biographical significance of work.

In contrast, the second way of coping with the altered work situation accentuates the private sphere of life over the work life. Conceptually, this "professional detachment" ideology is based on a dissociation between actual work and subjective aspirations toward work. Work is perceived as a job offering no opportunities for personal development; as a result, it is not an area for personal investment. On the contrary, all the truly important things in life happen outside of the professional world. The subjective detachment from work makes the individual more or less immune from the rapid changes of work tasks and of work conditions in general brought about by the introduction of new technologies. As in the professional attachment ideology, work is not conceived of as a lifelong commitment, but rather as a flexible arrangement. This subjective account of work thus provides the resources for organizing one's life around the time spent outside official work obligations. It is sustained by the (symbolic) acceptance of one's work capacity as a commodity that is not tied to one's identity. This interpretation of work as being dissociated from one's "real life" makes it possible to have no expectations, aspirations, or claims toward work in the sense of it being meaningful or fulfilling. In this kind of work intepretation, the relationship between social commitment and individual interests is biased in favor of individualism.

Brock and Vetter point out that these opposite accounts of the meaning of work in one's life find their supporters in quite different occupational positions within the printing industry. The professional attachment ideology tends to find adherents among workers in workplaces upgraded as a result of the introduction of new technologies. The professional detachment ideology is the preferred interpretation pattern of workers whose workplaces have been downgraded by the application of the computer-controlled technologies.

These two emerging accounts of work approximate the two end points of a continuum of possible biographical meanings for work.[26] Each differs from the old model which provided a symbolic structure integrating the social demands of the public with the individual interests of the private life. The two new symbolic structures of work are characterized by either a fusion or a dissociation of work and private life. One emphasizes work as the central life interest; the other focuses on nonwork time as the most valued sphere of life. In neither model is the relationship between the individual and society structured to integrate the different spheres of life using an overall, long-term perspective. The organization of one's work life as a biographical perspective no longer involves the commitment to a choice once made but, rather, the flexibility to adjust to changing circumstances. Moreover, the new models differ from the old one in that they are individualized forms of coping with the experience of work and of giving meaning to it. The concept of work as a collective enterprise encompassing corresponding responsibilities and identifications is abandoned in favor of a rational calculability of individual investments and returns.

The next section assesses the extent to which shifts in the cultural representations relate systematically to structural changes in the educational, occupational, and family spheres. An examination of the dynamic interplay between the rationalization of social action and exchange and cultural individualism permits conclusions with regard to observed changes in the social and individual organization of the life course.

## Social Dynamics between Rationalization and Individualization: Destandardization of the Life Course?

It is a basic assumption of sociology that societal rationalization and the ideology of individualism are ongoing, mutually reinforcing processes in modern society. Progressive rationalization involves further elaboration of the individualist ideology, and changes in the increasingly complex conceptions of the individual ease the way to further rationalization of social organization. The more the individual is integrated into the rational social structure, the more new elements of the self (i.e., needs, motives, interests, capacities, and competencies) are discovered (cf. Meyer et al., 1981; Meyer, 1986a) that reshape the cultural representation of the individual in the private and public realms of life. The recent expansion of higher education, for example, prolongs the amount of time individuals spend in bureaucratically defined learning situations dominated by the ideology of individual achievement. This facilitates the ascription of new capacities and dispositions and fosters the development of highly individualized identity patterns. Similarly, the contemporary accelerated rationalization of work demands greater flexibility on the part of the individual, enhancing the value of dispositions and competencies that are responsive to rapidly changing work tasks and the shifting marketability of particular professional qualifications. In the same way, changing family relations, especially the gradual dissolution of the traditional family as a lifelong institution, reinforce the norm of individual independence and are accompanied by notions of lifelong personal growth and self-exploration. The emergence of life-span psychology (Baltes & Brim, 1980) may be regarded as a professional account of shifts in the social reconstruction of the individual that emphasize the individual's capacity for change across the entire life span. Similarly, Lerner (1984) coined the term "human plasticity" to express the possibility of change at all stages of the individual life cycle, thus challenging the well-established assumption that early childhood experiences are the most important determinants of adult personality.

The progressive discovery of human personality in turn involves new forms of institutionalization that further the rationalization of social action and exchange. New concepts in socialization theory, for example, give rise to the current emphasis on continuous education and corresponding forms of institutionalization (e.g., institutionalized professional updating, universities for the elderly, recurrent education).[27] Shifts in the social construction of women's role in society (particularly definitions of women's role revised to include their autonomous participation in the labor force) ease the way for further monetarization of the home economy (cf. Meyer et al., 1981) and contribute to the increasing individualization of female life courses (Beck-Gernsheim, 1982, 1983, 1986). In a similar way, contemporary health movements emphasize everyone's right to a healthy life, thus stimulating the transformation of these new socially constructed needs into economic commodities and political rights.

We may interpret the trends toward discontinuity and flexibility in status/role sequences over the individual's lifetime and increasingly individualized life course patterns as a partial destandardization of the life course regime. This results from the high level of societal rationalization and individualization, and their dynamic interplay, in advanced industrial society. Analytically, we may distinguish three ways in which these destandardizing effects are produced.

First, accelerated rationalization of the economic sphere (see the discussion in this chapter, "The Changing Structure of Occupational Careers" and "Rationalization of Lifetime: The Impact of New Information Technologies") undermines the "institution" of the lifelong occupation for which qualifications have to be acquired *once* over a lifetime. The rapid shortening of the cycles of technological innovation challenges the life course sequencing of "preparation-activity-rest" (Kohli, 1983, 1985a), that is, the "education-work-retirement lockstep" (Best, 1980) which has given the life course its highly standardized form. Continued updating of professional qualifications, retraining, and various forms of flexible work schedules will contribute to "flexible life scheduling" (Best, 1980) and are likely to give rise in the long run to altered sequencing of positions and roles. These changes do not imply that the links between educational credentials and occupational positions cease to follow the logic of institutionalized status allocation. I assume, however, that the phases of standardization, that is, the temporal validity of linkages between educational and occupational status, have shortened. As a consequence, status/role sequences over an individual's lifetime in the public realm of life show increasing diversification, which either may be predominantly imposed externally on the individual (i.e., growing discontinuity) or which may reflect deliberate biographical strategies (i.e., increasing flexibility).

Second, structural and cultural individualization of the life course has reached such a high level in advanced industrial society that the formerly tight coupling between social class and the sociocultural milieu encompassing shared values, action orientations, common styles of life, and collectively defined biographical prospects (Beck, 1983) has greatly eroded. In Weberian (Weber, [1922] 1968) terms, the association between class (the market position) and status group (a collectivity bound together by a common worldview and style of life) is becoming looser and looser; furthermore, these sociocultural milieus are becoming diffuse and amorphous. The unraveling of social class and its accompanying culture renders any given sociocultural collectivity progressively less capable of determining individuals' orientations and behaviors. Individuals are less and less immersed in corporate groups that restrict action by their tradition and history; traditional ways of organizing life become obsolete. Thus, life situations, value and action orientations, and lifestyles show an increasing differentiation and pluralization. Particularly, the diversification of family life may be interpreted as a result of the lack of structural and cultural support for the traditional (bourgeois) family (Hoffmann-Nowotny, 1987). Thus, it is the successful institutionalization of the life course in advanced industrial society on which the present individualizing departure rests (Kohli, 1985b).

Third, the partial destandardization of the life course may be attributed to the tensions inherent in the conflicting relationship between institutionalized and noninstitutionalized elements of the life course. The logic of the social organization of individual life introduces a separation of the public from the private life sphere (see Chapter 1, "The Institutionalization of the Life Course"). In this dimension of the life course, a high degree of standardization may be a prerequisite for its partial destandardization. When there is a high degree of public institutionalization, the private life and action sphere may no longer be regarded as dependent on the institutionalized elements of the life course (Held, 1986). The influence of traditions and customs on the structuring of the life course is being replaced by an increasing range of biographical options, particularly within the noninstitutionalized sphere of the life course, for scarching for and experimenting with new forms of social relations and social identification and for testing new biographical models. The increasing destandardization of the family life course, in particular, may be regarded as resulting from this process.

Overall, the life course regime in advanced industrial society is characterized by tensions inherent in the relationship between standardization and destandardization of the life course: Increasing bureaucratically determined status allocation coexists with growing discontinuity/flexibility and diversification of life course patterns supported by the shifting cultural imagery of the private and public spheres. Individuals confront these conflicting tendencies as they devise their plans and attempt to put them into action. Current transformations of the life course regime thus highlight the dialectics between action autonomy and action constraint. A way of conceiving of these action dynamics is outlined in the next section as a basis for drawing conclusions regarding probable shifts in the subjective construction of biographical perspectives and strategies.

### The Dialectics between Choice and Constraint of Individual Action

I conceive of the continuous societal rationalization and individualization as simultaneous processes that enhance and restrict the individual's scope of action in a dialectical way. Growing bureaucratization of the life course—through both age-grading and institutionalized mechanisms of status allocation—and recent enforced structural discontinuities in status/role sequences impose external restrictions on the subjective organization of action. The individual's scope of action becomes more and more formalized and standardized. At the same time, however, structural and cultural individualization severs traditional bonds, affiliations, and identifications. The individual is increasingly set "free" to act on his or her own behalf; he or she is no longer immersed in corporate groups that restrict action by their tradition and history. An increasing range of life spheres and life concerns thus is subsumed into the individualistic way of action (i.e., the assumption that action depends on the choices of the individual actor).[28] As a consequence, the individual's actions, as well as his or her understanding of him/herself and the social world, are believed to be determined by individual decisions and efforts. Actions are more frequently justified in terms of individual needs, motives, interests, and subjective experiences. Justification of one's actions does not, however, occur in an unstructured or undefined social space. The dominant cultural meaning system, that is, the public representations and images, provide the legitimation for individual action. Meyer (1986a) maintains that individuals do not "develop" as idiosynchratic persons, but rather as highly standardized and universalistic entities. This structural arrangement simultaneously enhances and restricts both the individual's scope of action and the range of images of him/herself and the social world.

For instance, the vanishing influence of traditions and customs provides opportunities to establish new forms of social relations which set altered conditions for social identification and identity construction (Beck, 1983, 1985). Identification with and commitment to particular social groups and collectivities gradually become *deliberate* projects: Alliances become selective. Bellah et al. (1985), for example, characterize such new kinds of alliances as "lifestyle enclaves," which they define as groups "formed by people who share some feature of private life. Members of a lifestyle enclave express their identity through shared patterns of appearance, consumption, and leisure activities" (p. 335).

Lifestyle enclaves differ radically from what Weber ([1922] 1968) calls the "Stand," which represents a social milieu specific to a particular social stratum. Whereas membership in the latter is based on social class position (encompassing cultural commonalities and shared traditions), membership in a lifestyle enclave is a deliberate undertaking. But such new forms of alliances and collective identifications need not be restricted to private aspects of life; they can extend as well to groups acting together politically. The so-called new social movements (Touraine, 1978) are good examples of such alliances. Whether individuals become involved more in private or more in public alliances depends on social, cultural, and personal factors.[29] Individualization of action and exchange thus does not preclude collective involvements on the part of the individual; it does change the conditions and forms of commitment, however.

While societal individualization widens the *potential* scope of action, increasing state regulation of social life steadily imposes more external restrictions on the individual. To put it in extreme terms: The potential for deliberate choice of action can only be applied within a narrowly defined frame of state control. The more social life comes to be controlled by state activities, the more it takes the form of a bureaucratic social structure. Under these conditions, individual action is not really governed by subjective imperatives, but rather by externally imposed goals and means. The logic of individual action tends to become a functionally rational adjustment toward externally set goals and means.[30] To the extent that these imposed goals differ from personally perceived interests and needs, individualized society tends to constrain the individual's scope of action.

This interpretation differs in some important respects from speculations about the future of Western society that are part of the currently fashionable discussion in the social sciences on "modernism and postmodernism."[31] A brief overview of this debate is presented below in order to clarify the approach taken here.

Although most scholars agree that Western society has undergone major social and cultural changes, there is less consensus over how to interpret these transformations. Major differences concern the individual's status in society and, as a consequence, the relationship between the social structure and the actor. Habermas's discussion of modernity and postmodernity and Bell's account of the coming postindustrial society provide particularly clear examples of divergent viewpoints.

Habermas's diagnosis of the present is explicit: "More or less in the entire Western world, a climate has developed that furthers capitalist modernization processes as well as trends critical of cultural modernism" (1984, p. 13; 1985).[32] These critical trends ultimately are conservative, he argues, because they surrender the "project of modernity." For Habermas, the project of modernity—the specific pattern of cultural development in modern society—has not yet been fulfilled (Habermas, 1981).

Following Weber, Habermas defines cultural modernity as the separation of a previously integrated culture (i.e., that of traditional society) into different value spheres—science, morality, and art. These spheres come to be institutionalized in modern society and then develop according to their own inner logic. Although this process should release "the cognitive potential of each of these spheres for the enrichment of everyday life, that is to say, for the rational organization of everyday social life" (Habermas, 1984, p. 9), it has not. The scientific sphere in particular has not fulfilled its purpose. The professional culture grows ever more distant from the layman's culture while simultaneously increasing its influence over the layman's perception and interpretation of the world. More and more, professional culture is regarded as the only legitimate form of knowledge (science) and of expression (art), because the former develops according to the rational principle of science and the latter according to professional aesthetic standards. As a result, professional culture involves the rapid devaluation of the layman's culture. This contributes to the alienation of the modern individual and to the growing impoverishment of everyday life.[33] According to this view, the separation of value spheres did not contribute to the enrichment of everyday life, but rather resulted in alienation and cultural impoverishment.

Habermas further assumes that the continuous process of rationalization in the economic and the political sphere—the development of large-scale economic organizations and of the administrative bureaucratic apparatus of the state—submerges the individual and destroys his or her everyday world. He refers to this process as the subordination of the life worlds (the spheres of communicative action centered on the reproduction and transmission of values and norms based on mutual understanding) to the imperatives of economic and administrative rationality. The penetration of life worlds by exogenous principles of rationality creates the conditions that prompt protest and discontent on the part of the individual.

These protests are, according to Habermas, reactions against the process of societal modernization; they express altered attitudes toward life and institutions such as work, consumption, and leisure. The adherence to hedonistic and narcissistic values and the lack of social identification and of obedience toward authorities represent new forms of cultural expression and identity formation. These new orientations and practices in the life world can, Habermas argues, eventually involve the emergence of institutions "which set limits to the internal dynamics and the imperatives of an almost autonomous economic system and its administrative complements" (Habermas, 1984, p. 11). Together with the reappropriation of the professional culture from the standpoint of the life world, these new cultural expressions are the only means for fulfilling the "project of modernity."

Such altered attitudes, motives, and needs in the contemporary period are thus for Habermas expressions of the individual's reactions *against* society. Individuals form their identity in opposition to society in order to defend their autonomy and dignity as human beings. In this view of the development of modern society, one side of the development pattern—the impact of societal rationalization on the individual—is overemphasized at the expense of the dialectical counterpart to the rationalization of society, that is, the social construction of an autonomous, responsible individual in the ideology of individualism. The unequal weight attributed to the two sides of societal development leads Habermas to conceive of the individual as being fundamentally alienated in the contemporary period, thus excluding the possibility that the altered images of the individual are part of the ongoing process of reconstructing individualism.

Bell's (1973, 1976) explanation of the social and cultural transformation of modern society—what he identifies as a transition to postindustrialism and postmodernism—is also incomplete. Postindustrialism is characterized, according to Bell, by a new relationship between scientific knowledge and the economic system, whereby the production of this knowledge tends to become the crucial prerequisite for economic growth. The increasing significance of scientific knowledge in the economic sphere and in the political system is accompanied by the emergence of new elites—the professionals. In postindustrial society, the authority relations between those who have decision-making powers and those who do not replace the long-standing divisions based on class ownership and control of the means of production. Traditional class conflict is giving way to social conflicts and cleavages between those who control the institutions of decision making and those who are dependent on this new ruling elite.

Although Bell assumes that these conflicts will cause problems in the emerging new society, he is more concerned with another phenomenon accompanying increased professionalization, the emergence of hedonistic and narcissistic values. Bell (1976) argues that the cultural sphere of everyday life has been penetrated by values such as the principle of unlimited self-realization and the demand for authentic self-expression. He maintains that these emerging values and the rational social organization prevalent in the economic and political system are contradictory. This shift toward hedonistic and narcissistic values is incompatible with the purposive, rational conduct of life predominant in the economic and political spheres. These new values undercut the discipline of professional life because they further the withdrawal from competition for social status and achievement. Bell warns that in the transition to a postmodern culture, individuals with hedonistic/narcissistic values could demolish the social order. To prevent such potential disorder, Bell advocates a more disciplined socialization, a process that would provide individuals with clearly defined identities and the existential security that they now lack.

Bell's interpretation of contemporary cultural and social changes as contradictory neglects the dialectical relationship between social structure and culture. The emergence of new individual needs and motives, as well as of altered attitudes toward different spheres of life, complements rather than contradicts the continuous rationalization of modern society. The social redefinition of personality stressing hedonistic and narcissistic values as intrinsic elements of the modern individual can be interpreted as a crucial mechanism to legitimize the consumption and spending patterns of an affluent society: In order to sell the myriads of goods, the economy has to rely on individuals who are not only willing to buy all the (unnecessary) products but who find their ultimate joy and fulfillment in consumerism—an attitude that requires a specific personality.[34]

Whereas Bell laments the socially disruptive potential of postmodern values, there are other theorists in different disciplines (e.g., Foucault, 1970; Derrida, 1982; Deleuze & Guattari, 1983; Lyotard, 1984) who welcome this fundamental rupture. One common denominator among the arguments of these "postmodern theorists" is of particular interest here. All contain references to the "end of man" or the "end of the subject," which they relate to the "end of history." The conception of an autonomous self is dismissed as pure fiction (Jameson, 1984).[35]

The changed status of the individual is expressed in new manners, habits, and behavioral patterns which can be found, according to postmodern theorists (cf. Lyotard, 1984), in contemporary scientific, artistic, and literary production, as well as in the social organization and interaction of everyday life. Postmodern society has experienced a shift from permanent institutions to temporary contracts in professional, cultural, emotional, and family domains. The postmodern habitus emphasizes immediate experience and gratification, the joy of the event that is created without any reference to preestablished rules, but out of endless invention of new games and "stories." [36] The pure play of differences is king: Anything may be said and done with equal validity. [37] All this amounts to a new shallowness in consciousness and behavior which ultimately results in "the subordination of everything to the finality of the best performance" (Lyotard, 1984, p. 45). In sum, postmodern theory offers a new view of the individual, with a new definition of his or her properties and relation to society. The theory exposes the notion of subjectivity (i.e., the unified and autonomous subject) as an illusion of modern society and celebrates instead the "random subjectivity" of the individual.

Although the postmodern perspective on the new status of the individual in society provides some useful insights into changing attitudes and behaviors, it also has blind spots. As Eagleton (1985, p. 70) notes, "It sometimes mistakes the disintegration of certain traditional ideologies of the subject for the subject's final disappearence." Similarly, Meyer (1986a) argues that throughout Western history discourse on "the end of man" is not so much a final dismissal of the individual as it is a rhetorical concomitant of the changing social definition of the subject. Thus, it may be concluded that postmodern theory redefines, under the guise of the "end of history" and the "end of man," the ideological imagery of the individual; it reconstructs individualism (to use Meyer's expression). Postmodern theorists, then, may be regarded as the professional advocates and precursors of forthcoming changes in modern society. They furnish society and its members with a professional account of the changes *within* the rationalized and individualized society to which individuals must conform in the near future. [38] They are not, as Habermas (1984) assumes, the new conservatives (i.e., advocates for some retrograde development of society), nor are they seers of the advent of a whole new type of society.

These different theoretical conceptualizations of the individual in advanced industrial society demonstrate the wide range of possible interpretations of societal development. The *hypostatization of the individual* in the conception of the subject as the main form of social reality marks one extreme, the *dismissal of the subject as pure fiction* in the notion of random subjectivity, the other. Both ways of looking at the individual are one-sided interpretations of social reality, insofar as they reify one element in the development of advanced industrial society and neglect the other.

In contrast to these views, I maintain that increasing rationalization and individualization of modern society may be characterized, from the actor's viewpoint, as the *proliferation of action alternatives*. Individuals can choose, in a growing number of life spheres, among a growing number of action alternatives. Yet these options show a specific form: They are formalized and, as such, standardized. The increasing freedom of action consists, in other words, in choosing among a greater number of predefined options.[39] This structural arrangement illustrates the dialectics between choice and constraint of individual action in advanced industrial society, whereby the greater diversity of options represents the enhancing element in the development of the individual's scope of action, the formalization and standardization the restricting aspect. Which of these dialectical tendencies gains ascendancy in the further development of modern society cannot be decided in advance. Since individuals dispose of the socially produced potential of intellectual insight into their own action as well as in the structure of the social world, they can use it to call into question established social interaction patterns and structural arrangements. The specific development patterns of modern society, then, are not rigidly determined, but rather are flexible, insofar as individuals actualize their potential for self-reflection.

### Destandardization of the Life Course and Biographical Perspectives and Strategies

To summarize, the trends toward growing discontinuity/flexibility and diversification of life course patterns affect the ways in which individuals organize and enact their lives. Specifically:

First, the greater diversity of life course patterns, manifested in the increased dispersion of actual trajectories, diminishes the likelihood of more or less identical career paths among individuals endowed with similar social attributes (i.e., social class, sex, age). As a consequence, the objective possibility of comparing various life trajectories declines. Individuals thus are less likely to experience and/or recognize their own trajectory as part of the "collective destiny" of the social group(s) to which they belong. At the same time, they are less constrained by the tradition (i.e., the value and action orientations) of such groups, thus increasing the likelihood of biographical perspectives and strategies formed on the belief that accomplishments depend on individual decisions and choices.

Second, this tendency is further supported by the broadened range of life events potentially open to purposive action. This makes the organization of everyday life more dependent on individualized accomplishments. Biographical self-reflection is also more often required, since the flexibility and diversity of trajectories multiply the occurrence of situations in which deliberate attention is called to one's life path. Under these conditions of high structural individualization of experience, individuals are likely to regard success or failure in the life course as due to their own choices and actions.

Third, in such a structural situation, the probability of constructing identities, biographical perspectives, and strategies centered around the individual increases. The belief that "one's self is one's only resource" (Swidler, 1980, p. 134) may be regarded as the core of such highly self-centered identity patterns. As plans and strategies become more and more objects of deliberate attention on the basis of the increasing flexibility of the life course, they are also likely to be less permanent, more fluid and transient, that is, more open to continuous reconstruction. The quest for identity becomes an ongoing project.

Fourth, as a consequence, individuals are likely to construct multidimensional identities in which a clear hierarchic ordering of elements is absent. Such identity structures are composed of many different elements, which may be assembled in different ways—over time and according to shifting internal and/or external requirements. The ability to shift the identity focus in a flexible way and to reorder the elements in new combinations results in a pluralization of identities in the individual's progression through different social contexts.

Fifth, increased discontinuity/flexibility in the configuration and sequencing of positions and roles tends, at the same time, to undermine the chances for anticipating and predicting the various trajectories and thus tends to reduce the likelihood of building up long-term, stable expectations. In this sense, it is considerably more difficult for the individual to induce his or her future from his or her present circumstances. Poorly delineated perceptions of one's future are equivalent to the internalization of diffuse expectations and aspirations. Either under- or overestimation of one's trajectories may then result. Discrepancies between expected and realized career paths may give rise, on one hand, to increased psychological problems as a result of self-blame and, on the other hand, to social conflicts (in instances where the unfulfilled projects are interpreted as problems of the social structure, i.e., structural blame).

Sixth, increased flexibility/discontinuity and diversification of life course patterns provides structural support for a logic of action oriented more toward the present than toward the future (Brose, 1982, 1984, 1985a). The individual's time horizon tends to shorten, and there is a greater emphasis on immediacy. Following Swidler (1980, p. 140), "current pleasures become more important than either future rewards or past commitments." The individual's logic of action focuses squarely on immediate gratification(s). The present is perceived as the "here and now," rather than as an element in the movement from the past to the future. Thus, individuals tend to adopt action orientations that highly value new experiences: Novelty becomes a value in itself.

# 3 Changing Passages to Adulthood

Thus far I have analyzed current processes in various institutional domains that modify the nature of the life course in contemporary society, thus altering the structural and cultural setting within which individuals plan and organize their lives. This chapter examines more closely how and to what degree the transition to adulthood is changing as a result of these larger social transformations. Here, I develop hypotheses about the changing structure of the transition to adulthood by briefly tracing the social construction of youth as an institutionalized life stage.

## The Social Construction of Youth

The emergence of youth as a distinct biographical state must be understood within the larger process of the gradual segregation of children from the adult world that has occurred with the development of modern society. Over the very long history of the "individualization of the child" (Gélis, 1986), which began in the sixteenth and seventeenth centuries, the previous (emotional) indifference toward children (evidenced, for example, by fairly widespread abandonment) was slowly replaced by a conception of the child as a needy, dependent, and malleable creature. Children have come to be regarded as qualitatively different from grown-up persons. They are not just "miniature adults;" they require both physical and moral care and protection. Children are perceived as needing guidance, and proper education is the way to provide it.

The growing attention paid to children in the late seventeenth century (Locke), and especially in the eighteenth century (Rousseau), led to the emergence of social institutions that slowly created exclusive spheres and separate positions for children. The spread of schools, spearheaded by religious groups in the eighteenth century, was a crucial element in this process. By the nineteenth century, schooling had become the nearly exclusive province of the state, culminating in the institutionalization of compulsory education. Along with jurisdictional control over schooling, the state progressively defined special rights and responsibilities for children, often embodied in welfare legislation, and established related protective agencies (e.g., orphanages, child care centers). Child-specific penal laws were accompanied by correctional and rehabilitation institutions. And the state began to closely regulate child labor.[1]

The slow transformation of the status of children with the development of modern society has been interpreted variously. Ariès (1962) emphasizes the progressive loss of children's functions through segregation from the adult world. He equates children's confinement to exclusive social spheres, protected by parents and particularly by (state-managed) educators, with increasing dependence, discipline, repression, and formal inequality. The opposite interpretation of this process is associated with de Mause (1974). Referring to the history of childhood in premodern times as a "nightmare" (p. 1), he views the discovery of the child as a separate and unique personality and the gradually increasing attention paid to the specificities of child development as providing children with greater protection, equality, and welfare.

The logic of the social organization of the life course in modern society (outlined in Chapter 1) dictates the involvement of both positive and negative elements in the progressive institutionalization of childhood. To subject children to (adult-defined and -controlled) "pedagogical childhood" in segregated institutions makes them more dependent on adults and precludes their participation in the adult world. The increasing emphasis on professional expertise in childrearing that has led to the widespread dissemination and popularization of the developmental theories of Freud, Piaget, and Kohlberg restricts the scope of action available to children. This narrowing produces "child ghettos," highly selective contexts with regard to the opportunities of experience and learning (cf. Hengst, 1981). On the other hand, the progressive institutionalization of childhood endows children with individual membership rights in society and promotes them to citizenship status in the larger society. Children cease to be conceived of solely as (family) dependents and come to be regarded as unique individuals. As such, they have rights to claim and responsibilities to fulfill, both of which widen their scope of action. As children aquire more membership rights, they become more similar to and thus more equal to adults.

The social construction of youth as a life stage can be understood as an outcome of the increasing differentiation of the status of child from the status of adult, a process that has created separate segments within the general category of childhood. As Ariès (1962) has noted, the progressive provision of schooling was crucial to the development of increased age-stratification in society. In this respect, both the institutionalization of compulsory education[2] and the abolition of child labor are key elements in the social construction of youth.[3] These two measures are mutually reinforcing. Child labor regulation keeps young people out of the job market and in schools where they can be shaped according to the appropriate model of childhood. Labor laws and compulsory education that came into force in the nineteenth century affected the working class in the industrializing nations dramatically. Working-class parents were forced to withdraw their children from the labor market and enroll them in schools, thus depriving the children of their autonomy, their economic independence, and their chances for participation in the adult world (cf. Platt, 1969; Gillis, 1974).

The progressive consolidation of youth as a *standardized* life stage took place with the expansion of full-time mass education, especially after World War II. In many Western nations, compulsory full-time schooling has been gradually extended to fourteen, fifteen, or sixteen years of age (cf. Gillis, 1974; Ariès, 1983; Collins, 1979; Hills & Reubens, 1983); similarly, rules regulating young people's labor-force participation have steadily increased the minimum age for (regular) labor-force entry.

Research on historical changes in the transition to adulthood (Modell et al., 1976; Hogan, 1978, 1980, 1981; Winsborough, 1979; Featherman & Sorensen, 1983) indicates that the boundaries of the life stage youth have become more clearly defined (in relation to chronological age) with its progressive consolidation in the first half of the twentieth century. Specifically, the time needed to complete the various status/role transitions has steadily shortened, and the sequential ordering has slowly assumed a quasi-normative chronology.

Most researchers (Hogan, 1978, 1980, 1981; Modell et al., 1976; Winsborough, 1979) have measured age-grading by the number of years it takes a predefined proportion of a cohort, usually the two middle quartiles, to complete a given role transition. Based on 1880 census records for Philadelphia and on 1970 census data for the United States, Modell et al. found that the age span during which transitions such as school completion, labor-force entry, independent residence, and marriage occur has shortened. Similarly, Winsborough, analyzing the transition to adulthood of a nationally representative sample of American men born between 1911 and 1941, reports that the duration of each transition (i.e., completing school, labor-force entry, and marriage) has shortened for the younger cohorts, indicating greater age-grading. Moreover, Winsborough observes time-related changes in the linkages of several transitions: The younger cohorts move more swiftly from the completion of school to labor-force participation as full-time workers. As a result, the duration of the overall transition to adulthood has decreased.

These results suggest more clearly defined age boundaries and a greater demarcation between youth and other life stages. In addition to these changes in time, other studies (Hogan, 1978, 1980, 1981) show an increasing standardization of early life transitions with regard to their sequential ordering.[4]

These studies have certain limitations, however. The models they propose cannot accommodate the possibility of role reversals in the transition to adulthood (see Featherman & Sorensen, 1983). For example, young people may return to school after having entered the labor force as full-time workers. In this respect, the widely applied definition of first job as the first full-time job after the latest school enrollment may produce an undifferentiated picture of the transition to adulthood. For young men, in particular, an important aspect of life may be the movement back and forth between school and full-time work (p. 107). To capture these possibilities, Featherman and Sorensen propose a time-use approach, focusing on the way in which young people allocate their time to various activities (e.g., schooling, working, parenting) between given ages.

The measurement of time allocation (e.g., on a monthly basis) is possible only with continuous event history data, however. Analyzing the time allocation of cohorts of Norwegian men between the ages of fourteen and thirty years born in 1921, in 1931, and in 1941, Featherman and Sorensen (p. 111) found that "educational attainment has increased, age at marriage and parenthood has declined." Moreover, these changes in time allocation have been accompanied by increasingly complex age-stratification patterns. While men born in 1921 perform one role between ages seventeen and twenty-four, that of the unmarried worker, the 1931 and especially the 1941 cohorts' engagement in different activities has become more finely age-graded. The several transitions involved in the overall transition to adulthood have moved closer together, but the transition period has become more differentiated internally.

With respect to between-group differences, the chronological age at which this short period of role transitions occurs varies greatly with social characteristics, especially with class background, educational status, and sex (Hogan, 1982; Marini, 1978, 1984c; for reviews see Hogan, 1985; and Hogan & Astone, 1986). With the progressive consolidation of youth as a life stage, two well-delineated types of patterns emerge: a short-term youth with a rapid transition to adulthood at an early age for most children with lower social class background (typified by the image of the young worker), and a long-term youth accompanied by an extended transition to adulthood at a later age for most middle- and upper-class children (typified by the image of the bourgeois student).[5] Mobility between these two class-based types of youth was minimal until recently. These well-defined trajectories from childhood to adulthood thus gave rise to clear-cut frames of reference for the construction of identities and biographical perspectives. Studies of youth identities and lifestyles (Baacke, 1972; von Onna, 1976; Clarke et al., 1979) confirm the entrenchment of youth subcultures in the social class background of young people.[6]

In sum, the progressive consolidation of the life stage youth resulted in the gradual standardization of the transition to adulthood. Adult role entry became a *short period of transition* in which new positions and roles were assumed. These role and status changes showed a sequential ordering of events that provided a high *visibility* and *predictability* for early life transitions. Consequently, the transition to adulthood marked a *discontinuity*.

Eisenstadt (1956) defined the adult role entry as a well-defined status passage although, as a transitional phase inserted between childhood and adulthood, it is characterized by social indetermination. Whereas the child is totally integrated into and dependent on the family, adolescents gradually overcome family dependence, but they do not yet possess the fully autonomous existence of adults. Young people are located in social positions virtually outside of the "social universe." Metaphorically speaking, they are in training and waiting rooms, preparing for their future in the professional world (Ariès, 1983). Structurally speaking, young people overcome this period of indetermination by gaining economic autonomy through integration into the labor force and by acquiring emotional independence through the formation of their own families.

### The Increasing Obsolescence of Youth as a Well-Defined Status Passage

This vision of the transition to adulthood as a well-defined status passage is severely challenged by social and cultural developments in the larger society over the last two decades (cf. Buchmann & Vuille, 1985). I argue that these changes have contributed to a partial destandardization of the transition to adulthood. Transition patterns have become more extended, diversified, and individualized. These new modalities of adult role entry are the result of several interrelated processes, outlined briefly below.

Over the last two decades, the life stage youth has been simultaneously extended and narrowed. These opposing tendencies tend to accelerate the temporal disconnection of different events in the transition to adult status and contribute to the blurring of age boundaries. In many Western nations, compulsory full-time education has been extended, while the age of majority has been lowered and penal responsibilities are being imposed earlier in life. Young people thus are granted access to political and cultural autonomy at an earlier age. Their economic independence, however, is structurally postponed to a later age, which, for a steadily growing proportion of a birth cohort, greatly exeeds the age of majority (cf. Chamboredon, 1983; Hornstein, 1985).

Within the social sciences, it has become fashionable to discuss the prolonged economic dependence of a proportion of youths in terms of a new life stage, postadolescence (Keniston, 1968, 1971; Gillis, 1974; Jugendwerk der Deutschen Shell, 1982). According to these authors, postadolescence represents a new type of transition to adulthood. It is characterized by the discrepancy between the full psychological, social, and political autonomy of young persons and their simultaneous economic dependence. Postadolescents are adults except for the fact that they are economically dependent on others. This allegedly new structural situation gives rise to altered cultural expressions of young people who participate in this life stage. Postadolescents are said to value highly a lifestyle that emphasizes openness, immediacy, and change and to adhere to a time perspective that focuses on the present rather than on the future.

The authors who defend the idea of postadolescence regard the extension of schooling as the major factor contributing to the establishment of this new life stage. They link the invention of postadolescence to the transition of industrial society to postindustrial society. Postindustrial society's heavy reliance on technology induces the necessity of extended schooling for a substantial part of the young generation. Thus, the likelihood for participation in this new life stage depends on the family's social class status: Young people with higher social class background are more likely to participate in this new life stage. These authors conclude that the unequal access to postadolescence introduces a new form of social differentiation just at the moment at which the generalized access to the life stage youth has been realized. In my view, the concept of postadolescence as a new life stage is a foreshortened interpretation of the current transformations. It overlooks the fact that, from a sociological standpoint, the condition of schooling and/or professional training has always been the discriminatory feature of the youth status (cf. von Onna, 1976; Buchmann, 1983; Tully & Wahler, 1983, 1985). Thus, I prefer to argue that the rapidly increasing temporal disconnection of different events in the transition to adulthood helps to extend, to diversify, and to individualize the life period of becoming an adult—both in structural and cultural respects.

At the cultural level, the temporal extension of youth is accompanied, on one hand, by the de-structuring of child-specific and youth-specific spheres and modes of experience (cf. Hengst, 1981; Baethge, 1985). Particularly as recipients of media information and as consumers, although still segregated in separate institutions at the structural level, youths participate in the adult world at ever-younger ages. On the other hand, the distinction between youth status and adult status is gradually blurred as the adult culture rapidly usurps the values of youthfulness. Increasingly, adult lifestyles may be characterized as pseudo-youth subcultures (Held, 1986).

At the structural level, the extension of time needed for *stable* professional integration contributes to the dissolution of adult role entry as a well-defined status passage (Galland, 1984b, 1985a, 1985b; Gurny et al., 1984). For a considerable proportion of youths, stable integration into the labor force comes to be replaced by repeated cycles of retraining and interrupted labor-force participation. This likely tendency, besides contributing to the partial destandardization of the passage to adulthood, challenges the sequencing of the life course (see Chapter 2, "Social Dynamics between Rationalization and Individualization"). In this respect, retrained (or unemployed) youths and retrained (or unemployed) adults become, structurally speaking, alike. The aggravated competition for educational credentials and good jobs, however, may create new forms of family dependency. Young people's likelihood of turning down a job that does not meet their needs and interests depends on how well they are backed up by the family's material and symbolic support (Kloas et al., 1985).

These opposing tendencies at the structural and cultural level have been discussed by several authors as indicative of the the "decline" of the life stage youth (von Trotha, 1982) and even as the "disappearance of childhood" (Postman, 1982) or the "end of youth" (Elkind, 1979). These authors argue that, over the last fifteen years, the behavioral differences between youth and adults have drastically diminished. In a growing number of life spheres (sexuality, political behavior, etc.), young people behave like adults or claim the same rights as adults. Moreover, von Trotha (1982, p. 271) regards the decoupling of the status as a student from the age status as the major determinant of the obsolescence of the life stage youth. Being a student is no longer unambiguously associated with a certain age, as changes in the occupational sphere make professional updating increasingly more necessary. Adults thus return to school and act as students. He concludes that the status of the student has been transformed into an occupational status. Its holder is thus not set "free" from the responsibilities of the adult world, but, on the contrary, the status as a student confronts him or her with the demands of the adult world. I would argue, however, that this structural situation and its concomitant behavioral manifestations are indicative more of the dissolution of adult role entry as a well-defined status passage, that is, of a particular mode of becoming an adult, and less of the obsolescence of the life stage youth as such. The increasing individualization of the life stage youth discussed below further supports this interpretation.

With the recent expansion of the welfare state, children and youths have been rapidly integrated into the process of societal individualization by acquiring many membership rights in the larger society. Social welfare legislation and social policies address the child and the youth directly as holders of rights and as recipients of services and benefits (Riedmüller, 1981). As a result, children and youths become more directly integrated into the larger society and cease to be regarded solely as family dependents; they come to be viewed as subjects with individual rights. In this process of individualization, children/youths and parents become (structurally) more alike. The popularity of childrearing models that emphasize socialization styles based on mutual consent between parents and children (cf. Hengst, 1981; Sachse, 1986) reflects this tendency. Although mediated by the family's social class background, interaction patterns between parents and children also are increasingly defined on the basis of equality ("partnership") and less on the basis of obedience ("parental authority"; Rosenmayr, 1985). This accelerates children's independence by teaching them earlier and more thoroughly to behave as individual actors, to make their own decisions, to feel responsible for their actions, and to claim their rights.

This process is a structural prerequisite for the spread of the individualistic culture among youths that has occurred over the last decade. Increasingly, young people claim the right to define their own lifestyles and legitimize their ideas, plans, and actions on the basis of their own needs, motives, and interests (cf. Fuchs, 1983; Baethge, 1985; Rosenmayr, 1985). The greater emphasis on individualized criteria (e.g., spontaneous experience) in explaining and/or in evaluating action alternatives loosens youths' adherence to the value and action orientations defined by the sociocultural milieu of the family, thus resulting in a proliferation of juvenile value and action orientations and lifestyles (see Chapter 2, "Social Dynamics between Rationalization and Individualization"). Overall, the increasing individualization of the life stage youth at the structural and cultural level is likely to contribute to a greater variety in transition patterns to adulthood.

The empirical data presented in the chapters that follow allow us to test some aspects of this general hypothesis. The investigation focuses on two cohorts of white American high school graduates and examines how their lives unfold in the educational, occupational, and family domain over the first four years after high school. The analysis in this second half of the book compares the ways in which members of the high school class of 1960 and those of the high school class of 1980 plan their future and accomplish role transitions and status changes.

# From the 1960s to the 1980s: Differing Life Conditions and Life Experiences in the Transition to Adulthood

# 4

# The Sociohistorical Context of the High School Classes of 1960 and 1980

The opportunities and restrictions individuals encounter in their lives depend greatly on time- and place-specific circumstances. Thus, to understand the 1960 and 1980 senior cohorts' expectations and behaviors in their transition to adulthood, we need some knowledge of their childhood experiences. Under what circumstances did they gain their first impressions of the world? What early occurrences have shaped their current outlook on life? These experiences must be examined in relation to the broader social context and in terms of the intimate family milieus. In this chapter, I briefly trace the economic, political, and cultural circumstances in the United States that provided the crucial experiences during these two cohorts' formative years. Sensitivity to the cohort members' historical location underscores the conceptual relationship between historical time and the aging process. This relationship is outlined below; it provides the necessary analytic background for describing the sociohistorical context of the 1960 and the 1980 senior cohort.

## Historical Time and the Aging Process

Analyzing two cohorts who experience the same (social) event—high school graduation—at more or less the same chronological age, but at different times in history, highlights various dimensions of age and their relation to time, as illustrated in Table 4.1. Chronological age refers to biological and psychological development, using birth year as the point of reference. Based on the social meanings attached to chronological age, social age locates individuals in life stages and assigns roles (including tasks, rights, and obligations) and allocates status (including access to goods, power, and prestige). Annalistic age relates the birth year to historical conditions and events, underscoring the formative influence of history in the aging process.

Each of these three analytical dimensions highlights elements in the progression of the life course which may be individually examined. It is, how-

91

Table 4.1
Dimensions of Age and Their Relations to Time

| Principle of Classification | Dimensions of Age | Relation to Time |
|---|---|---|
| Relational (birth) | Chronological age (I am 24) | Development time (aging process) |
| Functional (age groups) | Social age (I am a pensioner) | Social time (life stages) |
| Historical (historical events) | Annalistic age (I was born in the Great Depression) | Historical time (historical location) |

ever, the interplay among these dimensions that is of greatest relevance to a comprehensive sociological analysis of the life course. For example: In what ways do particular historical circumstances and events foster or inhibit the assumption of family roles or participation in the labor force? And: What effects do such conditions have on psychological development? Figure 4.1 relates the three dimensions systematically.[1] The vertical axis represents chronological age, while the horizontal axis refers to annalistic age. The *diagonal* bars represent cohorts of people born in the same cal-

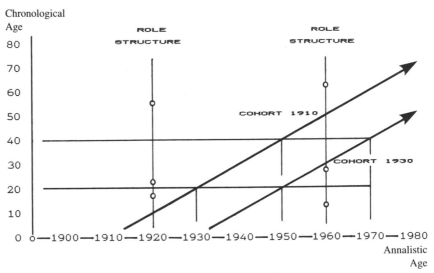

Figure 4.1. Interplay among chronological, social, and annalistic age.

endar year, moving through history as they grow older. *Vertical* bars are used to represent social age. They indicate the ways in which social roles and statuses are allocated or ascribed to people according to chronological age at a given historical time.

People in each cohort thus experience a unique slice of history, that is, specific constellations and sequences of states and events in the demographic, economic, political, and cultural development of society. These states and events, by influencing life chances, shape the way people age socially, biologically, and psychologically. As members of each cohort progress differently in social space and time, they induce, in turn, social and cultural change in different institutional spheres. By using this perspective to analyze the sociohistorical context in which the graduates of the high school classes of 1960 and 1980 grew up, we may gain an impression of the two cohorts' real life chances and prospects.

### The Impact of Historical Differences on the 1960 and 1980 Cohorts

The demographic characteristics of one's cohort are important, particularly its initial size. Being a member of a huge or a small cohort may affect life chances considerably, especially in relation to economic circumstances and with regard to the size of successive cohorts. A comparison of the cohort sizes since 1935 reveals that the graduates of the high school class of 1960 and of 1980 experience quite different cohort conditions. Table 4.2 shows that young people graduating from high school in 1960 belong to a fairly small birth cohort (taking 1940 as a proxy) surrounded by equally small cohorts. By contrast, those who graduate in 1980 are members of a huge cohort, preceded by equally huge cohorts, but followed by declining (birth) cohort sizes.

These cohort conditions are additionally important because they coincide with opposing tendencies in the economy and with different political climates. Most members of the 1960 senior cohort were born in the middle of World War II (i.e., 1942); they experienced their formative years in a period of economic upswing and an increasingly expanding economy. They came of age in the early 1960s, in a period of economic prosperity. In 1960, the year they graduated from high school, "the United States had just enjoyed the most prosperous year in [its] history" (Hodgson, 1976, p. 7). As members of a small cohort, their career opportunities were plentiful. By contrast, by the time the members of the high school class of 1980, predominantly born in 1962, had barely reached their teens, the economy

Table 4.2
Live Births from 1935 to 1970

|  | 1935 | 1940 | 1945 | 1950 | 1955 | 1960 | 1962 | 1965 | 1970 |
|---|---|---|---|---|---|---|---|---|---|
| Number (thousands) | 2,377 | **2,559** | 2,858 | 3,632 | 4,097 | 4,258 | **4,167** | 3,760 | 3,731 |
| Rate (per thousand) | 18.7 | 19.4 | 20.4 | 24.1 | 25.0 | 23.7 | 22.4 | 19.4 | 18.4 |

*Source: Statistical Abstract of the United States* 1986. Table 81; and 1978, Table 78.

had severely declined and remained depressed until the early 1980s, when many cohort members were seeking to enter the labor force (Wolfe, 1981). Thus, this cohort has had to struggle against unfavorable economic conditions, and as members of a huge cohort, they must face aggravated competition in the labor market.

The shift from economic prosperity to recession was also accompanied by political and cultural changes. It is reasonable to assume that the Cold War and McCarthyism shaped the early political consciousness of the 1960 senior cohort. The conservative political climate fostered by the zealous commitment to anticommunism and the "timid conformity" that characterized the nation's cultural and intellectual life (Hodgson, 1976, p. 45) slowly vanished by the end of the 1950s. It was replaced by a new conception of society embodied in Kennedy's "New Frontier" and in Johnson's "Great Society." Hodgson (p. 491) maintains that in the years just before and just after 1960, American politics and society were characterized by consensus, a shared vision of "an affluent society with growing abundance, and one that was steadily being transformed for the better by science and technology" (p. 8).

By contrast, the early political experiences of the 1980 senior cohort members were shaped by deep internal political and social cleavages over the Vietnam War, racial unrest, social inequality, and student protest. Culminating in the second half of the 1960s, these issues overshadowed the entire decade of the 1970s. The manifold internal problems were coupled with the decline of American leadership in the world. Yet the 1970s are also the decade of the "new social movements"—women's liberation, the ecology movement and antinuclear protests, the emergence of minority cultures, ethnicity, regionalism, and so forth (cf. Carroll, 1982)—which inspired the nation's political and cultural life. In a depressed economy, however, the ideas and ideals advanced by these movements were no match for the growing appeal of a conservative ideology whose main function was to "project optimism" (Hodgson, 1986). The promise to restore "both pride in the American past and optimism about the American future" (Hodgson, 1986) brought the conservative ideology to political power in the same year the 1980 senior cohort graduated from high school.

These economic, political, and cultural circumstances in which the graduates of the high school class of 1960 and of 1980 experienced their formative years were mediated by the family milieu. Historic experiences of the parent generation of the 1960 and the 1980 senior cohorts helped shape the value and action orientations within the family. Conversely, structural characteristics of the family affect socialization processes, which in turn may exert an influence on the younger generation's life course prospects. Thus, it is useful to know something of the 1960 and the 1980 senior cohorts' family milieus.

Most (58.1 percent) of the fathers of the 1960 senior cohort were born between 1911 and 1920, and another 20 percent were born between 1906 and 1910. Thus, the Great Depression was likely the major experience that shaped their younger years (Elder, 1974). Given childhood experience with severe national and individual deprivation, the fathers of the 1960 senior cohort might not have trusted the wartime boom and the postwar economic recovery. If the economy had failed so utterly once, who was to say that it would not do so again? It is reasonable to suppose that insecurity regarding long-term economic prospects influenced the basic value orientations in these families and thus shaped the early socialization experiences of the 1960 senior cohort members.

Although the birth year of the 1980 senior cohort fathers was not surveyed, we may reconstruct it by using a secondary source—husband's median age at birth of first and last child in the corresponding decade.[2] Thus, we can assume that most fathers of the 1980 senior cohort members were born between 1929 and 1937. They therefore came of age in a period of recovery and economic prosperity. Moreover, by the time the 1980 senior cohort members were born, their fathers had experienced a long time of economic progress, giving them some confidence in economic stability. This optimism is likely to have shaped the family milieus in which the 1980 senior cohort members experienced their first decade of life.

Comparing the economic situation at the time the parents and their children in each cohort come of age, we observe an inverse relationship: The 1960 senior cohort members start their work lives in a prosperous economy, while their parents faced the depressed economy of the 1930s. By contrast, members of the 1980 senior cohort who do not pursue higher

Table 4.3
Family Situation and Number of Siblings at the Time of High School Graduation

| Family Situation | 1960 Cohort (%) | 1980 Cohort (%) | Number of Siblings | 1960 Cohort (%) | 1980 Cohort (%) |
|---|---|---|---|---|---|
| Both mother and father | 85.5 | 79.3 | None | 6.1 | 3.3 |
| One parent | 7.0 | 12.0 | 1 | 9.8 | 19.8 |
| Parent/ stepparent | 4.4 | 6.0 | 2 | 22.6 | 27.4 |
| Other situation | 3.1 | 2.7 | 3 | 22.5 | 20.5 |
|  |  |  | 4 or more | **39.0** | 29.0 |
| Total | 100.0 | 100.0 | Total | 100.0 | 100.0 |
|  | (812) | (867) |  | (868) | (849) |

*Note:* $\chi^2 = 15.48$, df $= 3$, $p = .01$      *Note:* $\chi^2 = 53.7$, df $= 4$, $p = .000$.

education enter the labor force at a time of recession and unemployment, while their fathers started their work careers in a time of economic progress. These differences in major life experiences between parents and their children have broad implications.

Socialization experiences are also shaped by the internal structural relations of the family. Of particular interest is whether the 1960 and 1980 senior cohort families differ with respect to the number of parents present in the home and in the number of siblings. Table 4.3 reveals that most 1960 and 1980 senior cohort members were living in homes with both parents present at the time they graduated from high school. Members of the earlier cohort are slightly more likely to have been brought up in a complete family. We find greater differences between the two cohorts in the number of siblings: Approximately 40 percent of the 1960 senior cohort have four or more brothers and sisters, whereas almost 30 percent of the 1980 senior cohort members live in a two-child family, and another 20 percent are the only child. For the 1960 cohort members, then, it was much more common to grow up in moderately large families.

The cultural climate of the family is influenced by the parents' education and occupation, which in turn influence their aspirations for their children. Table 4.4 shows that one out of two 1960 cohort fathers (the majority of whom were born between 1906 and 1920) did not graduate from high school. In the 1930s, the completion of secondary education did not yet constitute a standardized stage in the educational trajectory (as it did for

Table 4.4
Educational Attainment of the 1960 and 1980 Senior Cohort Parents at the Time of Their Children's High School Graduation

| | Father[a] | | Mother[b] | |
|---|---|---|---|---|
| Educational Attainment | 1960 Cohort (%) | 1980 Cohort (%) | 1960 Cohort (%) | 1980 Cohort (%) |
| Less than high school | **47.2** | 18.9 | 39.0 | 13.6 |
| | (349) | (157) | (300) | (116) |
| High school graduation | 24.5 | 30.4 | 35.1 | 45.6 |
| | (181) | (253) | (270) | (387) |
| Noncollegiate/some college | 12.6 | 24.6 | 16.0 | 25.1 |
| | (93) | (205) | (123) | (213) |
| College graduation | 9.5 | 13.7 | 6.1 | 10.6 |
| | (70) | (114) | (47) | (90) |
| Advanced college degree | 6.4 | 12.4 | 3.8 | 5.1 |
| | (47) | (103) | (29) | (43) |
| Total | 100.2 | 100.0 | 100.0 | 100.0 |
| | (740) | (832) | (769) | (849) |

*Note:* Numbers in parentheses are numbers of subjects; this convention is used in subsequent tables and figures.
[a]$\chi^2 = 154.09$, df $= 4$, $p = .0000$.
[b]$\chi^2 = 132.40$, df $= 4$, $p = .0000$.

the parents of the 1980 cohort members). Higher education—a regular college degree or an advanced college degree—was a mark of outstanding achievement for the 1960 cohort parents. As Hodgson (1976, p. 53) maintains, "To graduate from college was still, in 1940, to hurdle one of the most significant class barriers in American life." For the 1980 senior cohort fathers and mothers alike, some college attendance had become fairly commonplace.

Similar educational attainments on the part of fathers and mothers of the two cohorts had no equivalent occupational returns (see Table 4.5). More than half (57.3 percent) of the 1960 cohort mothers had not been working for pay in the three years preceding the high school graduation of their child. Only a minority of the 1960 senior cohort members thus had the experience of a "working mother" while they were in their teen years. For the 1980 senior cohort members, the reverse is true: Only one out of four mothers was a housewife in the three years before their children were surveyed. Most of the working mothers were clericals and were employed mainly in low-paid, highly sex-stereotyped jobs. The changing distribution

Table 4.5
Occupational Position of the 1960 and 1980 Senior Cohort Parents at the Time of Their
Children's High School Graduation

|  | Father[a] | | Mother[b] | |
|---|---|---|---|---|
| Occupation | 1960 Cohort (%) | 1980 Cohort (%) | 1960 Cohort (%) | 1980 Cohort (%) |
| Professional | 6.3 | 15.3 | 5.6 | 9.9 |
|  | (47) | (109) | (44) | (69) |
| Managerial | 11.3 | 18.5 | 1.4 | 4.0 |
|  | (84) | (131) | (11) | (28) |
| Teaching | .7 | 1.6 | .4 | 6.7 |
|  | (5) | (13) | (3) | (47) |
| Technical | 2.7 | 3.3 | .4 | 1.6 |
|  | (20) | (31) | (3) | (11) |
| Proprietor | 18.8 | 13.1 | 1.9 | 2.4 |
|  | (140) | (100) | (15) | (17) |
| Craftsman | 23.0 | 16.5 | 1.3 | 1.4 |
|  | (171) | (119) | (10) | (10) |
| Clerical | 6.6 | 8.1 | 14.6 | 30.4 |
|  | (49) | (54) | (114) | (212) |
| General labor | 30.6 | 23.6 | 17.1 | 18.5 |
|  | (227) | (178) | (133) | (129) |
| Housewife[c] | — | — | 57.3 | 25.0 |
|  |  |  | (446) | (174) |
| Total | 100.0 | 100.0 | 100.0 | 99.9 |
|  | (743) | (735) | (779) | (697) |

[a]$\chi^2 = 61.67$, df = 7, $p = .0000$.
[b]$\chi^2 = 200.51$, df = 8, $p = .0000$.
[c]Had not worked for pay in the past three years.

of fathers' occupations indicates, on one side, the declining importance of
self-employment and, on the other, the increasing professionalization of
the occupational world. Although the shifts are not marked, they nevertheless point to permanent changes in the occupational structure.

This sketch of the sociohistorical context and the family milieus of the
1960 and 1980 senior cohort provides the necessary background for investigating changes in the transition to adulthood in general and shifts in the
educational, occupational, and family trajectories in particular. In the next
chapters, the analysis is focused on these latter three areas because they

represent the major social institutions within which individuals' biographical trajectories unfold. They are also the institutions most affected by major social changes over the last two decades (see Chapter 2). In exploring the two cohorts' life plans I begin by looking at these young people's high school expectations regarding education, work, and the family.

# 5 Biographical Orientations and the Passage to Adulthood in a Changing Society

When young people begin to devise their own plans regarding their educational attainment, initial career goals, and future families, they do so within a particular frame of reference, one constituted by the institutionalized elements of the life course discussed in Chapter 1. Individuals' biographical prospects take shape through socialization into particular social groups that equip them with skills, habits, and worldviews; acquaint them with the structural chances of their social position; and transmit some notion of what is within reach and what is unattainable in life. Finally, previous life course experiences and past personal attainments play a major role in an individual's decision to evaluate and possibly reshape his or her plans and actions.

Empirical investigation of such life course–related ideas, which I label "biographical orientations," may be done variously. Following my conception of the structure of the life course in modern society (see Chapter 1), I distinguish between status- and time-related biographical expectations regarding the areas of education, occupation, and the family. The former refer to the social ranks of the positions individuals hope to attain; the latter encompass the "timetables" they develop for major life events.

In practice, of course, these two types of expectations are not completely independent. Age at marriage, for example, usually depends on age of completing school. Conversely, time-related life course expectations include a status aspect; the right timing of particular life events may serve as a status-enhancing strategy. The accelerated obsolescence of professional qualifications, for instance, underscores the problem of the right timing of investments for acquiring new professional abilities and competencies.

In this study, time- and status-related biographical expectations are measured at the point of high school graduation. Although this choice is imposed by the data sets, high school graduation is an objectively defined career step. High school seniors are urged to think about educational and occupational investments, which in turn structure family-related life events.

100

Educational expectations are measured on a five-category scale: high school diploma; noncollegiate postsecondary education (i.e., vocational training) or some college education (i.e., community college; some regular college, but no degree); four-year college degree; and advanced college degree. Professional expectations are coded by type of expected occupation, using the scale developed by Flanagan et al. (1979). Expected timing of marriage and expected number of children serve as measures of family-related life course expectations.

## Continuity and Change in Status Expectations and Anticipated Timing of Life Events

The rapid expansion of higher education over the last three decades suggests that the 1980 cohort's educational status expectations should be considerably higher than their 1960 counterparts'. The comparisons presented in Table 5.1 support this assumption, but they also reveal a steplike rise in educational expectations rather than a linear one, suggesting continuity as well as change.

The proportion of 1980 cohort respondents expecting to leave school permanently after high school graduation has decreased, while the proportion of those planning to pursue noncollegiate or some college education has increased.[1] Considerably more 1980 cohort seniors expect to attain an advanced college degree. This goal seems to have replaced the four-year college degree as the educational status standard. Moreover, we observe a shift toward acquiring some postsecondary education (noncollegiate or junior college), which suggests a drop in the status of the high school diploma.

The data in Table 5.1 also illustrate a more pronounced change in women's educational plans, so that the observed global shifts are due mainly to diminishing sex differences in status expectations. In the early 1960s, two out of three women expect either to leave school after high school graduation or to receive postsecondary education below the college degree level. And only 6.5 percent of all women project the possibility of attaining an advanced degree. Women in the 1980s, however, plan educational careers similar to those of men: One out of four women (and men) expects to attain a four-year college degree; and one out of five plans to go to graduate school.

Rising female educational expectations in the 1980s may express more than an increasing desire for further education; they may reflect as well women's decreasing chances in the labor market (Barnhouse-Walters,

Table 5.1
Educational Expectations at High School Graduation

| Educational Expectations | Cohorts[a] | | 1960 Cohort[b] | | 1980 Cohort[c] | |
|---|---|---|---|---|---|---|
| | 1960 (%) | 1980 (%) | Men (%) | Women (%) | Men (%) | Women (%) |
| High school graduation | 26.3 (201) | 18.1 (155) | 18.9 (66) | 32.6 (135) | 21.6 (84) | 12.8 (71) |
| Noncollegiate/some college education | 29.6 (226) | 34.5 (295) | 23.5 (82) | 34.8 (144) | 29.9 (130) | 39.9 (166) |
| College graduation | 31.7 (242) | 26.1 (223) | 38.4 (134) | 26.1 (108) | 25.7 (111) | 27.5 (112) |
| Advanced college degree | 12.3 (94) | 21.3 (182) | 19.2 (67) | 6.5 (27) | 22.8 (93) | **19.8** (89) |
| Total | 99.9 (763) | 100.0 (855) | 100.0 (349) | 100.0 (414) | 100.0 (418) | 100.0 (437) |

[a]$\chi^2 = 38.8$, df $= 3$, $p = .000$.
[b]$\chi^2 = 55.4$, df $= 3$, $p = .000$, Cramer's V $= .27$, gamma $= .38$.
[c]$\chi^2 = 5.1$, df $= 3$, $p = .16$, Cramer's V $= .08$, gamma $= -.01$.

1984; Ostner, 1984; Allerbeck, 1985). Women may be using schools as "waiting rooms" until they perceive greater labor market opportunities. The greater proportion of women planning to pursue some noncollegiate or some college education short of a four-year degree supports this interpretation: Men with a high school diploma may be more likely to find a job, thus relegating women to schools.

Although the occupational expectations of the members of the 1960 and the 1980 cohorts differ in many important respects, they show significant overlap, as well (see Table 5.2). Respondents are inclined to focus on more rather than less prestigious jobs, especially on professions. This might be partly attributable to the fact that only white high school graduates are included in the samples. Yet we observe great differences in the proportions of 1960 and 1980 cohort respondents who expect to be professionals, to be in elementary and secondary teaching, or to work as general laborers. The 1980 cohort seems to perceive the occupational structure as polarized: A higher proportion of respondents expect either to become professionals or to be locked into low-prestige jobs (i.e., general laborers).[2] And, in fact, global shifts in the occupational structure show a decrease rather than an increase in unskilled labor. Moreover, the late 1950s and early 1960s were

Table 5.2
Type of Expected Occupation at High School Graduation

| Expected Occupation | Cohorts[a] 1960 (%) | 1980 (%) | 1960 Cohort[b] Men (%) | Women (%) | 1980 Cohort[c] Men (%) | Women (%) |
|---|---|---|---|---|---|---|
| Professions[d] | 31.3 | 39.8 | 48.2 | 16.6 | 37.3 | 42.2 |
|  | (226) | (335) | (162) | (64) | (153) | (182) |
| Technical work | 2.6 | 9.2 | 2.9 | 2.3 | 11.6 | 6.8 |
|  | (19) | (77) | (10) | (9) | (48) | (29) |
| Teaching[e] | 15.8 | 4.0 | 7.7 | 22.8 | 1.5 | 6.4 |
|  | (114) | (34) | (26) | (88) | (6) | (28) |
| Managerial work | 10.8 | 7.8 | 18.2 | 4.4 | 9.2 | 6.6 |
|  | (78) | (66) | (61) | (17) | (38) | (28) |
| Proprietor | 2.4 | 6.2 | 5.1 | — | 9.1 | 3.3 |
|  | (17) | (52) | (17) |  | (37) | (14) |
| Crafts | 5.6 | 8.5 | 11.6 | .3 | 16.5 | .9 |
|  | (40) | (72) | (39) | (1) | (68) | (4) |
| Clerical work, sales | 20.9 | 10.2 | 1.5 | 37.8 | 2.3 | 17.7 |
|  | (151) | (86) | (5) | (146) | (9) | (63) |
| General labor | 3.7 | 13.2 | 4.5 | 3.1 | 11.7 | 14.7 |
|  | (27) | (111) | (15) | (12) | (48) | (63) |
| Housewife/ not working | 6.9 | 1.1 | .3 | 12.7 | .8 | 1.4 |
|  | (50) | (9) | (1) | (49) | (3) | (6) |
| Total | 100.0 | 100.0 | 100.0 | 100.0 | 100.0 | 100.0 |
|  | (722) | (842) | (336) | (386) | (410) | (431) |

*Note*: For entire table df = 8 and $p < .001$.
[a] $\chi^2 = 232.2$.
[b] $\chi^2 = 331.1$, Cramer's V = .64, gamma = .44.
[c] $\chi^2 = 144.0$, Cramer's V = .41, gamma = .01.
[d] Includes semiprofessions.
[e] Includes elementary and secondary school teaching.

periods of rapid economic expansion, whereas from the mid-1970s onward, economic trends have been downward. Thus, there are grounds for the assumption that 1960 cohort respondents, having grown up in a period of long-term economic prosperity (see Chapter 4), tend to overestimate their occupational chances compared to their 1980 counterparts, who are faced with economic recession.

Women in the 1960 cohort perceive their occupational opportunities as highly restricted. They must have internalized to a great extent the sexual division of labor in the occupational world. About half of them anticipate either going into elementary or secondary teaching or becoming a secretary or a clerical worker. This suggests that two clearly delineated professional paths exist for white women in the 1960s. One trajectory is open to well-educated women: teaching (20.7 percent) either in elementary schools (57.5 percent) or secondary schools (42.5 percent)[3]; for less-educated women: jobs in lower-level white-collar occupations (clerical work/sales, 34.3 percent). Moreover, one out of ten women "escapes" to a third solution—housewife. These women do not even expect to participate in the labor force.

The professional prospects of eighteen-year-old women in the early 1980s look quite different. Less than 2 percent does not expect to join the labor force; the career path of completing school and getting married (cf. Hamilton & Wright, 1975) has become obsolete. More than 42.2 percent of the women expect to work as professionals. Closer examination of this category shows, however, that, to a much greater extent than men, women expect to work in occupations that could be labeled as semiprofessional (i.e., nurses, social workers, librarians): 73.7 percent of the women fall into this category and only 58.2 percent of the men.[4] Given these status differences *within* an occupational group, the somewhat unexpected greater proportion of women anticipating professional careers becomes plausible.[5]

These status differences within the professions also explain in part the smaller sex differences in occupational expectations in the 1980 cohort. New occupational positions have appeared over the last decades, especially at middle levels of the occupational structure; that is, technical and semiprofessional occupations (cf. Ostner, 1984; Pincus, 1980). In addition, the correlation between educational title and occupational position has become more closely defined in recent years. Since 1980 cohort women tend to increase investments in postsecondary education, they are likely to gain better access to the diversified middle levels of the occupational structure. Both factors tend to reduce sex differences in occupational expectations.

At first sight, it is also surprising that 48.2 percent of 1960 cohort men expect to work as professionals, compared to only 37.3 percent among their 1980 cohort counterparts. As noted earlier, I suspect that the robust economy facing young men in the early 1960s inspired them to overestimate their occupational chances.

Sex differences in type of occupation illustrate the extent of sex segregation in the occupational structure and thus best capture gender-based *role* differentiation. Sex differences in occupational prestige tap the social appreciation and the social esteem of different types of work and thus reflect the gender-based *status* differentiation. As Sewell et al. (1980, p. 552) note, "Prestige or socio-economic status metrics do not adequately reflect important aspects of sexual inequality in labor market positions," but I use these indicators for comparative reasons.

To detect shifts in gender inequality in occupational status, I assign the Treiman prestige score to expected occupation (cf. Treiman, 1977). Table 5.3 shows that 1980 cohort women on average not only anticipate more prestigious jobs than their 1960 counterparts, but their goals also slightly surpass men's.

The respondents' orientations toward education and occupation depict their expected public life courses. Timing of marriage and expected number of children reflect the aims of their private lives. Since these realms are not fully independent, shifts in the public life course such as those apparent between the 1960 and 1980 cohorts can be expected to affect the private sphere. Specifically, I assume that changing educational and occupational plans change some aspects of the family life course. In the fourth year after high school graduation, for instance, approximately two-thirds of all 1960 respondents and less than half of the 1980 seniors expect to be married[6] (see Figure 5.1). Again, shifts in expected marital behavior are attributable mainly to women's changing biographical orientations, which result in diminishing sex differences in marital expectations. The assimilation of male and female marital expectations indicates, moreover, that women's life plans are less fixated on marriage and the family. These changes in educational and occupational career plans may intensify the problem of coordinating different life spheres, with the result that both the timing and the number of children may be altered.

Project TALENT does not provide information on expectations regard-

Table 5.3
Treiman Prestige Scores for Expected Occupation at High School Graduation

|  | 1960 Cohort[a] | | 1980 Cohort[b] | |
|---|---|---|---|---|
|  | Men | Women | Men | Women |
| Mean | 55.4 | 46.4 | 52.0 | 52.2 |
| [sd][c] | [12.3] | [10.8] | [14.7] | [14.5] |
|  | (381) | (426) | (410) | (431) |

[a]Eta $= .36$, $p = .0000$.
[b]Eta $= .01$, $p = .879$.
[c]Standard deviation figures appear in brackets; this convention is used in subsequent tables and figures.

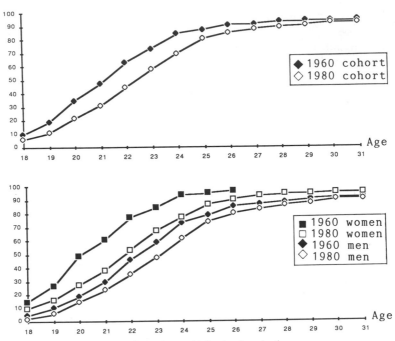

Figure 5.1. Expected timing of marriage at high school graduation.

ing the timing of children. However, data from the follow-up survey in 1971 make it possible to determine when 1960 cohort respondents bore their first children. Based on empirical evidence that age at first marriage is closely linked to age at first birth (cf. Hoffmann-Nowotny, 1987), I hypothesize that the period of time between high school graduation and parenthood has increased among 1980 cohort members as a result of marriage postponement. It is only in the seventh (for men) and eighth (for women) year after high school graduation that an equal proportion of 1960 and 1980 cohort respondents either has or expects to have a child. Once again, the greatest shifts are among women, and, again, the trend is toward traditionally male expectations, thus reducing sex differences in the timing of parenthood.

Both data sets provide information on expected number of children. Table 5.4 shows a trend toward smaller families. The majority of 1980 cohort respondents expect two children. By contrast, we find approximately equal proportions of respondents anticipating families with two,

Table 5.4
Expected Number of Children, at High School Graduation

| Expected Number of Children | Cohorts[a] | | 1960 Cohort[b] | | 1980 Cohort[c] | |
|---|---|---|---|---|---|---|
| | 1960 (%) | 1980 (%) | Men (%) | Women (%) | Men (%) | Women (%) |
| None | 6.3 (43) | 10.3 (86) | 9.9 (30) | 3.4 (13) | 11.5 (46) | 9.2 (40) |
| One | 4.0 (27) | 5.9 (49) | 4.6 (14) | 3.4 (13) | 5.9 (24) | 5.8 (25) |
| Two | 27.0⟶ 51.7 (184) (432) | | 32.0 (97) | 23.0 (87) | 54.6 (220) | 48.9 (212) |
| Three | 29.2 (199) | 21.1 (177) | 29.7 (90) | 28.8 (109) | 20.1 (81) | 22.1 (96) |
| Four or more | 33.5 ⟵ 11.0 (228) (92) | | 23.8 (72) | 41.3 (156) | 7.9 (32) | 14.0 (61) |
| Total | 100.0 (681) | 100.0 (836) | 100.0 (303) | 99.9 (378) | 100.0 (402) | 100.0 (434) |

[a]$\chi^2 = 165.1$, df $= 4$, $p = .0000$, mean for 1960 $= 2.8$, for 1980 $= 2.2$.
[b]$\chi^2 = 32.2$, df $= 4$, $p = .0000$, Cramer's V $= .22$, gamma $= .32$, mean for men $= 2.5$, for women $= 3.0$.
[c]$\chi^2 = 9.7$, df $= 4$, $p = .04$, Cramer's V $= .11$, gamma $= .14$, mean for men $= 2.1$, for women $= 2.3$.

three, and four children in the 1960 cohort. Comparing family size expectations by sex in both cohorts, two differences are striking: There is an increase in the proportion of women expecting to remain childless and a sharp decline in the proportion of men and women expecting a family of four or more children.[7] The fact that 41.3 percent of 1960 cohort women expect more than four children reveals how much the female life course was structured around the family.

This is no longer the case. Women in the 1980s expect to participate more fully in educational and occupational opportunities. I interpret the increasing correspondence in life course patterns between men and women as indicative of the growing individualization of the female life course. Women's public and private lives are structured less by ascribed membership in social groups (the family) and more by individualized investments (and rewards). Nevertheless, men continue to outdistance women in this process of individualization. We now examine how men's and women's social background affect the (changing) structure of the life course.

In advanced industrial society, the rapidly increasing institutionalization of the life course fosters the growing decoupling of an individual's socioeconomic position from his or her subculture integration. Given the fact that such positions are socially and individually recognizable and identifiable social entities only when they are linked to a common culture (i.e., common value and action orientations, common lifestyles), this process gradually sets the individual free from the group's value and action orientations. As a result, the scope of action widens, and conceptions of the life course become more individualized and diversified.[8]

If juvenile biographical orientations are now more individualized, we expect that in the early 1960s they were shaped more fully by social boundaries than in the 1980s. Using socioeconomic quartiles as indicators of the socioeconomic position,[9] in the 1960 cohort we should find similar biographical orientations in socioeconomic groups that form a sociocultural milieu, but very different ones in socioeconomic quartiles belonging to different sociocultural collectivities. By contrast, in the 1980 cohort, we should find evenly distributed differences among socioeconomic quartiles. I test this hypothesis using separate analyses of variance (by socioeconomic quartile) of respondents' expectations (at high school graduation) regarding timing of marriage and educational and occupational attainment (years of formal schooling and occupational prestige).[10]

The results, displayed in Table 5.5, demonstrate that social standing and biographical prospects for different life spheres are strongly associated for men and women in both cohorts. The higher men's and women's socioeconomic group membership, the more education they expect to attain, the higher the prestige of expected occupational position, and the later they expect to marry.[11]

As anticipated, type of association between social standing and biographical orientation varies between the two cohorts. This supports the hypothesis that both male and female biographical orientations are more marked by social barriers in the 1960 cohort and are much more individualized in the 1980 cohort. Not only are the differences among socioeconomic group means more evenly distributed in the more recent cohort, but the standard deviations are also generally larger than in the earlier cohort. The greater standard deviations, particularly regarding expected timing of marriage and occupational expectations, indicate more diversified (i.e., individually stratified) life course prospects.

Examining differences for the 1960 cohort in detail, we find that for men

Table 5.5

Analysis of Variance of Educational and Occupational Attainment Expectations and Expected Timing of Marriage

| | | 1960 Senior Cohort | | | | | | 1980 Senior Cohort | | | | | |
| | | Education | | Occupation[a] | | Marriage[b] | | Education | | Occupation[a] | | Marriage[b] | |
| Social Standing | | Men | Women | Men | Women | Men | Women | Men | Women | Men | Women | Men | Women |
|---|---|---|---|---|---|---|---|---|---|---|---|---|---|
| Low | Mean | 13.8 | 12.9 | 51.9 | 46.8 | 22.6 | 20.5 | 13.7 | 13.8 | 47.1 | 47.7 | 22.9 | 21.7 |
| | | [1.9] | [1.3] | [12.4] | [8.3] | [2.7] | [2.1] | [1.9] | [1.9] | [14.5] | [14.0] | [2.9] | [2.7] |
| | | (76) | (96) | (87) | (88) | (71) | (96) | (86) | (112) | (86) | (110) | (72) | (104) |
| Low-medium | Mean | 14.4 | 13.7 | 52.6 | 48.2 | 22.5 | 20.9 | 14.4 | 14.4 | 49.0 | 50.7 | 23.4 | 22.1 |
| | | [2.1] | [1.9] | [11.9] | [9.0] | [2.5] | [2.4] | [2.0] | [1.9] | [15.0] | [14.5] | [2.7] | [2.6] |
| | | (92) | (115) | (97) | (107) | (93) | (116) | (105) | (123) | (104) | (122) | (94) | (117) |
| High-medium | Mean | 15.4 | 13.9 | 57.3 | 48.7 | 22.7 | 20.7 | 15.2 | 15.3 | 53.4 | 53.4 | 23.7 | 22.5 |
| | | [1.9] | [1.9] | [11.6] | [8.6] | [2.5] | [2.0] | [2.0] | [1.9] | [13.9] | [14.2] | [2.6] | [2.7] |
| | | (92) | (123) | (101) | (106) | (85) | (118) | (121) | (111) | (121) | (110) | (107) | (106) |
| High | Mean | 16.2 | 15.3 | 59.4 | 52.1 | 23.7 | 21.4 | 16.4 | 16.3 | 58.3 | 58.6 | 24.6 | 23.4 |
| | | [1.8] | [1.8] | [11.7] | [10.2] | [2.2] | [1.9] | [1.8] | [1.8] | [13.1] | [13.2] | [2.7] | [2.5] |
| | | (89) | (80) | (95) | (76) | (86) | (80) | (99) | (86) | (95) | (85) | (87) | (80) |
| | Eta | .43*** | .41*** | .26*** | .20*** | .20** | .15* | .44*** | .44*** | .28*** | .26*** | .21*** | .22*** |
| Overall | Mean | 15.0 | 13.9 | 55.4 | 48.8 | 22.9 | 20.8 | 15.0 | 14.9 | 52.1 | 52.2 | 23.7 | 22.3 |
| | | [2.1] | [1.9] | [12.2] | [9.1] | [2.5] | [2.1] | [2.2] | [2.1] | [14.7] | [14.5] | [2.8] | [2.7] |
| | | (349) | (414) | (380) | (377) | (335) | (410) | (412) | (432) | (407) | (427) | (360) | (408) |

[a]Those who expect to be housewives excluded; 11.5 percent of the women in the 1960 cohort expect to be housewives.

[b]Those who don't expect to marry excluded. In the 1960 cohort 7.9 percent of the men and 2.6 percent of the women don't expect to marry, in the 1980 cohort, 9.3 percent of the men and 4.4 percent of the women.

* $p < .05$; ** $p < .01$; *** $p < .001$.

the lower two and the upper two socioeconomic quartiles seem to constitute sociocultural milieus which structure life course–related expectations. For the private life course, these boundaries of appropriate age at marriage are even more exclusive. They set off the highest socioeconomic quartile from the rest. The same pattern holds for all female life course expectations, reconfirming that even in the early 1960s the female life course was not highly differentiated. Higher education, more prestigious occupations, and later marriage were suitable expectations only for women of high social origin.

The 1960 cohort results suggest that subcultural milieus transmit and reflect structural chances (i.e., objective chances inherent within particular social positions) by shaping life course expectations. The objective chances of an individual's trajectory are transformed into subjective expectations regarding the future—into what Bourdieu (1975, 1978, 1984a) has called the probabilistic logic of action. In the 1980 cohort, by contrast, we observe more finely graded differentiations of male and female life course expectations. They still differ strongly by socioeconomic quartiles, but boundaries seem to be more permeable. Together with the higher standard deviations, these distributions indicate more individualized life course prospects, particularly for women.[12]

### Shifting Patterns in the Transition to Adulthood

Shifts in biographical orientations among young men and women of all social origins in the two cohorts may be interpreted as the subjective expression of changes in the social organization of youth and the passage to adulthood between the 1960s and 1980s. These new trends suggest the temporal extension of this life stage and the diversification and individualization of the entry into adulthood.

I test these assumptions empirically by using longitudinal data from both samples to evaluate respondents' life stage status four years after high school graduation. I use three measures of life stage status: completing school, marriage, and parenthood.[13] I interpret the number of status transitions as the extent of integration into the adult world.

In the fourth year after high school, the life stage status of 1960 and 1980 senior cohort members differs significantly. As predicted, a greater proportion of respondents in the more recent cohort had not yet experienced any of the three role transitions from youth to adult status, indicating a net extension of the life stage youth (see Table 5.6).

This extension is closely linked to increasingly longer periods of schooling for a growing proportion of an age cohort (Collins, 1979; Barnhouse-

Table 5.6
Life Stage Status, Four Years after High School Graduation

| | 1960 Senior Cohort | | | 1980 Senior Cohort | | |
|---|---|---|---|---|---|---|
| Role Transition | Cohort (%) | Men (%) | Women (%) | Cohort (%) | Men (%) | Women (%) |
| Youth status[a] | **25.0** | 35.3 | 16.9 | **35.1** | 37.7 | 32.6 |
| | (158) | (98) | (60) | (261) | (136) | (125) |
| Adult status[b] | **23.4** | 12.2 | 32.3 | **11.0** | 7.8 | 14.0 |
| | (148) | (34) | (114) | (82) | (28) | (54) |

*Note:* For 1960 and 1980 cohorts, $\chi^2 = 62.72$, df $= 3$, $p < .000$. For 1960 and 1980 cohort men, $\chi^2 = 8.77$, df $= 3$, $p < .05$. For 1960 and 1980 cohort women, $\chi^2 = 60.80$, df $= 3$, $p < .000$.
[a] No role transition completed (completion of schooling, marriage, parenthood).
[b] Three role transitions completed (completion of schooling, marriage, parenthood).

Walters, 1984); this, in turn, confirms the growing importance of formal education for structuring the life course (Hogan, 1981; Featherman & Sorensen, 1983). Furthermore, Table 5.6 shows diminishing differences between men's and women's participation in the youth status. This change is mainly attributable to women's increasing access to higher education, which causes a delay in their passage to adulthood. Note, however, that the distributions of *both* male and female life stage status suggest a prolonged passage from youth to adult status. For instance, although the proportion of male youths has changed only slightly, there is a smaller number of 1980 cohort men who assume full adult status. We may conclude that members of the younger cohort remain in intermediate stages between youth and adulthood considerably longer.

The progression into adulthood in the 1980s is not only a more extended process, it is also one of gradual integration rather than clear demarcation. These changes may signal the reversal of the trend towards accelerated timing and increasingly standardized sequencing of role transitions to adulthood, which characterized the development of modern society (Hogan 1978, 1980, 1981; Modell et al., 1976, 1978; Winsborough, 1979). It is therefore inappropriate to conceive of the transition to adulthood as a well-defined status passage (Eisenstadt, 1956). A more accurate conception would emphasize the diversification of the transition to adulthood that is accompanied by the pluralization of status/role configurations in advanced industrial society (Bilden & Diezinger, 1984; Buchmann, 1984; Fuchs, 1983; Baethge, 1985).

Comparison of 1960 senior cohort women from families of lowest and highest social background (i.e., lowest or highest SES quartile) with 1980 senior cohort women with similar family backgrounds demonstrates the greater accuracy of this revised conception: In each instance, the difference between the two cohorts in the number of women who maintain youth status is smaller than the difference in the number who make the transition to adult status (see Table 5.7). This trend is more pronounced for women of high socioeconomic status. An increasing proportion of these young people are, therefore, in an "in-between" phase in the transition to adulthood.

In looking at men's transition to adulthood, we should consider the impact of military service on timing of adult role entry. It should, however, be kept in mind that the social setting in which the 1960 senior cohort men had to cope with the problem of military service differs very much from that encountered by the 1980 cohort men. The military draft system, which was in effect in the United States around the period of the Korean War, Cuba crisis, and the Vietnam War, was abolished in 1973. By the time the 1980 cohort men began to be confronted with this issue, conscription had ceased to be in force. The 1960 cohort men, on the other hand, were faced with a compulsory enlistment system. For the men in the more recent cohort, therefore, military service is—as far as the institutional setting is concerned—a career option. By contrast, the 1960 men found themselves forced to confront, in one way or another, the problem of military service.

Table 5.7
Life Stage Status of Women from the Lowest and the Highest Socioeconomic Quartiles, Four Years after High School Graduation

| | 1960 Senior Cohort | | 1980 Senior Cohort | |
|---|---|---|---|---|
| Role Transitions | Lowest SES (%) | Highest SES (%) | Lowest SES (%) | Highest SES (%) |
| None | **6.3** | *42.6* | **12.7** | *59.1* |
| | (5) | (26) | (12) | (47) |
| One | 22.5 | 21.3 | 37.1 | 28.0 |
| | (18) | (13) | (36) | (22) |
| Two | 26.3 | 14.8 | 27.5 | 9.0 |
| | (21) | (9) | (27) | (7) |
| Three | **45.0** | *21.3* | **22.8** | *3.9* |
| | (36) | (13) | (22) | (3) |

For this reason, military service was much more of a compelling and vital question in the lives of the 1960 cohort men than it has been for the 1980 counterparts. This institutional change in the military system makes it somewhat difficult to compare the two cohorts with regard to the ways in which military service affects the timing of adult role entry. Nevertheless, we may ask about the role military service plays in the lives of the men in the two cohorts in the first few years after high school graduation.

The institutional change in the military recruitment system is reflected in the differing percentage of men in the two cohorts who plan to enlist into the armed forces. Asked at high school graduation about their plans regarding military service, about 40 percent of the 1960 cohort men said that they would enlist sometime.[14] By contrast, only 13.7 percent of the 1980 cohort men planned to do so. One year after high school graduation, 15.7 percent of the 1960 cohort men had been or were currently on active duty. This is the case for only 3.9 percent of the 1980 counterparts. Four years after high school graduation, 10.2 percent of the younger men had served in the regular armed forces ($N = 45$); in the elder cohort, the corresponding figure was 31.5 percent ($N = 63$) five years after high school graduation.[15]

The small number of 1980 cohort men with experience in active duty four years after high school graduation ($N = 45$) makes it somewhat difficult to compare the social background and the timing of adult role entry of these men with the corresponding characteristics of the group of men who lack this experience. These comparisons should therefore be regarded as suggestive. Consequently, the same applies to the corresponding intercohort comparisons. Among men in both cohorts who have been on active duty, we find a greater proportion of respondents who did not receive any college education, compared to those who have no military experience (70.9 percent versus 44.0 percent in the more recent cohort and 38.1 percent versus 29.1 pecent in the older cohort). With regard to the socioeconomic background of the family, very little difference may be observed in the 1960 cohort between men with and without military experience. By contrast, in the 1980 cohort, we find men from low socioeconomic background to be overrepresented in the group of respondents who have served in the regular armed forces (30.8 percent versus 19.9 percent in the lowest socioeconomic quartile). This difference may reflect the shifting status of being a member in the armed forces, owing to the institutional change from a draft system to a system of voluntary enlistment. Although we do not know for how long the 1980 cohort men will serve in the armed forces, the results suggest that for white men of low social origin military service in the 1980s may increasingly represent a career alternative to participation in the civilian labor force. Some further support of this interpretation can be found through comparison of marriage and parenting rates between men with and without military experience. Interestingly enough, a great difference is again found for the two cohorts. In the 1960 cohort, the proportion of married men who are members of the armed forces is smaller than that of their civilian counterparts (12.7 percent versus 32.1 percent). Likewise, men in the military are not as often parents as the civilians (7.8 percent versus 13.7 percent). In the 1980 cohort, by contrast, we find more married men among those who serve in the military than among those who do not serve (26.6 percent versus 18.8 percent), and 15.4 percent of the former have a child, compared to only 8.6 percent of the latter. Although the number of cases on which the analysis is based is very small, we may draw the tentative conclusion that military service in the 1980s accelerates the transition to adulthood, whereas it had slowed down adult role entry in the 1960s. This conclusion would also be in accord with the suggestion advanced above that military service in the 1980s may be regarded as a career alternative to the civilian labor force for men of low social origin who, as discussed earlier in this chapter, tend to marry earlier and to start families sooner. Today, the military is seen as a career choice, one that should generally be made relatively early, thus accelerating the progression into adulthood, whereas in the 1960s it was seen as a temporary phase which more or less interrupted career and family plans.

Most importantly, these suggestive comparisons do not contradict my hypothesis that the progression into adulthood in the 1980s has become a more extended process compared to the transition in the 1960s. This statement is based on the following reasoning. In the 1960s, participation in the military seemed to have slowed down adult role entry. Although the proportion of 1960 cohort men who serve in the armed forces is greater than that of the 1980 cohort men, we find nonetheless more men who assume full adult status four years after high school graduation among all male respondents of the older cohort (see Table 5.6). Conversely, the small number of 1980 cohort military members who experience an accelerated progression to adulthood do not greatly affect the finding that among the entire group of male respondents there are fewer men who have already experienced all role transitions to adulthood four years after high school graduation (see Table 5.6). In fact, if the results for the respective groups of men presented in Table 5.6 were not confounded with the effects of military service, they would be even more supportive of my hypothesis.

Furthermore, I assume that current transformations in life course structuring give rise to greater individualization in the transition to adulthood. In the early 1960s, the passage from youth to adult status was closely tied to social barriers that required a short-term youth linked to an early and rapid transition to adulthood for most children with low social background, and a long-term youth combined with a late and gradual transition to adulthood for most children of higher social origin (see Chapter 3). By the beginning of the 1980s, though, these distinct models of life stage participation were dissolving into more finely stratified patterns.[16]

Does the greater individualization of the transition to adulthood among both men and women render socioeconomic differences unimportant in structuring life course patterns? The answer is an emphatic "no." Socioeconomic position still greatly determines an individual's structural opportunities for educational and occupational attainment. The constraints linked to such a position have not declined with the development of modern society, they have merely changed (see Chapter 2). Socioeconomic groups have become less marked by boundaries and are much more finely graded. In this sense, current transformations give rise to more individualized membership in society and, as a consequence, to more individualized life course patterns. To test this hypothesis, I examine the number of completed role transitions in the fourth year after high school graduation by cohort, sex, and socioeconomic position (SES quartiles).

The results are displayed in Table 5.8. The group mean differences and standard deviations confirm that participation in the life stage youth and transition to adulthood in the early 1960s were marked by relatively fixed status boundaries, whereas the distribution at the beginning of the 1980s indicates a much more individually stratified participation pattern. I infer this from the recent cohort's more even distribution of group mean differences between SES quartiles. By contrast, we observe in the earlier cohort both small and large group mean differences between quartiles.[17]

For 1960 cohort men, Table 5.8 shows an apparent barrier between the two lower groups and the two higher ones. This indicates that, for a member of groups with lower social standing, the structural chances of experiencing a late and gradual transition to adulthood were very small, and vice versa for youths from families with higher social background. Among women in this cohort, only those from the highest socioeconomic quartile were likely to participate in an extended period of youth.

In the 1980 senior cohort, the association between social background and life stage status still holds. The chances of an extended period of youth and a late and gradual transition to adulthood continue to be unequally distributed, but, for both men and women, they seem to be more finely

Table 5.8
Number of Role Transitions Four Years after High School Graduation

| | | 1960 Cohort | | 1980 Cohort | |
|---|---|---|---|---|---|
| Social Standing | | Men | Women | Men | Women |
| Low | Mean | 1.52 | 2.10 | 1.25 | 1.60 |
| | | [.90] | [.96] | [.92] | [.98] |
| | | (65) | (80) | (70) | (98) |
| | Group mean difference from low-medium | .22 | .24 | .22 | .30 |
| Low-medium | Mean | 1.30 | 1.86 | 1.03 | 1.30 |
| | | [1.09] | [.99] | [.91] | [1.04] |
| | | (67) | (90) | (89) | (107) |
| | Group mean difference from high-medium | .46 | .11 | .19 | .33 |
| High-medium | Mean | .84 | 1.75 | .84 | .97 |
| | | [.92] | [1.05] | [.86] | [.97] |
| | | (68) | (96) | (108) | (97) |
| | Group mean difference from high | .35 | .60 | .40 | .39 |
| High | Mean | .49 | 1.15 | .44 | .58 |
| | | [.75] | [1.19] | [.67] | [.82] |
| | | (65) | (61) | (85) | (79) |
| | Eta | .40*** | .29*** | .32*** | .36*** |

***$p < .001$.

graded, without obvious barriers. I maintain that this reflects the more individually stratified life course patterns of the early 1980s.

This chapter focused on the biographical orientations in the two cohorts with regard to educational, occupational, and family choices, and on the overall transition patterns to adulthood four years after high school graduation. The succeeding chapters examine each trajectory separately in order to provide detailed accounts of their changing structures.

# 6

# The Increasing Prominence of Education in Everyday Life

The continuous expansion of education as an institution is a hallmark of modern society. In the United States (cf. Barnhouse-Walters, 1984; Boli-Bennett et al., 1985; Collins, 1979), by the end of the nineteenth century enrollment in primary school was nearly universal. After World War I, secondary school enrollment increased rapidly and reached near universality by the 1970s; and by 1984, 33.7 percent of white high school graduates were enrolled in college.[1]

Determining how the educational career opportunities of the members of the 1960 high school class differ from those of the class of 1980 is the primary objective of this chapter. Access to advanced education marks a turning point in the life history of young people because it sets the stage for a wide variety of subsequent biographical decisions and it has a considerable impact on future life chances. The first part of the chapter analyzes the progression of educational trajectories in the two cohorts and documents historical shifts in educational tracking over the last twenty years. A comparison of the educational attainment of particular social groups in the two cohorts in the second part of the chapter yields at least a tentative answer to the question of who profits most from the expansion of the American system of higher education.

## Changing Composition of Credentials and New Forms of Educational Tracking

The increasing prominence of schooling in people's lives signifies ever longer educational careers for a steadily growing proportion of a birth cohort. This process may be illustrated by comparing the amount of formal education the graduates of the high school classes of 1960 and 1980 have attained in the fourth year after high school graduation with each group's fathers' schooling. This approach has several shortcomings, however.

Since a considerable proportion of both 1960 and 1980 cohort respondents have not completed schooling in the fourth year after high school

117

graduation, we necessarily underestimate their educational status attainment.[2] By contrast, we tend to overestimate the educational attainment of the respective groups of fathers. Compared to fathers whose sons and daughters have not completed high school, fathers of high school graduates are likely to have received more schooling. On the other hand, since over- and underestimation occur in a systematic way and do not favor the expected changes, comparing the four series of data may provide useful insight.

I measure educational status using a four-category scale that takes into account the fact that not all 1960 and 1980 cohort respondents have completed schooling. The categories are: no postsecondary education; noncollegiate postsecondary education (vocational, trade, business, or other career training school); some college, but out of school and no regular college degree earned[3]; four-year college, either still attending or successfully completed. I recoded fathers' educational status to conform to these four categories. In particular, advanced college degrees are subsumed into the category "four-year college." Figure 6.1 shows the expected decrease in the proportion of lower educational credentials and increase in the rates of higher ones in the younger groups.[4]

The greatest shifts between the cohorts occur in the category of "four-year college," reflecting the expansion of higher education over the last twenty years.[5] The steady increase in noncollegiate vocational-technical education followed by a sharp decline in the most recent cohort implies a status loss of schools below college level that has accompanied the expansion of higher education. Even more than terminal vocational education in community colleges (see Pincus, 1980), certificates from noncollegiate vocational schools qualify individuals for middle-level jobs that involve modest skills and offer few opportunities for advancement. This type of education is thus likely to lead to "dead-end" jobs which (white) students in the 1980s try to avoid.[6]

The number and type of educational credentials in different age groups measures the outcome of schooling. By comparing 1960 and 1980 cohort respondents' educational status in the first and fourth year after high school graduation, we may observe how educational careers progress at different times. Figure 6.2 shows that the proportion of respondents with no postsecondary education decreases in both cohorts between the first and fourth year after high school graduation. The greater shift in the more recent cohort reflects the increasing likelihood of interrupted educational careers. In the 1980s, young people are more likely to go back to school after some time out. These results indicate that the decision to forego postsecondary

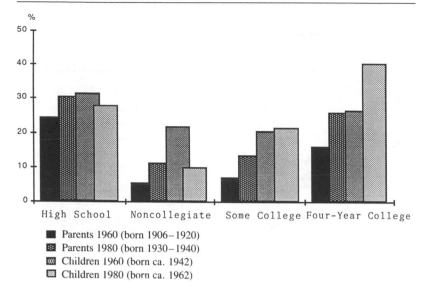

Figure 6.1. Educational status of respondents four years after high school graduation and of respective groups of fathers. (Distribution of fathers with less than four years of high school is not shown, so fathers' figures do not add up to 100 percent.)

education made at the time of high school graduation was more definite in the 1960s than in the 1980s. We may conclude that the more rigidly defined school participation patterns in the early 1960s have given way to a slightly greater flexibility in educational careers and a higher interchangeability of educational tracks.

This is not the only possibility, however. A second, and equally valid, interpretation has been advanced by Barnhouse-Walters (1984), who argues that young people in the 1980s return to school because of declining employment prospects in a "tight" job market (cf. the "warehousing function" of the school). In the early 1980s, the economy did not offer to newcomers to the labor market work opportunities that would constitute a real alternative to school. By contrast, the prosperous economy of the early 1960s put work and further schooling in meaningful competition.[7] These positive job prospects may underlie the more definite character of the decision to leave school for work among 1960 cohort respondents.

Although these explanations differ, both focus on external conditions that foster alterations in life plans and prospects. The greater flexibility of educational trajectories enhances individual decision-making opportunities and may thus contribute to less settled life plans among young people in

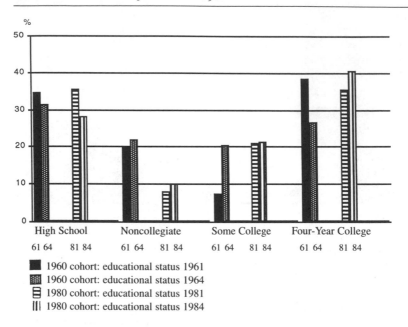

%

Figure 6.2. Educational status one and four years after high school graduation.

the 1980s. A tight job market also may produce changes in life plans, not so much by free choice as by necessity.

Figure 6.2 also reveals that the proportion of respondents included in the "some college" and "four-year college" categories in the first and fourth year after high school graduation varies by cohort. In the 1960 cohort, the greater proportion of respondents in 1964 who have received some college education means that this category is supplied predominantly by dropouts from four-year colleges (note the decreasing number of four-year college students in 1964). We may conclude that at the beginning of the 1960s, attending junior college and then continuing in a four-year college is a virtually nonexistent educational track.

By contrast, the equal number of respondents in the category "some college" in 1981 and 1984, accompanied by an increasing number in the category "four-year college," indicates that at least some respondents transfer from community to four-year colleges. Of course, there are also dropouts from regular colleges; unlike in the 1960 cohort distribution, however, they do not determine the rate of change. These distributions indicate a new form of tracking within higher education in the 1980s.[8]

Access to a regular college education is now less exclusive, educational tracks are less isolated from one another, and they offer more flexibility.

The rather modest rate of increase in the category "four-year college" suggests, however, that college transfers apply only to a minority of two-year college students. Other studies show that approximately 80 percent of these students do not transfer (see Pincus, 1980), but instead are channeled downwards toward terminal vocational programs.[9] These statistics bolster critics' contentions that community colleges fulfill the function of "cooling out" rising educational aspirations, particularly among working-class young people. Nevertheless, as an institutionalized track, these colleges foster the ideology of open access to higher education based on merit and talent.

### Access to Higher Education: Who Profits from the Educational Expansion?

Sex differences in educational attainment may be expected to decline, given the gender-based shifts in educational expectations documented in Chapter 5. I examine the amount of schooling of both 1960 and 1980 cohort men and women in the fourth year after high school graduation using the same educational categories as in the previous analysis. Figure 6.3 shows that women in the early 1960s had only limited access to post-secondary education: They normally completed schooling with high school graduation.[10] Male educational status attainment in the 1960s is a mirror image of the female distribution. Men are likely to attend a four-year college—almost 40 percent do so.

In the 1980s, women's educational opportunities have not only improved considerably, but sex differences in educational status attainment also have declined.[11] The expansion of higher education thus has not resulted in the reproduction of gender-based inequality in higher-level educational opportunities.

Among 1980 cohort men, there is a trend toward polarization of schooling: Men either leave school after high school graduation or they attend a four-year college. This pattern is attributable to the changing value of educational titles on the labor market. In the 1980s, a college degree is a necessary, although not sufficient, requirement for access to prestigious jobs. Educational degrees below college level have little influence on occupational status opportunities. Men who anticipate low chances of earning a college degree may decide to leave school permanently directly after high school graduation. They trade uncertain long-term chances of higher

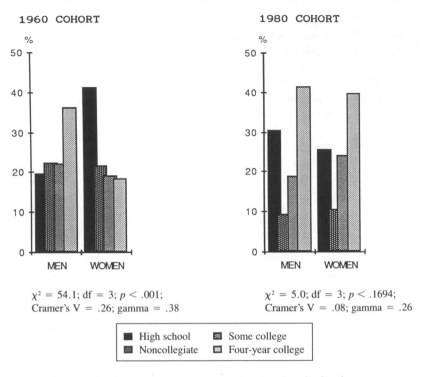

Figure 6.3. Educational attainment four years after high school graduation, by sex.

education providing access to prestigious occupational positions for more certain short-term opportunities for low-status jobs offering some income.

Examining the educational status attainment four years after high school graduation by the children's family background and in terms of the actual expansion of higher education may help determine whether social inequalities in educational opportunities have been reduced or reinforced over the last twenty years. At a more theoretical level, the task is to assess whether the expansion of higher education has fulfilled predominantly reproductive functions or whether it has acted as a vehicle for mobility.[12]

Theories about the reproductive function of education offer varying explanations for the greater educational success of children from economically privileged and well-educated families. In status attainment theory and research (e.g., see Blau & Duncan, 1967; for an overview of different models of status attainment, see Bielby, 1981), the general underlying argument is "that parents with prestigious jobs are able to use their (socio)economic resources to get good educations for their children, which in turn enable children to get prestigious jobs" (Robinson & Garnier, 1985, p. 251). Alternatively, Bowles and Gintis (1977) stress the ideological function of the educational system, which inculcates the acceptance of inequality. For example, differences in occupational opportunities based on educational titles are presented as being the result of merit and talent.

A third approach, and the one I find most persuasive, is associated with Bourdieu and his collaborators (Bourdieu, 1977a; Bourdieu & Passeron, 1977; Bourdieu & Boltanski, 1978). These theorists emphasize the symbolic significance of educational credentials.[13] By conferring educational titles, schools certify "cultural capital" (i.e., the tastes, skills, and habits of the dominant class), transforming what are essentially class attributes into universally recognized abilities and competencies. Accordingly, the educational system's main function is the public recognition of a class-specific subculture. Since upper-class children are more familiar with the abilities and competencies of this subculture and possess them to a greater extent, they have advantages in school over children from economically and culturally less-privileged families. The upper-class family's cultural capital is transferred to the child as educational capital. This in turn provides access to highly valued occupational positions because it enhances the individual's bargaining power in the negotiation between "purchasers" and "sellers" of labor (Bourdieu & Boltanski, 1975).

Bourdieu's theory helps explain why the acquisition of higher educational titles has become the prevailing strategy for the self-preservation of *all* factions of the dominant class (i.e., capital and business owners, cultural elites) over the last few decades. Increased demands for equality of educational opportunity and for meritocratic principles in allocating prestigious positions in the 1950s and 1960s partly illegitimized the capital and business owners' direct transfer of their heritage. In addition, the increasing separation of ownership and management of firms undermined the validity of the direct reproduction strategy. These factors prompted the economically privileged faction of the upper class to begin to invest more in the education of their children in order to transmit their heritage (Bourdieu & Boltanski, 1978). This gradual and more subtle intergenerational transmission of economic capital by means of acquiring educational titles eventually will replace more direct transfers.

The intensified use of schools by the economically privileged faction of the upper class threatens the social value of a higher educational title which, by definition, is linked to its scarcity. The changed approach to reproduction of the business class thus forces classes that have traditionally used higher educational credentials for their reproduction (i.e., cultural elites, managers) to increase investments in their children's schooling. To guarantee their children's future, these classes must seek even higher educational credentials in order to maintain the scarcity of persons with the highest educational qualifications.

Yet, in order to fulfill their reproductive function, schools must offer lower-class children some chances of mobility. It is this upward mobility that demonstrates the equality of educational opportunity and the significance of merit and talent, thus ensuring the viability of these principles and the schools which institutionalize them.

These theoretical considerations lead us to expect all families in the 1980s to have increased investments in their children's schooling, with the greatest change occurring among families of high social standing and the least among socially disadvantaged ones.[14] The data confirm these expectations. Using the family's socioeconomic status as a measure of economic capital, economically privileged groups have invested more in their children's educational careers than economically disadvantaged groups. And using the father's educational status as a measure of the family's cultural capital, college-educated families have increased investments in their children's schooling to a higher degree than have culturally disadvantaged families.

Respondents from all social origins attained (on average) more education in the 1980s than in the 1960s (see Figure 6.4). The stability of the Cramer's V coefficients suggests that, despite an expanded system of education, social inequalities in educational opportunities have remained fairly stable. The gamma coefficients, however, indicate that the family's socioeconomic status in the 1980s has a stronger impact on educational status attainment than in the 1960s. This apparent contradiction is an artifact of the measures themselves. Cramer's V expresses the "general trend" in the strength of a relationship between two variables; the gamma coefficient is very sensitive to deviations in single categories.

The higher value of the gamma coefficient in the 1980 cohort is a reflection of the larger proportion of respondents of highest socioeconomic status in the "four-year college" category on one side, and of respondents of lowest socioeconomic status in the "high school diploma" category, on the other. This is compatible with my hypothesis that, although all families have improved in educational status attainment, economically privileged groups have increased investments in their children's schooling more than economically disadvantaged ones. Given that I am particularly interested in the single-category deviations the gamma coefficient is designed to

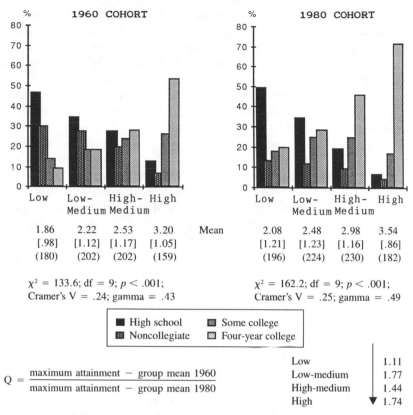

Figure 6.4. Educational status attainment four years after high school graduation, by socioeconomic position.

capture, it is a more appropriate measure for interpreting the data than Cramer's V.

Additional support for my hypothesis emerges when I compare the average amount of schooling between corresponding SES quartiles of the two cohorts. To calculate these group means, I coded the educational categories as follows: "no postsecondary education" equals one; "noncollege postsecondary education" equals two; "some college" equals three; and "four-year college" equals four. Because of probable floor and ceiling effects, the direct comparison of group means by calculating either the difference or the ratio between the 1960 and 1980 group means in each SES quartile may produce errors [15].

To control these effects as much as possible, in each SES quartile, I divide the 1960 cohort difference between the *maximum educational status attainment* (i.e., the value of four, signifying that *all* SES quartile members would attend a four-year college) and the group mean by the corresponding 1980 cohort difference (the formula is displayed in Figure 6.4). The higher the SES quartile, the larger the value of this ratio, thus indicating the disproportionate increase in educational opportunities among children from well-to-do families. Since all four values are greater than 1.0, we may conclude that families of all social origins have profited from the expansion of higher education, but economically privileged ones have done so more than the economically disadvantaged counterparts.

Using the same analytical methods, I find similar trends when examining the educational status attainment by father's education (used as a proxy for the family's cultural capital). In spite of probable ceiling effects, we observe the greatest improvement in educational opportunities among respondents whose fathers have college degrees (see Figure 6.5). This group also has the greatest value of the ratio between the 1960 and 1980 cohort "distance from maximum educational attainment." In fact, educational chances of respondents from families that have accumulated less educational capital than a college degree have not improved. This empirical evidence supports the hypothesis that educated families in particular have increased investments in their children's schooling.

Moreover, the shifts in educational opportunities by father's education confirm my hypothesis that particular educational titles have been devaluated as a result of the expansion of higher education. Declining values of educational degrees mirror a concomitant loss in the social value of the cultural capital that these degrees represent. For example, 1980 cohort respondents from families with an educational status below a four-year college degree have about the same educational chances as the corresponding 1960 cohort respondents—despite the expansion of the educational system. We may conclude that these families have accumulated less cultural capital than the corresponding 1960 cohort families. In fact, the 1980 families have experienced downward mobility, which is passed on to their children. They are therefore less able to transmit to their children the abilities, competencies, and skills that are necessary for educational success.

To examine changes in social inequalities of educational opportunities between the 1960s and 1980s in more detail, I compare the level of educational attainment in the lowest and the highest SES quartile in both cohorts. Likewise, I assess the educational careers of respondents in both

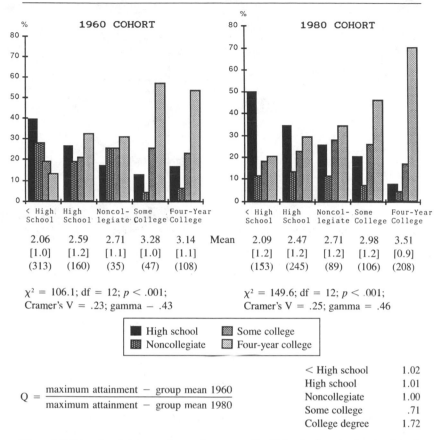

| | 1960 COHORT | | | | Mean | | 1980 COHORT | | | |
|---|---|---|---|---|---|---|---|---|---|---|
| 2.06 | 2.59 | 2.71 | 3.28 | 3.14 | | 2.09 | 2.47 | 2.71 | 2.98 | 3.51 |
| [1.0] | [1.2] | [1.1] | [1.0] | [1.1] | | [1.2] | [1.2] | [1.2] | [1.2] | [0.9] |
| (313) | (160) | (35) | (47) | (108) | | (153) | (245) | (89) | (106) | (208) |

$\chi^2 = 106.1$; df $= 12$; $p < .001$;
Cramer's V $= .23$; gamma $- .43$

$\chi^2 = 149.6$; df $= 12$; $p < .001$;
Cramer's V $= .25$; gamma $= .46$

| ■ High school | ▨ Some college |
|---|---|
| ▨ Noncollegiate | ▨ Four-year college |

$$Q = \frac{\text{maximum attainment } - \text{ group mean 1960}}{\text{maximum attainment } - \text{ group mean 1980}}$$

| < High school | 1.02 |
|---|---|
| High school | 1.01 |
| Noncollegiate | 1.00 |
| Some college | .71 |
| College degree | 1.72 |

Figure 6.5 Educational status attainment four years after high school graduation, by father's education.

cohorts whose fathers have not graduated from high school in relation to the school achievements of respondents from college-educated families.

Using the same measures and the same coding as in the previous analysis, I calculate the trend of educational attainment in each group[16] and then compare the groups' slopes. Slopes of similar inclination represent equal structural opportunities for schooling. The more dissimilar the slopes between corresponding groups are, the more educational opportunities have changed. A steeper slope in the 1980 cohort group indicates improved chances; conversely, a flatter slope represents a decline in educational opportunities. The steeper slopes in the left-hand side of Figure 6.6 indicate

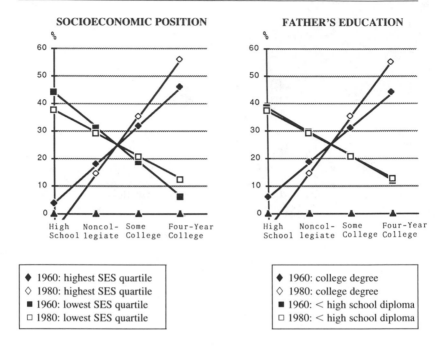

SOCIOECONOMIC POSITION

FATHER'S EDUCATION

| | |
|---|---|
| ◆ 1960: highest SES quartile | ◆ 1960: college degree |
| ◇ 1980: highest SES quartile | ◇ 1980: college degree |
| ■ 1960: lowest SES quartile | ■ 1960: < high school diploma |
| □ 1980: lowest SES quartile | □ 1980: < high school diploma |

Figure 6.6. Trends of educational attainment four years after high school graduation, by socioeconomic position (lowest versus highest SES quartile) and by father's education (less than high school diploma versus college degree).

that both lower and higher socioeconomic groups in the 1980 cohort have better educational opportunities. Economically privileged groups, however, have gained much more than economically disadvantaged ones; for the latter, structural chances have improved only slightly.

The trends of educational status attainment by fathers' education show that the educational opportunities of 1960 and 1980 cohort respondents whose fathers have not completed high school are about the same. Given the rapid expansion of the educational system, the participation of children from culturally disadvantaged families is below average. By contrast, children raised in families possessing a high amount of cultural capital (i.e., college-degree holders) have improved their position remarkably: The slope for the group of 1980 cohort respondents is much steeper than that of the corresponding 1960 group. Their level of participation in the expanding educational system is above average. Again, the conclusion is the same—it is the families of higher social standing who have profited most from the educational expansion.

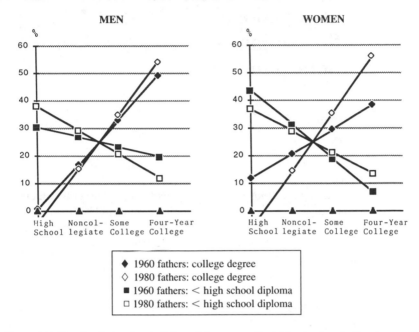

Figure 6.7. Trends of educational attainment four years after high school graduation, by sex and father's education (less than high school diploma versus college degree).

Breaking down the groups of both poorly educated and well-educated families by sex and then calculating male and female trends of educational attainment reveals that women from culturally privileged families have improved their educational status attainment (see Figure 6.7). These women are on equal footing with the corresponding group of men in the same cohort, indicating that sexual inequalities in education have disappeared at upper levels of the social hierarchy. Educational opportunities for women raised in families with low cultural capital have improved to a lesser extent. They have caught up with men of identical family background who, in turn, have lost ground compared to corresponding men in the 1960 cohort. Educational expansion has enhanced the structural chances for all women (although the extent of the improvement depends on the educational background of the family), but men from culturally disadvantaged families remain at the margin of the educational system.

The likelihood that the effects of unequal improvement in educational opportunities will spill over into the employment arena is examined in the next chapter, which focuses on the changing linkages between educational credentials and occupational positions.

# 7

## Occupational Choices: Somethings Old and Somethings New

The transition from school to work is a major milestone in the juvenile life course. By entering the labor force, young people gain economic independence and find their own position in the social hierarchy. The first full-time occupational position is likely to set the course for future biographical decisions and thus to have far-reaching consequences for other life course chances and prospects. The status and role changes that are associated with entering the labor force are also analytically significant in that they represent a strategic point at which to investigate the social structuring of the linkages between phases of the life course. The *point of entry* into the occupational structure reveals how well youths' educational investments have paid off, allocates them to particular positions in the social hierarchy, and structures their future work careers. Moreover, the *extent* to which they participate in the labor force provides insight into the sequencing of the completion of school and the start of work.

By comparing both the passage from school to work and the initial stage of work careers between the early 1960s and 1980s, we gain a deeper understanding of the ways that patterns in the transition to adulthood have changed in recent years. This analysis shows some of the modifications in the transition from school to work that have been brought about by the social change in the educational and the occupational system discussed in Chapter 2. The short-term nature of my empirical data precludes a full-scale investigation of recent shifts in the structure of occupational careers. A more restricted undertaking is possible, however. Here we study changing male and female labor-force participation patterns, trace the shifting exchange relations between educational title and occupational position, and analyze the changes that occur in the patterns governing the determinants of the initial status attainment in the occupational career.

The available information on work-related topics in the empirical data permits measurement of the respondents' employment and occupational status only at selected points in the life course. This restriction is imposed by the Project TALENT career data because they are not continuous event histories (i.e., the data provide no information about the sequence of occupational positions from the time respondents entered the labor force until the point when they were last surveyed); rather, they focus only on discrete points in the respondents' work lives.[1]

## Male and Female Labor-Force Participation Patterns

Despite the steady increase in female labor-force participation over the twentieth century,[2] women's work careers have been discontinuous: Women work before childbearing, leave the labor force, and return after their children have grown up. This sequence creates the "double-peak" pattern of female labor-force participation (cf. Treiman, 1985, p. 215), a pattern that persisted until the late 1960s. Since then women have become more likely to remain in the labor force after marriage and childbearing. If continuous labor-force participation becomes the norm for women, both the timing and sequencing of roles will become increasingly similar for men and women. These changes may ultimately affect both sexes' mobility patterns and occupational and earning careers.

Men's work histories have always been much simpler than women's: Most men work nearly continuously from the time they leave school until retirement. Reviewing trends in cross-sectional age participation profiles, Treiman (1985) concludes that male labor-force participation patterns have changed little in recent years. The only exception is that, on average, men start their work careers later because they spend more years in school.

Transition patterns from school to work are of interest in terms of both timing and employment status. Studies based mainly on male samples (Hogan, 1978, 1980, 1981; Winsborough 1979) show that in the 1950s and early 1960s, a man's first *full-time* job in the civilian labor force began promptly after the completion of school.[3] Female transition patterns for the same time period are similar, except that a considerable proportion of women never joined the labor force, suggesting that they passed directly from school to marriage (Hamilton & Wright, 1975).

Newer studies (cf. for the United States: Hills & Reubens, 1983; for France: Galland, 1984a, 1985a; Pialoux, 1979; for Australia: Sweet, 1983) show alterations in these patterns in the 1970s and early 1980s. Transition from school to work begins to blur as a greater proportion of students join the labor force.[4] Furthermore, the economic situation in the 1970s and 1980s no longer ensures full-time employment after completing school.[5] As a result, full-time job seekers entering the labor force for the first time are at greater risk. Finally, structural transformations of the work force affect the likelihood of finding a full-time job. Both accelerated use of new technologies and altered employment strategies contribute to increasing numbers of part-time jobs.[6]

In order to assess these shifts, I compare the extent of male and female labor-force participation by level of education in both cohorts (distinguishing between full-time and part-time employment). I measure employment status in the first and fourth (1980 cohort) or fifth (1960 cohort[7]) year after high school graduation. Figure 7.1 reveals that part-time employment has become more prevalent in the 1980s: Among men and women at each educational level, we find a greater proportion of part-time workers. This is the case in the first and in the fourth year after high school graduation. Of particular interest are the considerable shifts in part-time work over the last two decades, both at the lower and upper levels of education.

Although they are out of school, 1980 male and female high school graduates engage to a greater extent in part-time employment. This may reflect both altered attitudes toward work and declining opportunities for full-time jobs.[8] Part-time work is also more frequent among 1980 cohort four-year college students, at both time points. The greater tendency of students to hold jobs makes the transition from school to work a more gradual process.

The striking differences between male and female labor-force participation patterns in the 1960s disappear by the 1980s, except that slightly more women than men engage in part-time work. This convergence in male and female labor-force participation patterns at the initial stage of work careers is only one aspect of the changes that have occurred over the last twenty years, however. Among women with no postsecondary education in both cohorts, the proportion of respondents employed full time in the first year after completing school is the same; then, this figure drops by half in the earlier cohort, but decreases only slightly in the more recent cohort. This pattern suggests that work careers were only a marginal part of the female life course in the 1960s: Barely every third woman with a high school diploma was employed full time in the fifth year after high school graduation.

Moreover, female labor-force participation in the 1960s depends strongly on education. Higher educational status, particularly a college degree, fosters employment.[9] In the 1980s, we find equal proportions of women employed full time at all educational levels.[10] Extended labor-force participation (at least for some years after completing school) is now the norm for females—independent of educational status.[11]

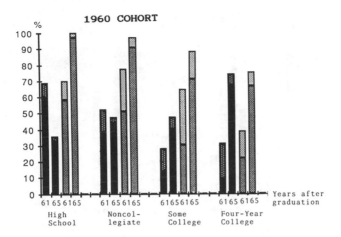

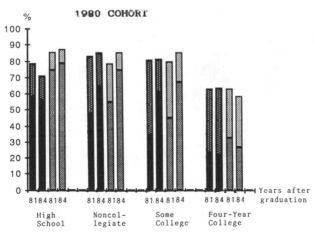

Figure 7.1. Labor force participation one and four/five years after high school graduation.

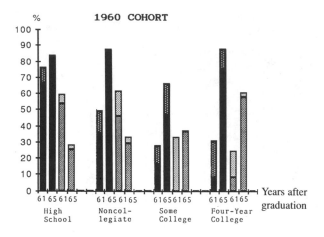

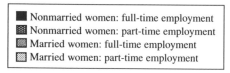

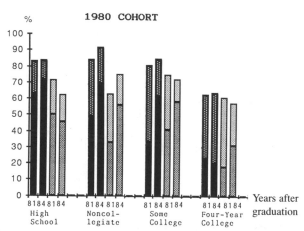

Figure 7.2. Female labor-force participation one and four/five years after high school graduation.

Whether the majority of these women will remain in the labor force during childrearing cannot be answered directly with my data, owing to the respondents' low age at the time of the last survey. Some assessment of the significance of the family for female work careers can be made, however, by examining women's labor-force participation by educational level and marital status.

At all educational levels, married women in both cohorts participate less in the labor force than do nonmarried women (see Figure 7.2). In the early 1960s, however, marital status preempts female work careers to a greater extent. Moreover, whether married women in the 1960s work depends strongly on the extent of their education; participation does not vary considerably with level of education in the 1980s. This suggests, again, that working outside the home is becoming an integrated part of the female biography.[12]

Women's lives in the 1960s and 1980s differ not only in the extent to which marriage excludes employment, but also with respect to employment status. Nonmarried women in the early 1960s tend to be employed full time, especially in the fifth year after high school graduation. Although part-time employment is not common in the 1960s, married women are more strongly represented in this category compared to single women. In the 1980 cohort, by contrast, we find elevated and equal proportions of married and nonmarried women with part-time employment. Although part-time employment is still strongly correlated with particular social groups (e.g., youth, women), these findings suggest that such jobs are an increasingly important part of the labor market structure.[13]

## Devaluation of Educational Credentials

I argued earlier (see Chapter 2, "Contradictory Effects of Education as a Credentialing System") that rapidly rising demands for higher education and increasing investments in educational credentials over the last twenty years have led to an inflation of educational titles and a consequent decline in their value on the labor market. According to Collins (1979, p. 191), "the credential system went into a state of explicit crisis" in the late 1960s and early 1970s.[14] The value of educational investments thus becomes increasingly ambiguous.

On one side, specific credentials promise less of a payoff than previously, which affects the individual's willingness to make educational investments; on the other, the possession of higher educational credentials is still a necessary condition for access to better jobs. In practice, strong pressures to invest in higher education remain in force. Two (structural) reasons foster the "individual rationality" of such investment: the strong negative correlation between unemployment rates and years of education and the consistent decrease in the number of jobs requiring only unskilled labor. As Pincus (1980, p. 344) has observed, these conditions make it "easy to conclude that the solution to unemployment is for individuals to acquire skills by getting more education; if they do not, they have only themselves to blame." Finally, the dominant ideology encourages rising demands for education by legitimizing differences in occupational outcomes based on education as resulting from merit and talent.

The increasing level of schooling among the population has outpaced shifts in job skill levels: Educational requirements have been rising faster than the skill levels of available jobs (Rodriguez, 1978; Burris, 1983).[15] Educational upgrading of occupations—which is the equivalent of the devaluation of educational credentials—signifies that the *same* jobs require more education than previously. By contrast, increases in job skill levels mean that the occupational structure is changing such that occupations demanding more skills and thus more education are required.

Several studies have examined the extent to which the increased education among labor-force participants is attributable to changes in skill levels or to educational upgrading within occupations. According to Folger and Nam (1964), who investigated educational trends in the labor force for thirty-five- to fifty-four-year-old white males between 1940 and 1960, "about 85 percent of the rise in educational attainment may be attributed to increased educational levels within occupations, and only 15 percent to shifts in the occupational structure from occupations requiring less to occupations requiring more education" (p. 29). Replicating Folger's and Nam's study for the 1950–1970 period, Rodriguez (1978, p. 61) finds that in the 1960s "educational upgrading accounted for 75 percent of the increase in education. Thus, 25 percent of the increase in education during this decade is due to shifts in the labor force from occupations requiring less to occupations requiring more education." Shifts in the occupational structure in this later period, then, are more important than in the two previous decades.

Examining the educational levels at which the upgrading is most pronounced, Rodriguez concludes that most of this rise in the 1960s "occurs in the middle educational levels, suggesting that current perceptions of a crisis in the labor market for higher education miss the more crucial situation in the middle educational levels and the middle skill occupations"

(p. 55). Pincus (1980) draws a similar conclusion for the 1970s. Preparing students mainly for middle-level jobs, the economic payoff of the rapidly expanding terminal vocational education programs in community colleges during this decade is modest, at best. Similarly, Burris (1983) reports higher rates of overeducation (i.e., the excess of educational attainment relative to the amount of education necessary in the present occupation) for workers aged thirty-five and under with thirteen to fifteen years of education than for those with a regular (four-year) college degree.[16] He maintains that the rise in overeducation is attributable to "an increase in the number of students attending community colleges (or who otherwise complete less than four years of postsecondary education) without achieving jobs which utilize any skills beyond those which are typically taught in high school" (p. 459).

Employers' hiring strategies are a key mechanism for effecting educational upgrading within occupations (Pincus, 1980). Comparing studies of educational requirements employers have set at different periods, Collins (1979, pp. 5ff.) shows that the minimum educational standard of employees has risen steadily between the 1940s and 1970s at all major occupational levels (i.e., unskilled, semiskilled, skilled, clerical, managerial, and professional). This "credentials inflation" makes employers believe that those with higher educational credentials perform jobs better than those with lower ones.

In general, employers prefer to hire the more educated applicants, relegating the less educated to semi- or unskilled slots. Changing employment strategies tend to set new minimum standards of education required to access the labor market segment offering better jobs. Rising levels of education thus change the rate of conversion of educational titles into occupational positions. By definition, then, some individuals will not receive the expected payoff for their educational investments, fostering a crisis of expectations. Yet, "as long as employers continue to allocate preferred jobs to those who are relatively better educated, there will be constant pressure for increased education, independent of the skill requirements of jobs or changes in the rate of economic return" (Burris, 1983, p. 455).

In order to test this assumed relationship between credentials inflation and the devaluation of educational titles on the labor market, I compare the prestige of full-time occupational positions by level of education and sex in the two cohorts. My test includes only the lower educational titles (i.e., high school diploma, noncollegiate postsecondary education, and some college education) because a considerable part of 1980 cohort respondents are still in school (four-year college). This is a major limitation, as the

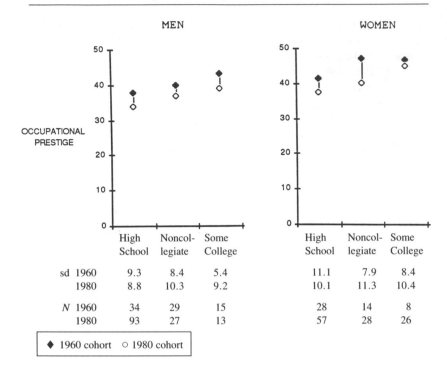

Figure 7.3. Occupational prestige of full-time job four/five years after high school graduation (Treiman prestige scores).

greater likelihood of the devaluation of lower credentials ought to be tested against the higher probability of stable values of higher educational titles (liberal arts degree and advanced college degree).

Using Treiman's prestige scores, I measure the occupational status of 1980 cohort respondents in the fourth year after high school graduation, and that of 1960 cohort respondents in the fifth year. Figure 7.3 shows that the average prestige of full-time jobs has declined at each level of education, both for men and for women.[17] Although the differences are not dramatic, their consistency suggests the devaluation of educational titles between the 1960s and the 1980s. Not only has the high school diploma lost much of its previous prestige, but the more diffuse categories of "noncollegiate postsecondary education" and of "some college education"[18] have also been devalued on the labor market. These categories include both shorter and longer training periods (e.g., a few weeks, months, or years) and more and less prestigious curricula (i.e., terminal vocational versus liberal arts curriculum in community colleges). The declining rate of conversion—despite the great variety of programs and curricula—suggests the *social* depreciation of educational credentials below the four-year college degree level.

To further evaluate this hypothesized devaluation, I compare in Table 7.1 occupational status *expectations*, again using Treiman's prestige scores, by *expected* level of education, as measured on a four-category scale (high school diploma, noncollegiate postsecondary education/some college education, four-year college degree, advanced college degree). This comparison is only a proxy based on the rationale that individuals internalize the relationship between "title and jobs." Professional counseling in high school, for example, provides young people with information about the jobs available to them on the basis of given educational attainments. Moreover, they perceive what their older peers or their older siblings have attained on the basis of particular credentials. Finally, most young people are aware of the occupational expectations their parents have for them, and

Table 7.1
Treiman Prestige Scores of Expected Occupational Position

| Expected Level of Education | Prestige Score of Expected Occupation | | | |
| | 1960 Cohort | | 1980 Cohort | |
| | Men | Women | Men | Women |
|---|---|---|---|---|
| High school | 47.5 | 40.2 | 41.7 | 41.3 |
| diploma | [10.9] | [8.5] | [11.0] | [11.6] |
| | (63) | (132) | (79) | (68) |
| Noncollegiate/some | 51.6 | 45.4 | **45.8** | **46.6** |
| college education | [11.4] | [9.7] | [12.1] | [13.3] |
| | (78) | (138) | (126) | (161) |
| Four-year college | 59.5 | 52.8 | 57.2 | 57.6 |
| degree | [9.3] | [9.8] | [11.2] | [10.4] |
| | (133) | (108) | (107) | (109) |
| Advanced college | 63.8 | 53.3 | 64.4 | 64.0 |
| degree | [10.5] | [9.0] | [13.1] | [11.7] |
| | (67) | (27) | (90) | (87) |
| Eta | .49 | .49 | **.59** | **.56** |

*Note: p* = .0000 for each column.

they, too, are based on a perception of the status connections between education and occupation at a given time.

We find that for men the social value of educational credentials below the liberal arts degree has declined, whereas college degrees have remained fairly stable. For women, lower educational degrees have not lost their value, whereas expected college degrees are associated with much higher occupational status.

Let us consider the pattern for women first. Those in the 1980 cohort expect a better payoff for given levels of credentials than do their 1960 counterparts. We may assume that they perceive the occupational structure as more accessible. However, the *actual* occupational opportunities for women with educational credentials below the college degree do not correspond with their expectations—they are considerably lower (see Figure 7.3).

This inconsistency arises partly from the fact that *all* women are included in the analysis of expectations, but only about 35 percent of the 1960 cohort women below college degree level are employed full time in the fifth year after high school graduation, while the corresponding figure is about 60 percent for 1980 cohort women. Thus, there are grounds for the assumption that, among the 1960 cohort women, those who remained in the labor force for some years started out with higher expectations and better jobs than women who left. Reexamination of occupational status expectations in the two lower educational categories based on the number of 1960 cohort women employed full time supports my assumption for women with high school diplomas and disproves it for those with noncollegiate postsecondary education.[19] Thus, we may cautiously conclude that the high school diploma, in particular, has decreased in value for women, too.

Nineteen-sixty cohort women expecting a liberal arts degree or an advanced college degree have considerably lower occupational status expectations than their 1980 counterparts[20]; the latter have status expectations very similar to those of the males.[21] Based on their expectations, well-educated women in the 1980s will have better access to higher levels of the occupational hierarchy than did women two decades ago.

The male trends are more clearly defined. In the 1980s, educational investments below the liberal arts degree have much less of a payoff than in the 1960s.[22] Men with such credentials in the early 1960s expected, on average, fairly good occupational chances, whereas their 1980 counterparts fall considerably behind. A new minimal educational standard seems to have been institutionalized for men: A college degree is now a necessary—but not a sufficient—condition for access to the labor market segment offering prestigious jobs. The college diploma is not a sufficient condition because the conversion of educational titles into occupational positions must be individually realized and, therefore, depends critically on the situation in the labor market (i.e., on the number of job offers) and on the number of competitors (i.e., on the number of particular degree holders).[23]

Although it cannot be directly inferred from the data, declining occupational chances for men without college education might be linked to changing sex ratios at lower levels of the occupational hierarchy over the last two decades. As more women remain in the labor force after marriage, jobs at the lower levels of the occupational hierarchy become gradually "feminized,"[24] and men with appropriate (higher) educational credentials move into middle- and upper-level job categories. Men with less education are thus left to compete with women for low-prestige, low-pay jobs. In the 1970s, these kinds of jobs grew much faster than better-paid "men's work" (Bird, 1979). In this respect, men's occupational prospects and careers in the 1980s depend more on success in school than they did in the 1960s.

### Labor Market Value of Credentials and Social Value of Degree Holders

These dynamics suggest that status and income attainment do not depend solely on educational credentials. Drawing on Bourdieu's thesis that the labor market value of educational certificates is related to the "social value" of the degree holders (see Chapter 1, "Social Structure and Action Strategies: An Outline of Bourdieu's Theory of Practice"), I examine sex differences in status and income attainment by level of education (i.e., high school diploma, noncollegiate postsecondary education, some college education) in both cohorts. Income attainment is measured by annual earnings of full-time jobs in the fourth (1980 cohort) and fifth (1960 cohort) year after high school graduation.[25] Occupational status is measured (as before) by the Treiman prestige score.

At each educational level in both cohorts, we find slightly higher occupational statuses for women and much higher annual earnings for men—a result confirmed by numerous studies (Figure 7.4; see Sewell et al. 1980). Educational investments provide a much higher economic return for men; women receive a small occupational status advantage.[26] Sex differences in status and income attainment seem to have remained fairly stable over the last two decades.[27] Women earn about 60 to 70 percent of what men do,

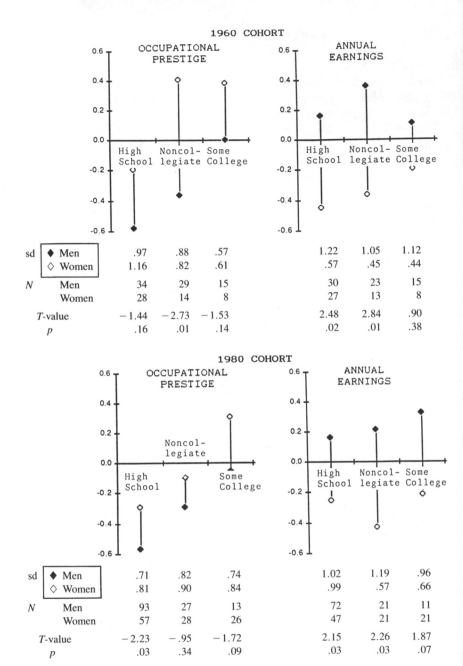

Figure 7.4. Occupational prestige and annual earnings of full-time jobs four/five years after high school graduation, by educational level and sex.

except for 1960 cohort women with some college education, who earn a bit more than this.[28] Despite the small number of cases on which the analysis is based,[29] these figures are consistent with those reported by Treiman and Hartmann (1981, p. 16), who find that the ratio of about 60 percent for women's earnings has held constant over the last twenty-five years.

The increasing sex difference in annual earnings of respondents with some college education may be linked to the status change in this category. Results presented in the last chapter showed that in the 1960s, this category consisted mainly of college dropouts, whereas it contains a much greater proportion of two-year college students in the 1980s. Thus, the increase in gender-based wage differentials suggests that women in the 1980s enroll to a greater extent than men in less prestigious educational programs, which lead to low-paying, sex-stereotyped jobs. Pincus's (1980) study of the social characteristics of community college students shows that women are overrepresented in the less prestigious terminal vocational programs, and men are more often found in the more prestigious liberal arts programs. Within terminal vocational training, there is a greater proportion of women in less prestigious programs.

Gender differences in earnings have often been based on claims that women tend to have much less work experience than men and moreover tend to have discontinuous work experience (Treiman, 1985). These criteria cannot explain wage differentials between male and female high school graduates in the initial stage of their work careers, however. Men and women at that point have about the same amount of work experience; moreover, jobs accessible to high school graduates do not require highly sophisticated skills. Thus, it is less actual and more expected work experience that discriminates against women. Specific job skills are acquired mostly on the job (Pincus, 1980). Depending on the type of job, such "on-the-job training" causes employers expenses which they try to minimize. In order to ensure the maximum return on their investment, employers rank potential employees according to the level of risk they represent. As women are more likely than men to interrupt work (and thus leave the company), hiring a female is likely to cause higher (long-term) expenses relative to hiring a male. Accordingly, although women possess the same formal qualifications as men, they are excluded from jobs with good income and promotional opportunities and relegated to dead-end and low-paying jobs within occupational groups.[30]

To provide greater insight into sex differences in annual earnings for full-time jobs at *all* levels of education, I present below men's and women's status and income attainment by level of education, using data from the

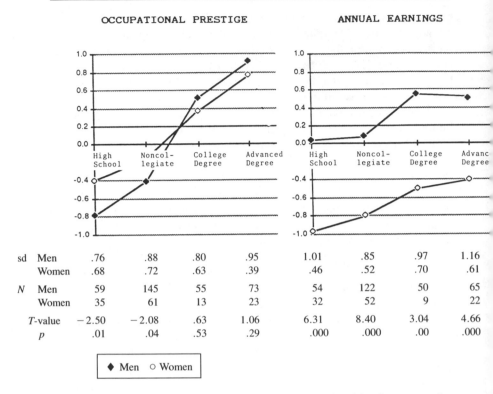

| | | OCCUPATIONAL PRESTIGE | | | | ANNUAL EARNINGS | | |
|---|---|---|---|---|---|---|---|---|
| sd | Men | .76 | .88 | .80 | .95 | 1.01 | .85 | .97 | 1.16 |
| | Women | .68 | .72 | .63 | .39 | .46 | .52 | .70 | .61 |
| N | Men | 59 | 145 | 55 | 73 | 54 | 122 | 50 | 65 |
| | Women | 35 | 61 | 13 | 23 | 32 | 52 | 9 | 22 |
| T-value | | −2.50 | −2.08 | .63 | 1.06 | 6.31 | 8.40 | 3.04 | 4.66 |
| p | | .01 | .04 | .53 | .29 | .000 | .000 | .00 | .000 |

◆ Men   ○ Women

Figure 7.5. Occupational prestige and annual earnings of full-time jobs eleven years after high school graduation, by level of education and sex.

1960 senior cohort eleven-year follow-up. Figure 7.5 shows that the status advantages of educational investments for females hold only at lower levels of the occupational hierarchy. Interestingly, sex differences in annual earnings are greater at these levels, too. If work experience was the major determinant of gender-based wage differentials, we would expect greater differences at higher-level jobs, which require more skills and work experience. The inverse relationship underscores the cumulative discriminatory effects of sex and low educational attainment.

## Titles and Jobs: Growing Dependency of Occupational Positions on Educational Credentials

Access to occupational positions is increasingly dependent on schooling, at the expense of job performance and on-the-job training (Lenhardt,

1985). Thus, formal education has an ever greater impact on the individual's allocation to a particular position in the social hierarchy.

Education's increasing influence results in the growing individualization of social positions because schooling emphasizes individualistic problem solving. Students come to conceive of themselves as independent actors and as isolated competitors. What is to be achieved in life is less defined by (ascribed) membership in a particular social group and instead is believed to depend more on individual action. It is in this sense that the rising influence of education is linked to the increasing individualization of both the life stage youth and the transition to adulthood.

The family's social standing has not, however, lost its importance in the process of status attainment and status inheritance. Rather, the way in which the family's social background is transmitted from generation to generation has undergone changes. As the empirical evidence presented in the last chapter shows, families of all social origins have increased investments in their children's schooling. To determine whether this heightened educational investment actually affects the children's placement in the social hierarchy requires an examination of occupational status attainment.[31]

A comparison of both cohorts' fathers' occupational status attainment with that of 1960 cohort male respondents in the *eleventh* year after high school graduation provides a measure of (the change in) the strength of the relationship between education and occupation over the last few decades. (The 1980 senior cohort is excluded from the analysis because too many respondents are still in school.[32]) I use a five-category scale for education (i.e., less than high school diploma, high school diploma, noncollegiate postsecondary education/some college education, four-year college degree, advanced college degree) and Flanagan et al.'s (1979) eight-category scale for the type of occupational position. This is the same approach I used for describing the respondents' occupational expectations (see Chapter 5, "Continuity and Change in Status Expectations and Anticipated Timing of Life Events").

Table 7.2 indicates that the allocation of occupational positions has become more dependent on educational status achievement.[33] This is only a rough test, however, because of differences in the career stages at which occupational status was measured in the three groups: 1960 male respondents' work careers are at the initial stage, whereas the 1960 and 1980 cohorts' fathers' work careers are already settled. Career stages are highly comparable between the two groups of fathers; moreover, the fathers have a similar average age and a similar age distribution. For the 1960 males, on the other hand, the relationship between educational and occupational

Table 7.2
Educational and Occupational Status Attainment, Gamma Figures

|  | 1960 Cohort Fathers | 1980 Cohort Fathers | 1960 Cohort Men |
|---|---|---|---|
| Strength of relationship between educational and occupational status | .45 ⟶ (681) | .51 ⟶ (708) | .55 (326) |

status is not likely to be confounded by occupational mobility experiences resulting from job performance. The stronger association in this group, therefore, might result from the greater impact of educational credentials on the port of entry into the occupational hierarchy than on later stages of the occupational career[34]. The available data do not allow me to test this possibility empirically. A proxy is an examination of the strength of the relationship between educational and occupational *expectations* among 1960 and 1980 senior cohort respondents.

Earlier I argued that individuals develop a sense of their occupational status chances by internalizing the relationship between titles and jobs. Table 7.3 displays the strength of this relationship for men and women in both cohorts, based on measures of expectations as reported at the time of high school graduation. I use the same scales as in the previous analysis. The data confirm my hypothesis: Educational and occupational status expectations are more closely linked among men and women in the 1980 cohort. The surprisingly strong association among 1960 cohort women stems from the closed occupational opportunity structure for women. Female professional expectations in the early 1960s focus on very few occupations, and these are perfectly matched with amount of schooling: Well-educated women expect to go into teaching[35]; women with low edu-

Table 7.3
Educational and Occupational Status Expectations at High School Graduation,
Gamma Figures

|  | 1960 Cohort | | 1980 Cohort | |
|---|---|---|---|---|
|  | Men | Women | Men | Women |
| Strength of relationship between educational and occupational status expectations | .46 (299) | .56 (319) | **.59** (402) | **.59** (425) |

cational status anticipate clerical and secretarial occupational positions. By contrast, 1980 cohort women's occupational expectations are much more diversified. Consequently, it is more the increasing dependency of occupational positions on educational credentials that explains the strong association among 1980 cohort women, and less the highly restricted occupational opportunity structure.

## Occupational Status Attainment: Direct versus Indirect Status Inheritance

As a final test of the hypothesis that the allocation in the social hierarchy and, by extension, the transition to adulthood are increasingly individualized processes, I investigate the relationship between family background and the respondents' educational and occupational statuses. In both cohorts, I assume a strong link between a respondent's family background and his or her status attainment. However, the increasing institutionalization of the life course through closer status connections between educational certificates and occupational positions changes the way in which family background affects status attainment.

I expect that an individual's occupational achievement has become less directly and more indirectly dependent on family background: The family's social standing is transmitted more indirectly through the child's education. The greater impact of credentials on the status attainment signifies an increasingly individualized social reproduction, since it is based in part on individual accomplishment. In this sense, status attainment has become less directly defined by membership in particular social groups, and as a consequence the placement in the social hierarchy is less marked by social status boundaries.

Path analysis provides a means of examining the direct and indirect impact of family background on occupational attainment. For men and women employed full time, separate regressions are run in both cohorts. In the first run, I include father's education (measured by years of formal schooling) and family income (using a six-category scale) as independent variables, and respondent's educational attainment in the fourth year after high school graduation (measured on a four-category scale: high school diploma, noncollegiate postsecondary education, some college education, and four-year college) as the dependent variable. In the second run, respondent's occupational position in the fourth or fifth year after high school graduation[36] is used as the dependent variable, and the variables of the first run serve as independent variables. The short-term nature of my empirical data underscores the provisional character of the present analysis. The fact that the respondents' occupational status attainment is analyzed in the fourth or fifth year after high school graduation, that is, at the initial stage of their work career, precludes a final judgment about the linkages between family background and status attainment. The occupational entry point, however, is indicative of occupational mobility chances in the future work career. For this reason, the results of the present analysis may be regarded as a proxy of the extent to which the family's social standing is transmitted to the offspring. Moreover, my primary analytic focus is comparative. Of particular interest is the way in which the linkages between family assets and the child's occupational status attainment may have changed over the last twenty years.

I include both family income and father's education in the analysis in order to examine the differential impact of the family's economic and cultural resources on the respondent's occupational attainment. Because of the closer status linkages between education and occupation, I would expect the family's cultural resources (father's education) to become more influential, both directly and indirectly. Conversely, I would assume that the family's economic resources (family income), which constitute the most visible direct transfer of the family's social standing, would have a diminishing direct effect. Nevertheless, because economically privileged groups have increased investments in their children's schooling in order to ensure their social reproduction[37], I would expect that family income would have an increasingly indirect effect on the child's placement in the social hierarchy. Figure 7.6 shows the direct effects of family background[38] and respondent's own education on occupational status attainment. The results for men and women are somewhat different.

For 1980 cohort men, the greater influence, not of family background, but of their own education on occupational success is consistent with my proposition of the increasingly closer linkage between educational certificate and occupational position. In this group, we also observe stronger direct effects of the father's education on the son's educational and occupational attainment. This supports my hypothesis that cultural resources have become more influential in status attainment. Conversely, for both the educational and the occupational achievement, the family's economic resources are more important for men in the 1960 cohort.

For women, the picture is less clear. First, the relative impact of a woman's own education on occupational position has diminished slightly. Second, in the 1980 cohort, father's education exerts only a slightly larger net effect on the daughter's educational attainment. By contrast, among the

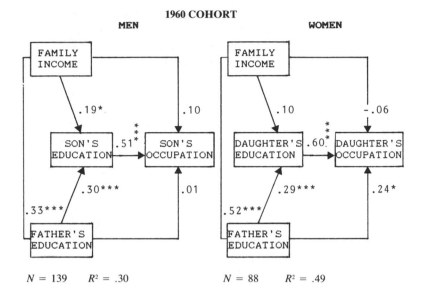

**1960 COHORT**

MEN                                                     WOMEN

$N = 139$      $R^2 = .30$                $N = 88$      $R^2 = .49$

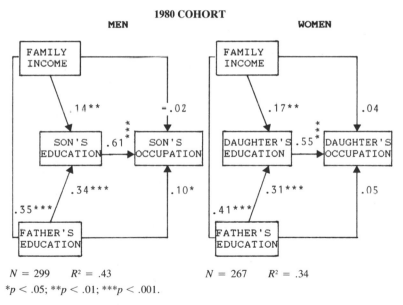

**1980 COHORT**

MEN                                                     WOMEN

$N = 299$      $R^2 = .43$               $N = 267$      $R^2 = .34$

*$p < .05$; **$p < .01$; ***$p < .001$.

Figure 7.6. Results of regression of son's/daughter's occupational status four years after high school graduation on son's/daughter's educational attainment and family background (standardized coefficients).

1960 cohort women, father's education strongly influences both educational and occupational status. Finally, we observe a stronger relative influence of family income on the 1980 cohort women's educational and occupational attainment. These findings provide only limited support for my hypotheses.

In interpreting these results, however, we must take into account the possibility that the 1960 cohort women's sample is biased. Compared to men in the same cohort, the much smaller number of cases indicates that full-time employment in the fifth year after high school graduation does not represent the modal female life situation in the early 1960s.[39] In fact, only 45 percent of all women are employed full time.[40] Moreover, educational attainment and female full-time participation in the labor force show a strong positive association: Only 32.6 percent of the women with a high school diploma are employed full time; 43.8 percent of those with noncollegiate postsecondary education are so employed. The percentage drops to 40.0 among those with some college education, and rises sharply to 67.2 for women with a four-year college education. As a result, well-educated women are overrepresented in the sample. This favors a strong link with occupational position, since educational and occupational status are more closely associated in the higher strata of the occupational structure. For this reason, I regard family background effects and the effect of women's own educational levels on their occupational achievements as over-estimated.[41]

Among 1980 cohort women, these two factors no longer apply: The rate of full-time participation in the labor force is much higher and it is not strongly affected by educational status. Hence, status attainment among 1980 cohort men and women looks very similar, indicating the increasing assimilation of male and female life course patterns in advanced industrial society.

In order to assess the magnitude of direct and indirect influences of both family income and of father's education on a respondent's occupational status, I decompose the total covariance by calculating the direct and indirect causal effects. The decomposition of the effects is shown in Table 7.4. All indirect effects of family background on respondent's occupational status attainment are larger in the 1960 cohort, with the exception of family income for the 1960 cohort women. This evidence suggests that the indirect transmission of the family's background is increasingly important. I interpret this as evidence of the growing individualization of the status attainment process.

Moreover, the covariance between family income and son's status attainment is stronger among 1960 cohort men, and it is composed of similar

Table 7.4

Direct and Indirect Effects of Family Income and Father's Education on Child's
Occupational Status Attainment, for Men and Women Employed Full Time
Four/Five Years after High School Graduation

| | Men | | Women | |
|---|---|---|---|---|
| Decomposition | Family Income | Father's Education | Family Income | Father's Education |
| | | 1960 Cohort | | |
| Total covariance | .25 ◀——— .22 | | .22 ———▶ .41 | |
| Causal: | | | | |
| Direct | .10 | .01 | −.06 | .24** |
| Indirect | .15 | .21 | .28 | .17 |
| Total | .25 | .22 | .22 | .41 |
| | | 1980 Cohort | | |
| Total covariance | .18 ———▶ .34 | | .22 ———▶ .27 | |
| Causal: | | | | |
| Direct | −.02 | .10* | .04 | .05 |
| Indirect | .20 | .24 | .18 | .22 |
| Total | .18 | .34 | .22 | .27 |

$*p < .05; **p < .01.$

magnitudes of direct and indirect causal effects. By contrast, among 1980
cohort men, family income exerts only an indirect effect; this is stronger
for the 1960 cohort men, however. This result confirms my assumption
that economically privileged families have changed their reproductive
strategies.

As expected, father's education and son's occupational position covary
much more among 1980 cohort men. The total covariance between these
two variables is divided between a large indirect and a smaller direct effect.
These results not only suggest a change in the way in which social positions are transferred, they also indicate a shift in the type of family assets
that ensure the transmission of social standing: namely, the growing importance of formal education.

The female pattern in the more recent cohort looks much like the male
one. Among 1960 cohort women, it is interesting to note the very large
direct and the fairly large indirect effect of father's education, and a strong
indirect influence of family income on status attainment. We may tenta-
tively conclude that the female status attainment process has always been

more indirectly dependent on family background. The greater differences between male and female patterns in the 1960s, however, may indicate different parental strategies for ensuring their sons' and daughters' social positions (Robinson & Garnier, 1985).

Alternatively, these differences may be related to the different ways in which men and women of the 1960 senior cohort conceive of the relationship between occupational life and family life in their biographies. The assimilation of the male and female patterns in the more recent cohort would then indicate diminishing differences between men and women in terms of the emphasis they place on family accomplishments, especially the timing of family events. This topic is examined in detail in the next chapter.

# 8 The Growing Diversity of the Private Life Course

In moving from the public world of education and work to the private world of marriage and the family, we encounter no fewer occasions for decision making, nor are choices less consequential in the future effects. The timing of marriage and, particularly, the timing of parenthood structure future family life in significant ways, and these decisions also impinge on future work careers, especially for women. The initial stage of the family career thus constitutes another strategic point for gaining insight into the patterns of entry into adulthood and into the structure of the life course as a whole.

To understand the ways in which young people in each of the cohorts handled the realities of marriage and parenthood, this chapter investigates the differing impact of gender, education, and family background on the timetables of marriage and parenthood in the 1960s and 1980s. How have the changes in American society that I have delineated in earlier chapters influenced the pace at which young people undertake these major transitions? Of special interest is whether or not shifts in the timing of marriage and parenthood are due solely to the recent greater prevalence of extended educational careers (discussed in Chapter 6). The changes in the educational and family trajectories emerge as partly independent from one another, thus strengthening my arguments about the changing structure of the life course in advanced industrial society. As argued earlier (see especially Chapter 2), family life exerts a great influence on the structure of the female life course. Accordingly, here I pay special attention to the way in which women coordinate the career lines of education, work, and family.

## The Timing of Marriage

Men and women in the 1980s both expect to and actually do marry later than young people in the 1960s. As the data in Table 8.1 demonstrate, four years after high school graduation, 41.4 percent of the 1960 cohort mem-

Table 8.1
Marital Status Four Years after High School Graduation, by Cohort and Sex

| | Cohorts[a] | | 1960 Cohort[b] | | 1980 Cohort[c] | |
|---|---|---|---|---|---|---|
| Marital Status | 1960 (%) | 1980 (%) | Men (%) | Women (%) | Men (%) | Women (%) |
| Never married | 58.6 | 73.2 | 73.3 | 45.7 | 80.4 | **66.2** |
| | (493) | (640) | (288) | (205) | (346) | (294) |
| Married[d] | 41.4 | 26.8 | 26.7 | **54.3** | 19.6 | 33.8 |
| | (349) | (234) | (105) | (244) | (84) | (150) |
| Total | 100.0 | 100.0 | 100.0 | 100.0 | 100.0 | 100.0 |
| | (842) | (874) | (393) | (449) | (430) | (445) |

*Note:* Chi-square test for marriage of 1960 and 1980 cohort women: $\chi^2 = 38.45$, df $= 1$, $p < .0001$. Chi-square test for marriage of 1960 and 1980 cohort men: $\chi^2 = 6.19$, df $= 1$, $p < .05$. Ratio of 1960 men to 1980 men $= 1.36$. Ratio of 1960 women to 1980 women $= 1.61$.
[a] $\chi^2 = 28.4$, df $= 1$, $p = .0000$.
[b] $\chi^2 = 64.8$, df $= 1$, $p = .0000$, phi $= .28$, gamma $= .53$.
[c] $\chi^2 = 21.7$, df $= 1$, $p = .0000$, phi $= .16$, gamma $= .35$.
[d] Including divorced, widowed, and separated cohort members.

bers have married, compared to 26.8 percent of the 1980 cohort.[1] The actions of both men and women contribute to this change. Although women still are more likely to marry in the first four years after high school graduation, the proportion delaying this step has grown, thus reducing sex differences in marital behavior. In 1964, every other woman was already married, compared with barely every third woman in 1984. Among men, one out of four in 1964, and one out of five in 1984, had married.[2]

The postponement of marriage is only partially explained by the emergence of new forms of living arrangements, such as cohabitation; 4.4 percent of the 1980 cohort members live together outside marriage. The rate is higher for women (5.8 percent) than it is for men (3.1 percent). The Project TALENT data do not include comparable information for the 1960 cohort, indicating that cohabitation was a statistically insignificant phenomenon in the early 1960s. Thus, we may cautiously conclude that the observed shifts in the organization of the private life course are attributable to both new forms of living arrangements and changing timetables for marriage.[3]

Although the average increase in age at first marriage seems to be an outcome of the expansion of the educational system, this is only partly true. If the later timing of marriage was largely a result of extended educational careers, we would expect the proportion of *married* men and women with *no* postsecondary education not to have changed between 1960 and 1980. Table 8.2 shows that this is not the case, particularly among women. Young people in the 1980s, even when they are out of school, are inclined to postpone marriage. On the other hand, as in the past, school attendance continues to be correlated with the postponement of marriage. In both cohorts, we find a very low proportion of four-year college male and female students who are already married. The fact that the marriage rate for 1980 cohort men in college is even lower than for the 1960 counterparts suggests the increasing effect of education on the timing of family life events.

Among 1960 cohort men and women in the first three educational categories, we find surprisingly little variation in marriage behavior. It is in the smaller, four-year category that sharp deviations appear. Thus, education and marriage are related in a "steplike" way. By contrast, the association in the 1980s shows a higher degree of linearity, although it is still four-year college attendance that most distinguishes marriage behavior. On one hand, the pace-setting influence of school attendance has increased,[4] so that the educational system homogenizes the temporal structuring of life events. On the other hand, later marriages among school leavers seem to indicate shifts in the transition to adulthood. While rapid exchanges of

Table 8.2
Marital Status Four Years after High School Graduation, by Educational Attainment and Sex

| Amount of Schooling | 1960 Cohort | | 1980 Cohort | |
| --- | --- | --- | --- | --- |
| | Men (% married) | Women (% married) | Men (% married) | Women (% married) |
| High school diploma | 34.8 | 71.6 | 30.8 | 59.9 |
| | (23) | (121) | (39) | (66) |
| Noncollegiate education | 34.7 | 65.2 | 27.2 | 42.8 |
| | (26) | (58) | (10) | (19) |
| Some college education | 29.1 | 50.0 | **20.3** | 34.1 |
| | (23) | (39) | (16) | (35) |
| Four-year college | **16.0** | **14.5** | **9.5** | **14.1** |
| | (20) | (11) | (16) | (24) |
| $\chi^2$ | 12.2 | 73.9 | 22.7 | 65.0 |
| df | 3 | 3 | 3 | 3 |
| $p$ | .007 | .0000 | .0000 | .0000 |
| Cramer's $V$ | .19 | .42 | .23 | .39 |
| Gamma | .29 | .55 | .43 | .58 |

roles and statuses (the completion of school promptly followed by marriage) characterized this passage in the early 1960s, transition is more extended in the 1980s. Since early marriages still occur, these changes in the transition to adulthood reflect a diversification of juvenile life course patterns.

A second source of influence in the observed trend toward later marriages is the family's social background. Social standing and educational attainment are, of course, interrelated. Nevertheless, findings reported by Marini (1978) indicate that social standing exerts an impact of its own on the timing of marriage—independent of the structuring effect of educational careers. Thus, it is important to assess the extent to which differences in the marital behavior of men and women reflect subcultural norms and ideologies regarding family life.

Table 8.3 reveals that the impact of the family's socioeconomic position (measured by SES quartiles) increases for women, while it diminishes for men. The low propensity of early marriage among men of lower social origin in the 1980s can hardly be attributed to the life course structuring effect of the educational system.[5] Rather, it reflects the changing structure of life course patterns in the passage from youth to adult status. In the 1980s, young people across all socioeconomic groups participate in the extended "in-between period," which in the 1960s had been the nearly exclusive province of children from socially privileged families.[6]

Declining effects of family background on male marital behavior are related as well to the disproportionately high marriage rate among 1960 cohort men of lowest social origin. This may reflect specific cultural attitudes toward males' early transition to adulthood at that time. Becoming an adult through early family formation indicates independence and thus confers status on men from socially disadvantaged families (cf. Bourdieu, 1984c). In this sense, early marriage could be regarded as a status-enhancing life course strategy for men from modest family background whose mobility chances through educational attainment are highly limited (Ostner, 1986).

The family's socioeconomic background differentiates women's marital behavior in the 1980s more than in the 1960s. In the earlier decade, variation in female marital behavior among the first three SES quartiles was minor, indicating the degree to which the female life course was structured around the traditional family career.[7] Alternatives to early marriage exist only in the highest SES quartile. Such alternatives become more accessible to women of all social origins in the 1980s, although among women from low-status families the traditional family career still dominates. In general,

Table 8.3
Marital Status Four Years after High School Graduation, by Social Standing and Sex

|  | 1960 Cohort | | 1980 Cohort | |
| --- | --- | --- | --- | --- |
| Social Standing | Men (% married) | Women (% married) | Men (% married) | Women (% married) |
| Low | 40.5 | **59.2** | **27.7** | 48.3 |
|  | (34) | (58) | (25) | (55) |
| Low-medium | 24.9 | **55.6** | 22.9 | 36.5 |
|  | (29) | (65) | (25) | (46) |
| Medium-high | 21.0 | **57.9** | 19.3 | 29.8 |
|  | (21) | (70) | (24) | (34) |
| High | 15.6 | 39.0 | 9.9 | 16.5 |
|  | (15) | (32) | (10) | (14) |
| $\chi^2$ | 16.5 | 9.3 | 10.4 | 23.7 |
| df | 3 | 3 | 3 | 3 |
| p | .0009 | .0257 | .012 | .0000 |
| Cramer's V | .21 ⟵——— .15 | | .16 ———⟶ .23 | |
| Gamma | .34 ⟵——— .16 | | .28 ———⟶ .36 | |

status-based marital behavior of women in the 1980s is similar to that of men in the 1960s. The considerable time lag with which this assimilation occurs suggests the gradual integration of the female life course into modern society: that is, into the realms outside the home.

In order to assess the degree to which milieu-specific norms of marital behavior override the pace-setting effect of schooling, I investigate the relationship between education and marriage in each SES quartile. The weaker the relationship, the more subcultural norms influence marital behavior. Conversely, the stronger the relationship, the more education determines the timing of marriage. I hypothesize that family career patterns dominated by subcultural norms represent the traditional life course structure, whereas those dominated by demands of schooling express the modern structure.[8]

On this basis, I expect a closer association between education and marriage with increasing SES quartile, since top levels of the social stratification system show a stronger integration into modern society. By contrast, lower socioeconomic groups are defined to a greater extent by common sociocultural milieus that prescribe value and action orientations, common lifestyles, and ideas of the probable and appropriate biographical destiny.

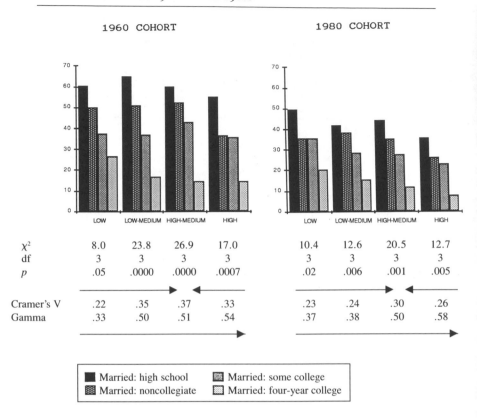

Figure 8.1. Marital status four years after high school graduation, by educational attainment and social standing.

The gamma coefficients in Figure 8.1 confirm these assumptions. Among respondents of both cohorts with a higher socioeconomic status background, the rate of marriage decreases with increasing educational status. In the lowest SES quartile, marital behavior varies much less with educational attainment. Using Cramer's V as the measure of association, however, the results are more complex. They show a stronger influence of milieu-specific norms at both lower and upper ends of the social hierarchy. In the lowest SES quartile, this relationship is attributable to the high marriage rate for four-year college students; in the highest SES quartile, it is attributable to the weak marriage propensity of respondents of high social status with no postsecondary education. Accordingly, a lower-class norm of early marriage and an upper-class norm of late marriage seem to exist—independent of educational status.[9] This possibility does not invalidate my initial assumptions; later timing of marriage among respondents of high socioeconomic standing with no postsecondary education does not undermine the postulated structuring effect of extended education.

## Timetables for Parenthood

I have demonstrated that men and women of all social origins in the 1980s expect to and do marry later. In addition, among those who expect to have children, anticipated family size is very small. These changes in biographical orientations are likely to affect the actual timing of parenthood.

Data in Table 8.4 show that, four years after high school graduation, approximately one-fourth of the 1960 respondents are parents, compared to only 13.7 percent of their 1980 counterparts. These differences are statistically significant using the chi-square test. Although fathers and mothers are the minority in both cohorts, the proportion has dropped almost by half, thus justifying the identification of delayed parenthood as a trend.

As expected, women in both cohorts are mothers significantly earlier than men are fathers, but sex differences have dropped greatly (cf. gammas for 1960, .50; and for 1980, .36). As the chi-squares demonstrate, the shift

Table 8.4
Parenthood Four Years after High School Graduation, by Cohort and Sex

| | Cohorts[a] | | 1960 Cohort[b] | | 1980 Cohort[c] | |
|---|---|---|---|---|---|---|
| | 1960 (%) | 1980 (%) | Men (%) | Women (%) | Men (%) | Women (%) |
| Parents | 26.0 ◄— | 13.7 | 15.2 | **34.9** | 9.3 | 17.9 |
| | (190) | (108) | (50) | (140) | (35) | (72) |
| Not parents | 74.0 | 86.3 | 84.8 | 65.1 | 90.7 | 82.1 |
| | (541) | (677) | (280) | (261) | (345) | (332) |
| Total | 100.0 | 100.0 | 100.0 | 100.0 | 100.0 | 100.0 |
| | (731) | (785) | (330) | (401) | (380) | (404) |

*Note:* Chi-square test for parent status of 1960 and 1980 cohort women: $\chi^2 = 29.62$, df = 1, $p < .0001$. Chi-square test for parent status of 1960 and 1980 cohort men: $\chi^2 = 5.36$, df = 1, $p < .05$. Ratio of 1960 men to 1980 men = 1.63. Ratio of 1960 women to 1980 women = 1.94.
[a] $\chi^2 = 35.4$, df = 3, $p = .0000$.
[b] $\chi^2 = 35.7$, df = 3, $p = .0000$, phi = .22, gamma = .50.
[c] $\chi^2 = 11.5$, df = 3, $p = .0000$, phi = .13, gamma = .36.

in timing of the first child is statistically highly significant for women, while it just reaches the 5 percent significance level for men. The more rapid decline for women also may be inferred from the comparison of the ratio between 1960 and 1980 cohort men with children (15.2% / 9.3% = 1.63) with the corresponding female ratio (34.9% / 17.9% = 1.94). Moreover, when this ratio is compared with the female marriage ratio (1.61; see Table 8.1), it is clear that women are even more inclined to postpone having children than they are to postpone marriage. Since the timing of family life events has changed much more for women than for men over the last twenty years, we may conclude that the previously rigid ascription of sequences and events of the family career loosened, resulting in a greater diversification in female life course patterns. These shifts reflect the increasing individualization of the female life course in advanced industrial society.

As with changes in the timing of marriage, the trend toward delayed parenthood is only partly due to the recent greater prevalence of extended educational careers. If changing social timetables of family life events were solely attributable to increases in years of schooling, we would expect the same proportion of parents among school leavers. Yet Table 8.5 shows that 1980 cohort respondents who are out of school also are more likely to postpone parenthood.[10]

Table 8.5
Parenthood Four Years after High School Graduation, by Completion of School

|  | 1960 Cohort[a] | | 1980 Cohort[b] | |
|---|---|---|---|---|
|  | Completed (%) | Not Completed (%) | Completed (%) | Not Completed (%) |
| Parents | **35.7** (159) | 4.8 (10) | 20.1 (91) | 3.4 (10) |
| Not parents | 64.3 (286) | 95.2 (199) | 79.9 (359) | 96.6 (285) |
| Total | 100.0 (445) | 100.0 (209) | 100.0 (450) | 100.0 (295) |

Note: Chi-square test of parent status for 1960 and 1980 respondents with completed schooling: $\chi^2 = 27.20$, df $= 1$, $p < .0001$. Chi-square test of parent status for 1960 and 1980 respondents with noncompleted schooling: $\chi^2 = 0.81$, df $= 1$, $p =$ ns.
[a]$\chi^2 = 69.5$, df $= 1$, $p = .0000$, phi $= .33$.
[b]$\chi^2 = 42.0$, df $= 1$, $p = .0000$, phi $= .24$.

Thus, these findings bolster my assumption that the transition to adulthood has changed from a short time involving various rapid status and role changes to an extended in-between period. Together with the increasing number of respondents postponing or excluding (6.8 percent) marriage and those expecting to remain childless (10.3 percent), my findings indicate the growing diversification of the transition to adulthood, a trend which may ultimately dissolve the boundaries between the life stages of youth and adulthood. The growing number of status/role configurations that are becoming socially acceptable reveals that social norms defining these life stages are eroding and that social definitions of youth and adult statuses are undergoing revision.

Similarly, the trend toward later parenthood may indicate that marriage and childrearing, traditionally closely linked, are becoming more separate. The loose coupling between marriage and parenthood suggests that the traditional conception of the family, with its emphasis on the role of procreation, is declining in importance. Comparing the number of respondents in 1960 and in 1980 who had a child in the first or second year of marriage substantiates this argument[11] (see Table 8.6). However, because these comparisons are based on very short time intervals, they are only suggestive, not conclusive.

Previous results suggest that postponing parenthood represents a general trend[12]. This would be strongly confirmed if the data showed that respondents from all social origins delay the birth of the first child. In Table 8.7 we find fewer fathers and mothers in each 1980 cohort SES quartile. The

Table 8.6
Childbirth in the First or Second Year of Marriage

|  | Childbirth[a] | |
|---|---|---|
|  | 1960 Cohort[b] | 1980 Cohort[c] |
| Year of Marriage | (%) | (%) |
| 1960 or 1980 | **60.5** | 50.6 |
|  | (55) | (20) |
| 1961 or 1981 | **57.1** | 43.5 |
|  | (48) | (23) |
| 1962 or 1982 | 37.5 | 34.5 |
|  | (30) | (20) |

[a] In year of marriage or year of marriage plus one.
[b] Cramer's $V = .43$ ($p < .001$).
[c] Cramer's $V = .34$ ($p < .001$).

Table 8.7
Parenthood Four Years after High School Graduation, by Social Standing and Sex

| Social Standing | Cohorts | | 1960 Cohort | | 1980 Cohort | |
|---|---|---|---|---|---|---|
| | 1960 (% parent) | 1980 (% parent) | Men (% parent) | Women (% parent) | Men (% parent) | Women (% parent) |
| Low | 36.1 | 23.4 | 26.0 | 44.9 | **15.9** | 31.2 |
| | (60) | (42) | (20) | (40) | (9) | (25) |
| Low-medium | 26.1 | 17.3 | 20.0 | 31.0 | 14.4 | 22.1 |
| | (47) | (36) | (16) | (31) | (13) | (24) |
| High-medium | 24.7 | 10.1 | 10.1 | 35.1 | 8.1 | 13.8 |
| | (47) | (22) | (8) | (39) | (9) | (14) |
| High | 17.0 | 4.2 | 5.2 | **30.0** | 3.5 | **7.4** |
| | (25) | (7) | (4) | (21) | (4) | (8) |
| Overall | 26.2 | 13.8 | 15.3 | 35.4 | 9.3 | 17.9 |
| | (179) | (107) | (48) | (131) | (35) | (71) |
| $\chi^2$ | 15.1 | 31.7 | 15.8 | 5.3 | 10.2 | 19.2 |
| df | 3 | 3 | 3 | 3 | 3 | 3 |
| p | .0000 | .0000 | .001 | .15 | .01 | .0002 |
| Cramer's V | .15 | .20 | .22 | .12 | .17 | .22 |
| Gamma | −.24 | −.43 | −.45 | −.13 | −.42 | −.42 |

*Note:* Ratio between cohorts, 1960/1980:

| | Cohorts | Men | Women |
|---|---|---|---|
| Low | 1.54 | 1.60 ⟵ 1.58 | |
| Low-medium | 1.51 | 1.72 ⟵ 1.40 | |
| High-medium | 2.45 | 1.22 ⟶ 2.93 | |
| High | 4.05 | 2.17 ⟶ 4.84 | |

greatest reduction is among women from families with high social standing: They are the trendsetters for the changing timetables within the female private life course.[13] The change in this group contrasts sharply with the very modest effect that family background exerts on the timing of motherhood among 1960 cohort women: 44.9 percent of the women from the lowest SES quartile are already mothers by the fourth year after high school graduation, compared with 30 percent of the women in the highest SES quartile. This suggests that, in the early 1960s, women of all social origins were more inclined to organize their life course around the family and thus were more likely to make a rapid transition from school to marriage and to parenthood.

The female distribution in the 1980s suggests that women are gradually adopting male life course patterns in this area, much as they are in the educational and occupational spheres. This wide-ranging time-lagged assimilation supports my assumption that, over the last twenty years, the female life course has experienced an accelerated integration into the structure of the institutionalized life course.[14]

So far, my analysis has been limited to assessing the impact of structural factors on the timing of parenthood. To examine the way in which subjective factors (i.e., biographical orientations) shape male and female life courses in early adulthood, I analyze respondents' family life plans. Various status- and time-related life course expectations (i.e., educational attainment, timing of parenthood) depend to some degree on the extent of family orientation. I assume that expected age at marriage (as reported at the time of high school graduation) measures the extent to which the family sphere provides the frame of reference within which respondents organize their life plans. The earlier young people expect to marry the more pronounced the family orientation. Conversely, later marriages are associated with a less pronounced family orientation; these young people invest resources and energies in other life trajectories, particularly in educational and occupational careers.

I assume that the degree of family orientation has a greater impact on female than male life courses. The social division of labor between the sexes more effectively precludes women than men from investing their resources and capacities in both educational/professional careers and in the family. Female life chances have always been more exclusively defined to include *either* marriage and motherhood *or* a professional career. Increasing access to higher education for women and growing, although fluctuating, integration into the labor force are slowly reducing the exclusiveness of female investments in either family or work. This trend makes it increasingly possible for women to assume roles both in the public and private life spheres.

To assess the way in which family orientation is shaped by social background and how this in turn structures public and private life course statuses, I conduct a path analysis, presuming the following cause-and-effect connections: Resources and opportunities of the family's socioeconomic position structure both family life prospects and educational status attainment. The way in which the family career is depicted in turn influences educational career outcomes, as high investments in one career to some extent preclude the allocation of resources to others. Double career investments are less likely for women, particularly for those in the early cohort (cf. Marini, 1984c). Finally, family orientation and educational status determine the likelihood of parenthood in the fourth year after high school graduation.

I test this causal structure by running separate regressions for both men and women, using, in the first run, educational status as reported in the fourth year after high school graduation as the dependent variable, and socioeconomic status of the family (SES index) and extent of family orientation surveyed at the time of high school graduation as the independent variables. In the second run, I include parent status surveyed in the fourth year after high school graduation as the dependent variable; variables from the first run serve as the independent variables. Figure 8.2 presents the standardized regression coefficients and the explained variance ($R^2$) for men and women in each cohort.[15]

Educational career exerts the largest (net) effect on the likelihood of having a child in the fourth year after high school graduation, except among the 1960 cohort men. The considerably stronger impact of education on the timing of motherhood supports my hypothesis that women experience more difficulties in integrating and synchronizing education and family life. Similarly, the subjective relevance of the family affects female educational attainment to a greater extent than it does male. As expected, the effect is smaller for 1980 cohort women. A strong family orientation no longer precludes women from attaining higher education. This supports the assumption that female life course statuses have become less ascribed. The scope of action available to women has increased, enhancing their opportunities for individual decision making.

In both cohorts, the direct effects of family orientation on the timing of parenthood for men and women are not easily interpreted. For 1960 cohort men, the effect is .20 net of social background and educational status, whereas it is .15 for women in the same cohort. For 1980 cohort men, it is only of minor importance (.12), while it assumes greater importance for women (.19). Increasing variation in family orientation among 1980 cohort women may explain its greater impact on the timing of children. Extent of family orientation and timing of parenthood are more susceptible to individual decision making, whereas a pronounced family orientation was more like an "ascribed" attitude among young women in the early 1960s. As such, it involved little opportunity for individual choice. The declining importance of family orientation among men is partly due to little variation in the dependent variable among 1980 cohort men[16] (even men even with a strong family orientation avoid parenthood in the first four years after high school graduation).

Interestingly, 1960 cohort men, unlike any other group, show a fairly

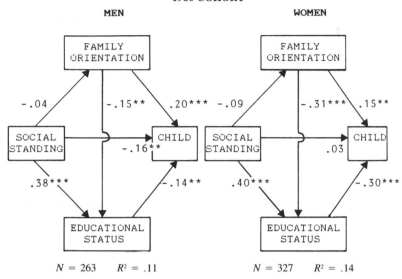

**1960 COHORT**

MEN       WOMEN

$N = 263$   $R^2 = .11$      $N = 327$   $R^2 = .14$

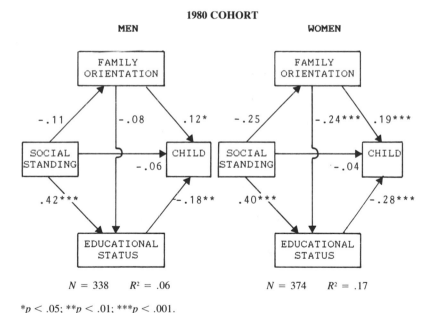

**1980 COHORT**

MEN       WOMEN

$N = 338$   $R^2 = .06$      $N = 374$   $R^2 = .17$

$*p < .05; **p < .01; ***p < .001.$

Figure 8.2. Results of regression of parenthood on social standing, family orientation, and educational status (standardized coefficients).

large net effect of parents' socioeconomic position on the likelihood of being a father. This suggests the existence of strong milieu-specific norms regarding the timing of parenthood for men in the early 1960s, mores that are not merely derivative of the status-based timing of educational and/or occupational careers.

The varying strength of the relationship between parents' social standing and family orientation in the two cohorts suggests that the way in which family background in the early 1960s shapes male and female family career prospects differs from its impact in the 1980s. In the 1960 cohort, for both men and women, there is little variation in this relationship; the distribution is highly clustered. Among 1980 senior cohort men and women, by contrast, family orientation varies with the socioeconomic standing of the family in a more linear and gradual way, which results in higher correlation coefficients. This type of distribution produces a highly individualized pattern. Although family orientations are strongly influenced by socioeconomic status, unlike in the clustered distribution, they are not shaped by well-defined social boundaries.

In order to assess the magnitude of direct and indirect influences of parents' socioeconomic position, family orientation, and educational status on the timing of parenthood, I decompose the total covariance into direct and indirect causal effects. The decomposition of effects is shown in Table 8.8. For men of both cohorts, social background and family orientation exert only small indirect effects on the likelihood of having a child in the fourth year after high school graduation. The path "social origin–educational status–parent status" ($-.09$) for 1980 cohort men is the only (minor) exception. By contrast, fairly strong indirect effects, particularly of the family's socioeconomic position, are found for women in both cohorts. Socioeconomic group membership structures the timing of family life events by strongly influencing female educational attainment. The stronger effect for 1980 cohort women indicates that family background tends to differentiate female life course patterns in the 1980s to a greater extent than in the 1960s. Moreover, we observe increasing values of direct and decreasing values of indirect effects of family orientation on the timing of motherhood: The distribution of effects for 1980 cohort women resembles the male one. In fact, it resembles the distribution of effects for the 1960 cohort men. This again supports the assumption of the time-lagged assimilation of male and female life course patterns. This shift in the relationship between direct and indirect effects shows that the influence of family orientation is becoming more confined to the family sphere and spills over less to other life spheres. This suggests that public and private

Table 8.8
Decomposition of Effects on Parenthood of Parents' Socioeconomic Position
(Social Origin), Family Orientation, and Educational Status

| Decompo-sition | Men | | | Women | | |
|---|---|---|---|---|---|---|
| | Social Origin | Family Orientation | Education Status | Social Origin | Family Orientation | Education Status |
| | | | 1960 Cohort | | | |
| Total covariance | −.22 | .22 | −.24 | −.12 | .25 | −.34 |
| Causal: | | | | | | |
| Direct | −.16** | .20*** | −.14** | .03 | .15** | −.30*** |
| Indirect | −.06 | −.02 | — | −.14 | .09 | — |
| Total | −.22 | .22 | −.14 | −.11 | .24 | −.30 |
| Noncausal (spurious) | — | — | −.10 | — | .01 | −.04 |
| | | | 1980 Cohort | | | |
| Total covariance | −.15 | .15 | −.22 | −.22 | .30 | −.37 |
| Causal: | | | | | | |
| Direct | −.06 | .12* | −.18** | −.04 | .19*** | −.28*** |
| Indirect | −.09 | .01 | — | −.18 | .07 | — |
| Total | −.15 | .13 | −.18 | −.22 | .26 | −.28 |
| Noncausal (spurious) | — | .02 | −.04 | — | .04 | −.09 |

$*p < .05; **p < .01; ***p < .001.$

life spheres in the female life course may be slowly becoming more balanced.

One finding in Figure 8.2 merits separate attention: The positive association between family background and parenthood for 1960 cohort women—a relationship not found in any other group. Although the relationship is very weak, the inverse sign reveals that higher social origin did not preclude women in the early 1960s from early motherhood. This is surprising in view of the negative association between social background and family orientation and the positive relationship between social background and educational status. It suggests the possibility of small interaction effects among these characteristics.

To test for the presence of these effects, I conduct a log-linear analysis based on 1960 cohort women, using dichotomized measures of the family's social background (low: first and second SES quartile; high: third and fourth SES quartile), of educational status (college versus no college education), and of family orientation (low: scores below average; high: scores above average). Table 8.9 presents the model coefficients and the chi-square likelihood ratio. In addition, I display the multiplied coefficients and the antilogs because I interpret the results as odds probability rather than as log odds probability. Accordingly, the effect parameters represent the net odds probability of being childless in the fourth year after high school graduation by dichotomized SES quartiles, family orientation, and educational status. These are greater than 1.0 if the probability is greater than average and less than 1.0 if the probability is less than average. The results confirm my suspicion: There is a significant interaction effect between social background and educational status.[17]

The grand mean or overall effect shows that the net odds probability of being childless is 3.67 to 1. Thus, it is much more likely that a woman will not assume the role of mother in the fourth year after high school graduation. For women of higher social status, for example, the odds probability is .80 to 1, other things equal; for women from families of lower socioeconomic status, it is 1.25 to 1. Stated in another way, the odds

Table 8.9
Net Odds Probability for 1960 Senior Cohort Women of Being Childless Four Years after High School Graduation by Social Background, Family Orientation, and Educational Status

| Model Coefficients | Coefficient | Coefficient × 2 | Antilog |
|---|---|---|---|
| Not mother (N-M) | .65* | 1.30 | 3.67 |
| N-M by social background | −.11 | −.22 | .80 |
| N-M by education | .37* | .74 | 2.10 |
| N-M by family orientation | .26* | .52 | 1.68 |
| N-M by social background and by education | −.15* | −.30 | .74 |

Notes: $\chi^2_{LR} = 1.19$, df = 3, $p = .756$.

| | |
|---|---|
| T(parent status) | 3.67 |
| T(social background)$_i$ | .80 for $i = 1$ (high) |
| | 1.25 for $i = 2$ (low) |
| T(education)$_j$ | 2.10 for $j = 1$ (college) |
| | .48 for $j = 2$ (no college) |
| T(family orientation)$_k$ | 1.68 for $k = 1$ (low orientation) |
| | .59 for $k = 2$ (high orientation) |
| T(social background/education)$_{ij}$ | .74 for $i = j$ |
| | 1.35 for $i \neq j$ |

*$p < .05$.

probability of being childless is 56 percent higher ($1.25 / .80 = 1.56$) for lower-status women compared with higher-status women. As with the regression analysis results, the findings in Table 8.9 indicate that college-educated women and those with weak family orientation are, other things equal, less likely to have children.

Of special interest is the interaction effect between social standing and educational status. This illustrates how women of different social origins integrate the public and the private sides of the life course. This interaction effect also sheds some light on the socioeconomic status-related significance of higher education for women at the beginning of the 1960s. For college-educated higher-status women and for lower-status women without college education, the net odds probability of being childless is *below* average; it is *above* average for women from well-to-do families without college education and for college-educated women of modest social origin. These results suggest that low social background precluded women in the early 1960s from investing their resources and abilities into both education and family. Higher education assumed a professional-career-oriented value for these women. If they attended college, they were likely to regard it as a channel for upward (occupational) mobility. Early motherhood would interfere with these "biographical calculations." The considerable amount of (scarce) resources a family of modest socioeconomic status must invest in a daughter's college education engenders expectations regarding future rewards.[18] By contrast, college education among women of higher social standing seems to be a matter of milieu-appropriate culture. Regardless of future use in the professional world, college education is required by the cultural standards of the family. Since college education does not preclude motherhood, we may conclude that college served higher-status women as a "milieu-appropriate" marriage market.[19] The fact that the interaction effects between social background and education have disappeared for 1980 cohort women suggests that education and family tend to become disentangled in the female life course, thus indicating a greater equality among different life spheres—at least in early adulthood.

The topic of equality among different career lines in the female life course is viewed from a different angle in the next chapter. There I compare the respondents' educational and occupational expectations at high school graduation with their actual situations four years later. By exploring the matches and mismatches in these outcomes across different social groups, we can assess how an individual's location in the social structure affects his or her sense of opportunities in life.

# 9 Outcomes of Biographical Projects: Social Dependency of Matches and Mismatches

In this chapter, I investigate the relationship between subjective and objective factors in the respondents' life courses, giving special attention to the degree of correspondence between (high school) expectations and outcomes (four years later) in particular social groups. I assume that social groups, by helping to shape their members' biographical orientations, convey a sense of both the opportunities and barriers for particular positions and roles. Theoretical considerations also lead us to expect this conveyance to be more complete when social groups are characterized by well-defined boundaries and high internal homogeneity with regard to value and action orientations and lifestyles (see Chapter 1). By contrast, social groups lacking these characteristics are likely to structure their members' perception of career opportunities in a more diffuse way, resulting in looser associations between expectations and outcomes. Subjective expectations that either under- or overestimate given chances are thus more likely.

Drawing on Bourdieu's work (1975, 1978, 1984a), in Chapter 1 I argued that individuals relate their own life chances in different spheres (e.g., educational and professional attainment, marriage opportunities) to the "collective destiny" of the social groups to which they belong. Socialization into particular social groups equips individuals with certain skills, habits, and worldviews (i.e., the habitus); acquaints them with the chances inherent in their social position; and helps them develop—more unconsciously than consciously—a sense of what is and what is not within their reach. Individuals tend to align their action strategies with their subjective perception of their own social position, thus following what Bourdieu has called the probabilistic logic of action. This process makes it likely that individuals will contribute to the reproduction of a given social structure.

The validity and utility of these ideas are tested first by investigating outcomes of respondents' educational plans, and then by a comparison of occupational expectations and respondents' actual positions.

170

## Outcomes of High School Educational Plans

We know that both educational expectations and educational status attainment are highly determined by social standing. To assess the relationship between educational expectations and outcomes in different socioeconomic groups, I use a T-test, comparing in each SES quartile the group mean of respondents' educational expectations as reported at the time of high school graduation with the group mean of educational status attainment in the fourth year after high school graduation. For both variables, I use the same four-category scale of education (1 = no postsecondary education; 2 = noncollegiate education; 3 = some college education—out of school and without a degree; 4 = four-year college education).

In Table 9.1, the lower correspondence between expectations and out-

Table 9.1
Educational Expectations at High School Graduation and Educational Status Attainment Four Years Later, by Social Standing

| Social Standing | | 1960 Cohort | | 1980 Cohort | |
|---|---|---|---|---|---|
| | | Expectation | Attainment | Expectation | Attainment |
| Low | Mean | 2.03 ◄––► 1.85 | | 2.25 ◄––► 2.09 | |
| | | [1.2] | [1.0] | [1.2] | [1.2] |
| | | (158) | | (191) | |
| | T-value | 2.43 | | 2.45 | |
| | p | .016 | | .015 | |
| Low-medium | Mean | 2.47 ◄–– 2.26 | | 2.70 ◄–– 2.47 | |
| | | [1.3] | [1.1] | [1.2] | [1.2] |
| | | (186) | | (221) | |
| | T-value | 2.96 | | 3.49 | |
| | p | .004 | | .001 | |
| High-medium | Mean | 2.87 ◄–– 2.53 | | 3.16 ◄–– 2.98 | |
| | | [1.2] | [1.2] | [1.1] | [1.2] |
| | | (193) | | (224) | |
| | T-value | 4.55 | | 2.99 | |
| | p | .000 | | .003 | |
| High | Mean | 3.54 ◄–– 3.22 | | 3.64 ◄––► 3.54 | |
| | | [.9] | [1.0] | [.8] | [.9] |
| | | (149) | | (178) | |
| | T-value | 4.32 | | 1.93 | |
| | p | .000 | | .06 | |

comes in the 1960 cohort, particularly in the two upper SES quartiles, suggests the lower objective and subjective relevance of educational credentials for occupational careers at that time. In the 1980s, by contrast, the exchange relation between occupational status and educational credential has become more closely defined, thus engendering more firm educational goals. In addition, the higher correspondence in the two upper SES quartiles of the 1980 cohort may be partly attributable to the greater proportion of respondents expecting to attain an advanced college degree compared to their 1960 counterparts (21.3 percent versus 12.3 percent). Consequently, a greater proportion of 1980 cohort respondents are very likely to attain at least a four-year college degree.

Although all respondents expect on average more education than they attain, levels of correspondence differ by socioeconomic status in both cohorts.[1] In the 1960 senior cohort, and even more so in the 1980 senior cohort, expected and attained educational status are much more closely matched at both lower and upper ends of the social hierarchy than in the middle ranges. Low status discrepancy in the lowest socioeconomic quartile may result from internalizing the restricted opportunity structure. This involves a self-fulfilling prophecy whereby the subjective perception of the social structure as offering only very limited objective mobility chances fosters low educational expectations, which are reproduced in low status attainment, and which confirm in turn the restricted structural chances of such social positions. This process helps reproduce the social hierarchy.

In the highest socioeconomic quartile, particularly in the 1980 cohort, the same social mechanism is at work—only in reverse. High educational expectations are transmitted by the subjective perception of an objectively unrestricted opportunity structure. Again, the correct estimation of one's chances is confirmed by high educational status attainment. Low standard deviations in the highest SES quartile for both expectations and outcomes indicate, moreover, that the anticipation of educational careers is very homogeneous in this group. It reveals the highly visible structural chances at the upper ends of the social hierarchy.

At middle levels of the social structure, particularly in the 1980 cohort, expectations and outcomes are less synchronized, indicating the heterogeneous structural chances associated with these ranges of the social hierarchy. The greater (objective) likelihood of either upward or downward mobility is reflected in respondents' over- or underestimation of probable educational careers.

This empirical evidence suggests the high stability of the social stratification system at lower and upper ends, both in the 1960s and the 1980s. By contrast, middle ranges of the stratification system are more unstable and engender some mobility in both directions. With regard to the question of whether the educational system transmits inequality from generation to generation or acts as a vehicle for mobility (see Chapter 6), we may again conclude that it does both. It fulfills its predominantly reproductive function at both lower and upper ends of the social hierarchy. It provides only very limited chances to children of the lowest social background and "cools out" the educational expectations of the majority of this group. By contrast, rising expectations of children from families of highest socioeconomic status are rewarded with corresponding educational titles. The educational system may act as a vehicle for mobility in the middle ranges of the social structure where it is perceived as more easily attainable (as indicated by higher educational expectations), but this group's expectations are only partially converted into corresponding educational credentials.

I narrow the focus now to examine the social-background-related chances of converting educational expectations into a particular educational degree. Using the same four-category education scale as before, I compare in each SES quartile the 1960 and the 1980 group mean of educational attainment in the fourth year after high school graduation, selecting respondents who expected to attain a four-year college degree at the time of high school graduation. Table 9.2 shows that 1980 cohort respondents of all social

Table 9.2
College-Degree Expectations at High School Graduation and Educational Attainment Four Years Later, by Socioeconomic Status

| | Educational Status in the Fourth Year after High School Graduation[a] | | | |
|---|---|---|---|---|
| | Low | Low-Medium | High-Medium | High |
| 1960 cohort | 3.00 | 3.28 | 3.21 | 3.51 |
| | [1.03] | [.88] | [.95] | [.82] |
| | (33) | (65) | (92) | (115) |
| 1980 cohort | 3.60 | 3.69 | 3.79 | 3.93 |
| | [.79] | [.70] | [.58] | [.31] |
| | (38) | (63) | (105) | (128) |
| $Q$[b] | 2.50 ◄──► 2.32 | | 3.76 ──► 7.00 | |

[a]Four-year college degree $= 4.0$.

$$^{b}Q = \frac{\text{maximum attainment} - \text{group mean 1960}}{\text{maximum attainment} - \text{group mean 1980}}.$$

origins have better chances of realizing their educational expectations. Both higher group means and much smaller standard deviations in all SES quartiles of the 1980 cohort support this interpretation. I believe that this result reflects the improved accessibility of higher education through the expansion of the educational system over the last twenty years and the greater (subjective) importance of educational credentials.

The extent of this improvement varies by socioeconomic group, however. This status-related differential cannot be inferred directly from the 1960 and the 1980 group mean difference in each SES quartile because of floor and ceiling effects resulting from different starting levels of educational attainment. To control these effects, in each SES quartile I divide the 1960 cohort difference between the maximum attainment (i.e., four, because of the coding) and the group mean by the corresponding 1980 cohort difference.[2] The highest socioeconomic quartile shows the largest value; the smallest ones are observed in the two lower quartiles. Thus, members of higher socioeconomic groups especially have profited from the educational expansion over the last two decades. This conlusion confirms earlier findings.[3]

To explore the reasons why 1960 and 1980 senior cohort men and women give up their college education plans, I use a regression analysis, with the likelihood of dropping out of college (i.e., the ratio between respondents who planned at the time of high school graduation to earn a college degree, but who have left college, and those who planned to and still attend college in the fourth year after high school graduation) as the dependent variable. The family's socioeconomic status, extent of family orientation (i.e., expected age at marriage surveyed at the time of high school graduation), and parent status are the independent variables.

I assume that family background influences the chances of finishing college in several ways. Families of higher social standing have at their disposal more socioeconomic resources for acquiring good education for their children. In this sense, they are able to purchase educational credentials. These families also provide their children with a cultural environment that fosters the development of abilities, skills, and habits that are highly compatible with the cultural and intellectual requirements that the educational system rewards with its credentials.

Moreover, I assume that the high subjective relevance of the family career and/or the actual demands of family life interfere most with educational plans, particularly among women. Given previous results, we would expect these factors to better explain the likelihood of dropping out of college in the earlier cohort than in the more recent cohort.

Table 9.3
Results of Regression of the Likelihood of Dropping out of College on Socioeconomic
Position (Social Background), Extent of Family Orientation, and Parent Role
(Standardized Regression Coefficients)

|  | 1960 Cohort | | 1980 Cohort | |
|---|---|---|---|---|
|  | Men | Women | Men | Women |
| Social background | − .19* | − .24** | − .16* | − .21** |
| Family orientation | .04 | **.21*** | − .03 | .02 |
| Parent role | .23** | .32*** | .16* | .28*** |
| $R^2$ | .11 | .21 | .05 | .14 |
| $N$ | 150 | 96 | 169 | 172 |

$*p < .05; **p < .01; ***p < .001.$

The standardized regression coefficients in Table 9.3 show that the effect of family background on the likelihood of dropping out of college has diminished slightly for both men and women. It still exerts a greater impact on women than on men, however. Over the past twenty years, social inequalities in access to higher education have lessened somewhat. The relatively strong effect of becoming a parent on the likelihood of giving up college education for 1960 cohort men may indicate economic necessity. The roles of breadwinner and student were not compatible.

It is worth noting that the subjective relevance of the family among 1960 cohort women significantly influences the likelihood of dropping out of college, net of the effects of both social background and presence of a child. Thus, in some respects, college attendance served women in the early 1960s as a marriage market.[4] The complete disappearance of this impact among 1980 cohort women indicates a shift in the female motivation for college attendance away from meeting well-educated men and toward the instrumental value of a college degree for a professional career.

## Outcomes of High School Occupational Plans

In forming occupational expectations, individuals are inclined to dismiss careers for which they think they lack the expertise, particular skills and habits, and, of course, educational credentials. Instead, they envision future careers in which they may make use of their existing abilities and qualities.

Viewing respondents' occupational expectations in this perspective, I anticipate that individuals who are integrated into social groups with well-defined opportunity structures will have highly realistic occupational plans. By contrast, membership in social groups in which mobility chances imply diffuse and uncertain futures (i.e., a high likelihood of either upward or downward mobility) will be more likely to engender occupational expectations that either over- or underestimate objective chances. As with the relationship between expected and attained educational status across socioeconomic groups, I expect to find at the bottom and at the top of the social stratification system a higher level of correspondence between occupational plans and outcomes than in the middle ranges.

To test this hypothesis, I compare respondents' occupational plans as reported at the time of high school graduation with the positions they hold eleven years later, using only the 1960 cohort data.[5] I measure the linkages between high school professional plans and occupational positions by the rank difference between type of expected and type of achieved occupation. Both variables are coded to reflect the status hierarchy between the occupations,[6] allowing definition of three types of occupational attainment: Respondents holding a job that ranks higher than the expected position are labeled as "overachievers;" "underachievers" are respondents with the opposite configuration. If the rank of the position corresponds with the expected status, respondents are labeled as "realizers." The analysis includes all 1960 cohort members with a full-time job in 1971.[7] This test is exploratory only; the data do not permit investigation of shifts in the relationship between expected and attained occupational status across socioeconomic groups. Table 9.4 shows that respondents with the lowest and the highest social backgrounds assess their structural chances in the occupational structure most accurately.[8] They do so for different reasons.

The range of occupational positions that respondents from lowest social origin perceive as accessible is restricted. Moreover, positions at the lower end of the occupational structure demand few formal requirements (e.g., educational credentials). Since both factors facilitate the comparison of one's own resources and assets with demands of probable occupational positions, they improve the visibility of structural chances and barriers. Future occupational positions that respondents of high social origin will be likely to hold are characterized by highly selective conditions of access. This is true for educational credentials, social skills, and personal qualities and abilities. Despite the broad range of qualifications they require, these occupations provide well-structured professional images and clear-cut career opportunities with which one's own abilities, resources, and assets

Table 9.4
Type of Occupational Attainment, by Socioeconomic Position (Social Background),
1960 Senior Cohort: Expectations in 1960 and Positions in 1971

| Type of Attainment | Social Background | | | |
| | Low (%) | Low-Medium (%) | High-Medium (%) | High (%) |
| --- | --- | --- | --- | --- |
| Underachiever | 43.6 | 41.6 | 47.2 | 37.3 |
| | (44) | (52) | (58) | (41) |
| Realizer | 34.7 ◄——— 32.8 | | 26.8 ———► 34.5 | |
| | (35) | (41) | (33) | (38) |
| Overachiever | 21.8 | 25.6 | 26.0 | 28.2 |
| | (22) | (32) | (32) | (31) |
| Total | 100.1 | 100.0 | 100.0 | 100.0 |
| | (101) | (125) | (123) | (110) |

Note: $\chi^2 = 3.75$, df $= 6$, $p = .7100$.

may be compared. These conditions enable respondents from families of high social standing to accurately apprehend their objective chances and to develop a good sense of successful investments.

The two "in-between" groups are less able to convey a sense of structural chances to their members. Respondents from the high-medium SES quartile in particular overestimate their chances—a reflection of strong upward mobility aspirations in this group. However, the objectively uncertain position of the middle levels in the stratification system results in a high rate of failure, that is, in the miscalculation of objective chances.

Using father's education as an indicator of social standing, Table 9.5 reveals that the uncertain social positions represented by father's educational status of "noncollegiate or some college education" are transmitted from generation to generation by means of the lowest rate of expected occupational status achievement and the highest rate of underachievement. Fathers with a little higher education but no degree seem to transfer their unachieved mobility aspirations to their children. Their children's strong drive for upward mobility may engender, in turn, unrealistic assessments of their own resources, abilities, and assets in relation to the demands of expected occupational positions. In a college-educated family, by contrast, the cultural and intellectual environment is likely to foster the development of abilities and skills that are necessary for an accurate apprehension of the relationship between investments and rewards.

In sum, families in different social groups are not in the same position

Table 9.5
Type of Occupational Attainment, by Father's Education, 1960 Senior Cohort:
Expectations in 1960 and Positions in 1971

| | Father's Education | | | |
|---|---|---|---|---|
| Type of Attainment | No High School Diploma (%) | High School Diploma (%) | Noncollegiate/ Some College (%) | Four-Year College (%) |
| Underachiever | 43.4 | 44.7 | **50.0** | 34.8 |
| | (82) | (47) | (27) | (24) |
| Realizer | **33.3** ◄——— | 28.6 | 22.2 ———► | **44.9** |
| | (63) | (30) | (12) | (31) |
| Overachiever | 23.3 | 26.7 | 27.8 | 20.3 |
| | (44) | (28) | (15) | (14) |
| Total | 100.0 | 100.0 | 100.0 | 100.0 |
| | (189) | (105) | (54) | (69) |

*Note:* $\chi^2 = 11.91$, df $= 6$, $p = .0641$.

to convey an accurate sense of the "possible" and "probable" future to their children. The higher the stability of the family's own socioeconomic position, the more secure the framework they provide for their children's biographical orientations: We observe high rates of intergenerational reproduction of social inequalities at both lower and upper ends of the social hierarchy.

Having established the connection between family background and aspirations and occupations, I turn now to gender effects. I suspect that the observed intergenerational reproduction pattern primarily reflects the male relationship between occupational expectations and outcomes. For women, higher rates of either over- or underestimating structural chances are more likely, since the pursuit of a professional career over many years did not represent an integral part of the female life course pattern at the beginning of the 1960s.

Separate analyses of 1960 cohort men and women yield an interesting result, presented in Table 9.6: Compared to women, men of all social origins attain less than they expect. Conversely, women of higher social origin are to a great extent overachievers. Thus, men are more likely to overestimate their occupational chances, whereas higher-status women, especially, underestimate them.

These results are not as surprising as they seem. We know from previous results that women employed full time eleven years after high school

Table 9.6
Type of Occupational Attainment, by Socioeconomic Position (Social Background) and
Sex, 1960 Senior Cohort: Expectations in 1960 and Positions in 1971

| | Social Background | | | | | | | |
|---|---|---|---|---|---|---|---|---|
| | Men[a] | | | | Women[b] | | | |
| Type of Attainment | Low (%) | Low-Medium (%) | High-Medium (%) | High (%) | Low (%) | Low-Medium (%) | High-Medium (%) | High (%) |
| Under-achiever | 48.1 (37) | 45.9 (39) | 51.7 (45) | 43.5 (37) | 29.2 (7) | 32.5 (13) | 36.1 (13) | 16.0 (4) |
| Realizer | **32.5** (25) | 25.9 (22) | 26.4 (23) | **36.5** (31) | **41.7** (10) | **47.5** (19) | 27.8 (10) | 28.0 (7) |
| Over-achiever | 19.5 (15) | 28.2 (24) | 21.8 (19) | 20.0 (17) | 29.2 (7) | 20.0 (8) | **36.1** (13) | **56.0** (14) |
| Total | 100.1 (77) | 100.0 (85) | 99.9 (87) | 100.0 (85) | 100.1 (24) | 100.0 (40) | 100.0 (36) | 100.0 (25) |

[a]$\chi^2 = 4.63$, df $= 6$, $p = .5909$.
[b]$\chi^2 = 11.06$, df $= 6$, $p = .0866$.

graduation are a highly selective group. They represent only about one-third (30.5 percent) of all women in the cohort; they include a higher proportion of unmarried women—32 percent versus about 20 percent in the whole cohort; and a much higher proportion of these women are unmarried and well-educated. Thus, the female sample is biased toward highly educated, unmarried, career women.

By contrast, the male sample is not biased in any particular direction. We know from earlier results that more than 90 percent of all married and unmarried men in the cohort have a full-time job in 1971.

The explanation for the high rate of underachievement among men, independent of social origin, lies in the economic development of the 1960s and the 1970s. These men planned their occupational careers in the early 1960s against the background of a still expanding economy. By the time their careers should have been settled—at the beginning of the 1970s—the long-term economic boom started to decline, thus reducing opportunities for good jobs. A sizable proportion of these men, then, are victims of changing economic conditions.

It could be argued that the same pattern should emerge for women. I would counter that women are aware of sex discrimination in the labor

Table 9.7

Type of Occupational Attainment, by Educational Status, 1960 Senior Cohort: Expectations in 1960 and Positions in 1971

| Type of Attainment | Educational Status | | | |
| | High School (%) | Vocational (%) | Some College (%) | Four-Year College (%) |
|---|---|---|---|---|
| Underachiever | **29.9** | 48.9 | 51.5 | 37.5 |
| | (26) | (43) | (51) | (51) |
| Realizer | 37.9 ◄——— | 25.0 | 23.2 ———► | **41.9** |
| | (33) | (22) | (23) | (57) |
| Overachiever | **32.2** | 26.1 | 25.3 | 20.6 |
| | (28) | (23) | (25) | (28) |
| Total | 100.0 | 100.0 | 100.0 | 100.0 |
| | (87) | (88) | (99) | (136) |

*Note:* $\chi^2 = 18.20$, df $= 6$, $p = .0058$.

market and tend to limit their occupational expectations in advance. Well-educated women thus may underestimate their structural chances. At the other extreme, the narrow range of occupational positions available to women from families of low socioeconomic status, in particular, indicates a well-defined (albeit highly restricted) opportunity structure, which may explain the high rate of female realizers in the two lower SES quartiles.

The type of occupational attainment does not depend on family background alone; it is also mediated by respondents' own educational attainment. Table 9.7 reveals that respondents with either no postsecondary education or with a college degree most often attain the expected occupational status. I attribute this to the well-defined "rate of conversion" inherent in these two types of educational degrees.

Interestingly, the proportion of underachievers for respondents with some college education is approximately the same as for respondents whose fathers acquired this level of education. This underscores the ill-defined occupational chances inherent in this type of educational status and supports the idea that the uncertainties associated with this status are transmitted from generation to generation.

# Conclusions

The data I analyzed show that for the members of the high school class of 1960, the passage to adulthood involves more rapid role transitions and status changes and shows much less variety in transition patterns than those found among the members of the high school class of 1980. Specifically, four years after high school graduation, 67.2 percent of the 1960 senior cohort members have left school, compared to 58.0 percent of the 1980 cohort; 41.4 percent of the earlier cohort have married, while only 26.8 percent in the more recent cohort have done so. Consequently, a greater proportion of the 1960 cohort members are already parents: 26.0 percent have a child, compared to 13.7 percent of the 1980 cohort members. The considerably larger proportion of 1980 cohort members with only high school diplomas who are neither married (55.7 percent versus 38.7 percent) nor have a child (79.9 percent versus 64.3 percent) strongly indicates that these shifts in the timing of family life events are not solely the outcome of the greater prevalence of extended educational careers. Rather, they suggest a greater complexity and diversity in transition patterns to adulthood. Using these role transitions as indicators of participation in particular life stages, I found that 23.4 percent of the members of the 1960 cohort had achieved adult status (i.e., completed all three status changes) compared to only 11.0 percent in the 1980 cohort. Conversely, 35.1 percent of the members in the more recent cohort had not yet experienced any of the three role transitions from youth to adulthood, while only 25.0 percent in the earlier cohort had not done so.

In the 1980 cohort, the greater likelihood of interrupted educational careers indicates that role reversals between school enrollment and labor-force participation have become more prevalent. Movements to and from school and labor force in the early 1980s suggest a somewhat greater flexibility in educational tracking, thus enhancing the individual's chances for revising educational career decisions. On the other hand, the return to

181

school may be less an indication of free choice and more a reflection of economic necessity induced by declining employment prospects. In either instance, these reversals indicate that, by the early 1980s, the transition from school to work had become a process of gradual integration rather than clear demarcation. The greater prevalence of labor-force participation (mainly part-time) among 1980 cohort members still attending school reinforces this tendency. The fact that, compared to 1960 cohort members, more members of the 1980 cohort who have left school also work part-time reveals, on one side, declining opportunities for full-time employment and suggests, on the other, altered attitudes toward work. Both tendencies contribute to a greater complexity and diversity in the transition patterns to adulthood.

These global shifts are attributable to actions on the part of both men and women. Although women continue to be more likely to leave school, to marry, and to become parents at earlier ages than men, over the last two decades female transition patterns have changed more than those of males. Consequently, sex differences in the passage to adulthood have greatly diminished. While the life courses of the 1960 cohort women were strongly organized around private life (i.e., the family), those of the 1980 cohort women show a greater balance between the public life sphere (i.e., educational attainment and labor-force participation) and the private one. Several results document this increasing integration of the female life course into realms outside the home: Women's educational opportunities have improved considerably. While women in the early 1960s had only limited access to postsecondary education, especially to a four-year college degree, equal proportions of men and women in the 1980s earn a four-year college degree. And, at postsecondary educational levels below the college degree, women have surpassed men.

This trend, however, may be less indicative of gender equality in educational chances and more of the continuation of sex discrimination on the labor market. Credentials inflation over the last two decades has resulted in the devaluation of educational titles below the college degree. My data show that the occupational status and income return of these educational certificates have declined. In the 1980s, a college degree is a more and more necessary (although not sufficient) requirement for preserving access to better jobs. Men in the 1980 cohort who anticipate little chance of attaining a college degree leave school directly after high school graduation because they can still find jobs. Women who do not expect to earn a college degree are relegated to school, where they make investments in noncollegiate postsecondary education or in terminal vocational education in community colleges, for which the improvement in future employment opportunities and economic payoff are doubtful. Thus, the social basis for female integration into the larger society continues to remain uncertain, despite some improvements over the last decades.

One such improvement is that, among 1980 cohort women, family plans no longer interfere with the attainment of higher education, while in the early 1960s, a strong family orientation greatly increased a woman's likelihood of dropping out of college. For women in the early 1980s, college is less likely to be perceived as a marriage market and more likely to be seen as a means for attaining a professional career. In addition, since marriage excluded employment for women in the early 1960s, full-time employment did not represent the modal female life situation. Consequently, educational status and female labor-force participation showed a strong positive association: Higher educational credentials fostered employment. Rapidly increasing female labor-force participation in the early 1980s that is much less directly associated with either educational or marital status suggests that a career in the labor force is becoming an integrated part of the female biography. The growing proportion of women who expect to remain childless (9.2 percent versus 3.4 percent) or to have two children at the most (48.9 percent versus 23.0 percent) and, consequently, the rapidly declining proportion of those who anticipate having four or more children (41.3 percent versus 14.0) strongly support this tendency. Overall, these results indicate that women's opportunities for dual career investments—in a professional career and in family life—have improved somewhat compared to women in the early 1960s.

The data show the persistent influence of socioeconomic position on the expected and the actual transition to adulthood: The higher the families' social standing, the more likely their sons and daughters are to expect a higher educational degree, a more prestigious occupational position, and a later marriage; and in fact, they experience an extended period of youth and a gradual and late transition to adulthood. While the constraints linked to the socioeconomic standing of the family have not diminished, the data indicate a change in the way in which these effects are produced. For the 1960 cohort men and women, the distributions of educational, occupational, and marital expectations, as well as of the actual adult role entry, are more clustered than are those for their 1980 counterparts. The latter are much more finely graded. Put differently, the 1960 cohort's biographical orientations and subsequent transition behaviors are greatly determined by social status boundaries, whereas the 1980 cohort's orientations and actions show more individually stratified patterns. These changes in the shape of the distributions suggest a decoupling of socioeconomic group membership and its accompanying culture: Socioeconomic position still exerts a strong impact on life chances, but it seems less capable of conveying corresponding value and action orientations.

Shifts in the intergenerational reproduction patterns of the 1960 and 1980 cohorts reveal similar trends, especially for men. In the more recent cohort, men's occupational status attainment is not only more closely linked to their own educational achievement, but it also is less directly and more indirectly dependent on the family's social standing. Because of the increasing relevance of educational credentials for status allocation, the family's cultural resources (as measured by father's educational status) become more influential, both directly and indirectly, while the family's material resources (i.e., family income) exert only indirect effects (these, however, become stronger). These results show a shift away from more direct social reproduction patterns and toward more subtle (i.e., indirectly determined and more finely stratified) ones.

To integrate these empirical findings, I developed a broad theoretical framework. Its major focus is the relationship between structural and cultural developments in modern society and the social structuring and individual organization of the life course. To avoid the pitfalls of previous studies where youth is examined as an isolated age group and shifts in juvenile orientations and behavioral patterns are not linked to social and cultural change in the larger society, the theoretical perspective proposed here combines a macrosociological perspective with an actor-oriented approach in the study of the life course.

I used the concept of institutionalization to describe the type of social organization of the life course in modern society: The chronology of life based on standardized age categories, institutionalized status allocation, and the highly organized cultural images of the life cycle regulate the individual's progression in social time and space. The life course becomes a sequential order of positions and roles, meeting the structural and cultural requirements of a progressive societal rationalization and individualization. In this process, individuals acquire ever more membership rights that create direct ties to the larger society, especially to the state. As individuals participate in markets, enter the political sphere as citizens, and become recipients of welfare, obligations to social collectivities (i.e., corporate groups) such as the family, local communities, or status groups gradually vanish and render social identifications and identity constructions based on membership in these collectivities increasingly obsolete. Instead, the institutionalized elements of the life course become the official, socially validated public identities which serve as the biographical frame of reference. These publicly acknowledged identities are somewhat split off from the notion of the private self rooted in the noninstitutionalized elements of the life course. It is in this sense that we may speak of the structural and cultural individualization of the life course in modern society.

Since the institutionalization of the life course is largely a product of the state, it follows the logic of state intervention, which orders the individual life according to universal, rational principles of law. Thus, the more the individual life course is state-regulated (e.g., through age-grading and bureaucratically defined status allocation and status linkages), the higher its formalization and standardization. The simultaneously increasing individualization and standardization of the life course with the development of modern society engenders a peculiar dynamic: Life is less constrained by traditions and customs and thus more susceptible to individualized action orientations; these potential individual choices, however, must be made within the context of standardized and bureaucratized life patterns.

I coupled this notion of the social organization of the life course to strategies of action individuals construct themselves, so that we might fully understand how individuals in different structural positions enact their lives and give meaning to them. Individuals develop their own strategies of action using the skills, habits, capacities, and competencies that they have acquired through socialization into the subcultures associated with particular social groups. They cope with the constraints set by the institutional framework of the life course by learning to value highly those life goals for which their cultural equipment is well suited, thus assuring the maximum return on their investments. The assessment of one's life chances is highly calculable and predictable when life trajectories assume a high level of standardization. Such trajectories provide a secure framework within which individuals may judge what is (socially) possible and what is unattainable against the background of their own resources (i.e., capital and assets) and competencies. Under such conditions, individuals tend to internalize and to respect the social limits encoded in the institutionalized trajectories. Conversely, they are inclined to exclude a priori those trajectories for which their resources and competencies are not well matched. Since highly standardized trajectories are easily discernible with regard to the resources, capacities, and competencies necessary to be successful, individuals who have similar resources at their disposal are likely to experience similar life trajectories. These conditions provide the structural background against which the individual's life course may be understood as inscribed in the collective history of the social group to which he or she belongs.

Over the last two decades, these highly standardized life trajectories have been "shattered" by structural and cultural developments in all major social institutions. In the educational system, the inflation and concomitant devaluation of educational credentials intensifies competition in school and results in the increasing decoupling of previously well-established (career) linkages between education and occupational opportunities, at the same time as the labor market is undergoing a long-term structural crisis. Educational investments thus assume an ambiguous meaning as their future returns become highly unpredictable. On the other hand, the structural necessity of investing in higher education exposes individuals for ever-longer periods to a social context dominated by highly individualistic action perspectives. In the occupational sphere, the declining "half-life" of the validity of professional qualifications due to shortened cycles of technical innovations intensifies the problem of professional updating, which induces a greater likelihood for both more discontinuous and more flexible occupational trajectories. As a result, the cultural image of a lifelong occupation, the qualifications for which are acquired once, becomes obsolete and is gradually replaced by notions of lifelong learning and job flexibility. These cultural shifts result in highly individualized biographical conceptions of work.

The trend toward greater complexity and diversity in life trajectories is perhaps clearest in the area of the family. The proliferation of living arrangements is accompanied by an imagery of private relationships that emphasizes personal development over the whole life course. Instead of the idea of lifelong commitment, the image of a lifetime of choice emerges, with an emphasis on spontaneous experiences. Consequently, the investment-and-reward balance of personal relationships is evaluated on a short-term basis rather than in terms of a life-cycle-encompassing concept of identity.

More flexible and discontinuous, and increasingly diversified and individualized, life course patterns have been discussed as effects of the mutually reinforcing processes of rationalization at the level of social organization and the elaboration of the ideology of individualism. They have reached such a high level in advanced industrial society that the tensions inherent in the dynamics of standardization and individualization result in a partial destandardization of the life course regime.

In this respect, the accelerated rationalization of the economic sphere challenges the tripartition of the life course, potentially dissolving the fixed scheduling of the major activities of education, work, and leisure. This may ultimately affect the social construction of time and modify the subjective experience and use of time. Specifically, competent coping skills with respect to the mediation between work time and nonwork time are likely to become important resources for the individual organization of action. Individuals' membership rights in society have increased rapidly over the last decades and are now extended to members of social groups previously characterized by a weak integration into the process of societal individualization (particularly women and children), thus providing strong structural support for individualistic action in an increasing number of life spheres. Specifically, accelerated societal individualization has fostered the progressive decoupling of socioeconomic positions from sociocultural milieus. Decreasing milieu-specific restraints on value and action orientations "encourage" biographical prospects assumed to depend on individual choice and accomplishment. This tendency in turn contributes to the presently increasing diversification of life course patterns. Furthermore, the high level of societal individualization provokes a decoupling of the public and private life course. The private action sphere thus is increasingly structured by action orientations based on quickly changing personal needs, moods, and interests. In sum, the partial destandardization of the life course in contemporary time broadens the range of life events potentially open to purposive action and simultaneously decreases the likelihood of building up long-term, stable expectations as the various life trajectories become less predictable and calculable. The partial transformation of the life course regime thus contributes to the formation of a highly individualistic, transient, and fluid identity and supports a logic of action oriented toward the present rather than toward the future.

Within this larger process, the transition to adulthood is transformed into a more extended, diversified, and increasingly individualized period. The rapid integration of youth into the process of societal individualization and the simultaneous extension and contraction of youth at the structural, institutional, and cultural levels increasingly blurs the distinction between youth status and adult status. Specifically, extended schooling for a steadily growing proportion of youths postpones economic independence, while the status of student simultaneously becomes dissociated from a particular age range as structural transformations of the occupational sphere increasingly necessitate the updating and "retooling" of the professional expertise of adults. Similarly, the structural crisis of the labor market impedes the stable professional integration of youths who therefore alternate between schooling and periods of uncertain, short-term labor-force participation. As the half-life of professional qualifications rapidly decreases due to the accelerated cycles of technological innovation, unemployment is likely to affect not only the lower and upper age strata (i.e., youths and older workers), but also the middle stratum, although, of course, the probability of unemployment is highly dependent on both professional qualifications and gender. Both youths and adults therefore find themselves in school for retraining, which makes them, structurally speaking, alike. Structural differences between youths and adults are also diminishing with regard to living arrangements; the proportion of one-person households in all age categories has rapidly increased, and marriage, in its legal form, has lost ground to cohabitation. Consequently, the age-heterogeneous group of "singles" and of persons living together outside marriage indicates a reversal of the trend toward more strictly age-organized life stages. This trend is supported, moreover, by the gradual de-structuring of age-specific spheres and modes of experience: Children and youths participate in the adult world as consumers in markets (media, fashion, etc.), while adults increasingly usurp the value of youthfulness in their lifestyles. With the expansion of the welfare state, children and youths have been rapidly integrated into the process of societal individualization and have acquired nearly similar membership rights in society as their parents. This fosters the spread of individualistic action strategies among youths and accelerates children's independence, thus rendering the sociocultural milieu of the family progressively less capable of determining juvenile value and action orientations.

Together, these structural and cultural changes over the last two decades have made youth as a life stage increasingly obsolete, while they have simultaneously extended it indefinitely. As a result of these opposing tendencies, transition patterns to adulthood in the contemporary period show a greater variety: They become less age-graded (i.e., more extended) and increasingly diversified and individualized.

Since the data I analyzed were neither collected for my purposes nor ideally suited to them, I was not able to investigate all of the issues raised in the theoretical part of this work. The interplay between the destandardization of the life course and the shifts in identity patterns, in particular, should be analyzed in more detail. By investigating the individual's time horizon and his or her subjective experience and use of time, the postulated greater emphasis on flexible, fluid, and highly individualistic identities could be assessed. To grasp these highly subtle changes in the formation of identities may also require other types of data and indicate the "structural limits" of survey data. More qualitative, in-depth data are needed, moreover, to better assess the impact of historical events on the aging process.

While the data largely support the arguments presented in this work, future research would profit from comparing the passage to adulthood in a cross-national perspective. Given the importance of structural and cultural developments in explaining the changing structure of the transition to adulthood, a cross-national approach could systematically rank countries on these dimensions and assess more thoroughly their impact on the transition patterns to adulthood and the accompanying juvenile orientations and behaviors. A cross-national perspective also would be an appropriate testing ground for further investigating the issue of age as a structuring principle of the life course in the future. Several findings in my study and some of my theoretical propositions suggest that life stages in the contemporary period have become less segmented with regard to chronological age. Much more research is needed, however, before we can confidently determine whether we are heading toward an age-irrelevant society (cf. Neugarten & Hagestad, 1976).

Finally, cross-national research could help clarify some of the major issues raised in this study. I viewed the institutionalization of the life course and the accompanying standardization and individualization as largely a product of the state. Thus, it is possible that the recent partial destandardization of the life course might be related to what some scholars have identified as the structural limits of the welfare state. A comparison of life course patterns in countries in which the state assumes a varying degree of responsibility would provide useful insight. These suggestions for future research should lead to further understanding of the changing structure of the life course in contemporary society.

# Appendix

This appendix provides some additional information regarding the global setup of the Project TALENT and High School and Beyond data sets, from which data were selected for the present study. Some related methodological issues will also be discussed here.

### Issues of Technical and Substantive Comparability

The empirical approach taken in this book is to compare two high school cohorts and to analyze subgroup variations within and between cohorts. In cohort comparison based on survey data, the "technical" comparability of the selected data sets is a fundamental requirement. I have already mentioned in the Introduction that both studies define their sample population in the same way. Here, I focus on the comparability of procedures used in sample selection. Students in each study were selected through a two-stage, stratified probability sample. The primary sampling units used were schools; students within selected schools constituted the second-stage units. Project TALENT used type of school (public, parochial, private) and geographical location (regions, major cities) as primary stratification variables in selecting schools. Within public schools further stratification was based upon school size and student retention ratio. The school probability sample consisted of 1,225 schools within which every student attending grades nine through twelve was selected. Schools in the High School and Beyond study were selected—with the exception of oversampled special strata (e.g., alternative schools, private Cuban Hispanic)—with probability proportional to estimated enrollment, resulting in a sample of 1,122 schools that was stratified by geographic location (regions, city), racial composition, and enrollment. Within each school, in general, thirty-six seniors and thirty-six sophomores were randomly selected. In addition, both studies have developed school and student case weights. Their use should lead to correct estimates of the population of each of the grade cohorts and correct estimates of subgroups within each grade of high school students.

The two studies differ, however, in some aspects of the post–high school follow-up survey procedures that are of relevance for the 1960 and the 1980 senior cohort comparison undertaken in this volume. While both studies utilized mailed questionnaires as the data collection technique, Project TALENT asked all of the students of each grade cohort to fill out the questionnaire. By contrast, High School and Beyond selected a stratified subsample of 11,500 base-year participants who were then seniors (i.e., about 40 percent of the initial senior sample). The study provides the corresponding follow-up weights to compensate for unequal probabilities of selection for the follow-up survey and to adust for the nonrespondents to these surveys. While High School and Beyond realized very high follow-up success rates (e.g., 94 percent for the senior cohort in 1982), Project TALENT suffered from a sizable loss of participants in each wave. In the one-year, five-year and eleven-year follow-ups for the different grade cohorts, response rates varied from over 60 percent to about 20 percent. In order to overcome the potentially serious bias introduced by the poor response rates, Project TALENT conducted special surveys of nonrespondents to each follow-up of each grade cohort. These surveys are generally based on respective representative samples of about 2,500 of those who did not return the questionnaires. In the different waves, the response rates to these special samples varied from 99.5 percent to 60.6 percent, thanks to intensive efforts to locate the selected individuals. The specifics of the Project TALENT data base raise some methodological problems. Wise et al. (1979, p. 45) state in the *Project TALENT Data Handbook* that the "unequal sampling and acceptance ratio in 1960 and the sizable number of nonrespondents to the follow-up surveys make it necessary either to select a self-weighted subsample or to use differential weighting of cases in order to obtain nationally representative statistics." The "Public Use File" of Project TALENT provides the first option of a self-weighted subsample that was realized as follows: "A self-weighted subsample is obtained by selecting each member of the subsample from the total sample, with probability proportional to his/her weight; that is, proportional to the number of individuals in the population he/she represents" (p. 50).

A further difference in the follow-up survey procedure between the two studies regards the timing of the successive survey waves. As depicted in Figure A.1, the participants in Project TALENT have been followed up

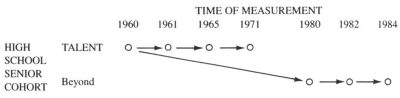

Figure A.1. Timing of survey waves in the selected data sets.

one, five, and eleven years after graduating from high school. High School and Beyond surveyed the 1980 senior cohort students two and four years after graduation, and additional survey waves are planned. These differences in the design of the follow-up surveys result from the fact that each study was undertaken independently from the other.

To handle the differences in the time span between the successive survey waves of the two studies, several strategies were indicated by the particular structures of the two data sets. Unlike the High School and Beyond data, Project TALENT life course data are not continuous event histories (i.e., the data are not a continuous record of various activities such as schooling, labor-force participation, etc. from the time respondents graduated from high school until the point when they were last surveyed); rather, they focus only on discrete points in the respondents' lives. This type of data dictated the strategy of comparing the two cohorts and subgroups within and between cohorts at selected points in time; specifically, high school graduation and again four years later. Accordingly, I used data from the two base-year surveys (i.e., 1960 and 1980) and from the High School and Beyond 1984 follow-up. To reconstruct the 1960 cohort respondents' life course–related data for the ideal year 1964 (i.e., four years after high school graduation), I relied on the eleven-year follow-up of Project TALENT, which provides a great deal of retrospective information regarding positions and roles (e.g., educational and occupational status, marital status, presence of children) for *all* students selected for the self-weighted subsample. A few comparisons referred to the first year after high school graduation. To make this comparison possible I reconstructed the 1980 cohort respondents' positions and roles from the High School and Beyond 1982 follow-up survey, which provides continuous event histories for relevant life areas.

Apart from the issues of "technical" comparability of the selection processes used in the two studies, the question of "substantive" comparability should still be addressed. Because the comparison is between two *school* cohorts (i.e., white graduates of the high school classes of 1960 and 1980)

TABLE A.1
Percentage of High School Graduates Eighteen Years Old, All Races

|  | Year of Graduation | | | | | | | |
|---|---|---|---|---|---|---|---|---|
|  | 1950 | 1955 | 1960 | 1965 | 1970 | 1975 | 1980 | 1983 |
| Percentage of 18-year-olds | 56.0 | 64.6 | **72.4** | 70.8 | 77.1 | 73.6 | **71.5** | 71.8 |

*Source: Statistical Abstract of the United States* 1986, Table 249.
*Note:* Figures are based on estimated resident population as of July 1.

rather than two *birth* cohorts (i.e., age groups), we need to know whether high school attendance until the senior year represents the normal career trajectory for the members of a given birth cohort (i.e., the eighteen-year-old persons). Using two senior high school cohorts as samples for studying changes in the entry into adult roles could be problematic, if the overwhelming majority of young people do not remain in school up to the senior year. Table A.1 shows that this basic requirement is met: The data (which include all races) reveal that the great shift in the rate of high school graduation occurred before 1960; approximately equal proportions of eighteen-year-old persons completed high school in 1960 and 1980.

Moreover, confidence in the overall comparability of the basic characteristics of the two school cohorts requires that the age distributions of high school graduates in 1960 and 1980 be stable. When samples of white persons in the 1960 and the 1980 senior cohort are broken down by birth year, it is clear that an overwhelming majority in both cohorts were born either in 1942 or 1962. Approximately 75 percent of each cohort are eighteen years old when they graduate from high school. In the more recent cohort, nineteen-year-olds are slightly overrepresented compared to the earlier cohort, in which we find a greater proportion of seventeen-year-olds. Comparison by birth year and sex reveals that the women in both senior cohorts tend to be younger than the men. White women are slightly more likely to graduate from high school when they are eighteen years old, as compared to nineteen years old for the men. Despite these minor differences, the age distribution of the two cohorts has remained fairly stable.

## Issues of Measurement and Analytic Procedures

The use of available data from sociological studies—one of which has been conducted more than two decades ago—confronts the researcher with the problem that the studies are shaped by the research techniques prevalent at their time. Such data sets reflect the developments of sociological theory and methodology over time. Especially when conducting comparative research at more than one time point, the use of such data can be associated with limited availability of indicators highly significant for the theoretical model. Choice of analytic techniques may be constrained as well. In addition, the fact that each study was undertaken independently of the other affects the range of theoretical and methodological options in several respects.

First, the types of data collected in Project TALENT and in the High School and Beyond study define the range of analytic techniques that may be applied in the present investigation. As has been mentioned before, Project TALENT did not collect continuous event histories of the activities in various life spheres from the time respondents graduated from high school until the point when they were last surveyed. Although High School and Beyond provides such data, I am limited to comparing the two cohorts at selected points in time and to using research techniques that are compatible with this kind of data.

Second, the foremost problem in comparative research based on secondary data is the availability of indicators of variables deemed to be significant for the conceptual framework. If such indicators are available, it is their adequacy that might pose new problems. These issues assume even greater importance in the present research because it is comparative. It was not always the case that both studies provided the indicators of variables necessary to empirically test certain theoretical claims. In other instances, it was the unsatisfactory indicator in one of the two studies that forced me to reduce the analysis to the smallest common denominator. Sometimes, the two studies did not use the same degree of differentiation in constructing the categories of an indicator, thus forcing me to collapse the categories. In light of the various possible factors that hampered the empirical analysis, the general strategy I adopted in analyzing the data was to focus on those substantial issues for which *both* data sets provided adequate, that is, valid and reliable, indicators. In some instances, this meant settling for less in terms of the range of substantial topics covered, in favor of the methodological defensibility of the analysis.

The design of the present study as well as the particularities of the two data sets imposed several requirements on the analytic procedures and techniques. The aim of the present study being a comparison of cohort processes and subgroup variations within and between cohorts, the basic research strategy involved a comparison of group statistics and statistical patterns. To address the main questions of the study outlined in the Introduction, several analytic techniques were required. Chi-square tests of statistical significance of alterations in cohort distributions have been employed to assess whether shifts in life course expectations and life course statuses between the 1960 and 1980 senior cohort respondents represent reliable, nonchance findings. Bivariate analysis of particular social characteristics and life course–related dimensions by cohort have been used to determine which social groups are most/least affected by shifts in life course expectations and status/role sequences. This entailed cross-tabular analyses and ordinal measures of association (gamma, Cramer's V, eta) for nominal and ordinal variables, correlational analyses (Pearson's r) for interval variables. Finally, to assess what kind of changes occurred in patterns governing the determination of life course–related expectations and statuses, multivariate analytic techniques have been used. Depending on the particular question asked and on the type of data involved, I employed regression, path, and log-linear analyses. These techniques are described in detail where they are first employed in this book.

# Notes

### Introduction

1. Both data sets were made available by the Interuniversity Consortium for Political and Social Research. The data for Project TALENT Public Use File, 1960–1976 (ICPSR 7823) were originally collected by John C. Flanagan, David V. Tiedeman, William V. Clemans, and Lauress L. Wise of the American Institutes for Research, Palo Alto, California; the data for High School and Beyond, 1980: Senior Cohort First and Second Follow-up (1982/1984) (ICPSR 8297) were collected by the National Center for Educational Statistics. Neither the collectors of the original data nor the consortium bear any responsibility for the analyses and interpretations presented here.

2. The number of cases the "Public Use File" of Project TALENT provides for high school graduates of other racial origin is very small; nonwhites are therefore excluded from the present study.

3. In contrast to Mannheim's ([1928] 1978) definition of a "generation," the concept of the cohort does not imply any common generational consciousness among its members, which Mannheim considers the result of a generation's similar position in historical time and thus of its similar historical experiences.

4. Reviewing design possibilities and problems in the analysis of transitions, Power (1983) distinguishes three models. The first is the cross-sectional design that tests different samples at the same point in time. The second model, the longitudinal design, requires testing of a given age or school cohort at different points in time; the third model is the time-lag design described above.

5. The twenty-year time span between the two cohorts makes it difficult to interpret such shifts as trends. To lessen the possibility that the time points selected are atypical, I reinforce the results (where possible) with time series data based on secondary sources (e.g., *Statistical Abstract of the United States*, publications of the National Center for Educational Statistics).

197

## Chapter 1

1. Western societies have differed significantly in terms of the scope and speed of rationalization and individualization. This issue lies outside my focus, which is limited to an examination of the developmental logic of modern society. For a comprehensive analysis of "the rise of Western rationalism," see Schluchter (1981).

2. It is important to keep in mind that the concept of rationality is two-dimensional: One dimension refers to the rational definition of ends, the other to the rational account of means. The first dimension captures the fact that ends are not predetermined, but rather are always open to question—and thus are susceptible to rational decision. The second dimension involves what Weber refers to as the technical aspects of rationality: The highest degree of rationality is found where the means selected to pursue given ends provide the highest level of calculability and efficiency.

3. Mayer and Müller (1986, p. 10) assert that "legal rationality establishes the individual as the prime holder of rights and duties and as the prime target of bureaucratic action."

4. Civil rights are a prerequisite for individual freedom. They comprise the liberty of the person; freedom of speech, thought, and faith; the right to own property and to conclude contracts; and the right to justice (Marshall, 1964). They are very important for the establishment of the market, especially the attribution of the formal right to a job of one's choosing. In this sense, the development of the rationalized economy is paralleled by the institutionalization of civil rights. As Janowitz (1980, p. 13) points out, "Civil rights undermined the economic forms of feudalism and made possible the contractual relations essential for the emergence of capitalism with the resulting economic growth." Consequently, the expansion of the rationalized polity cannot be understood as a simple reaction to the development of the rationalized economy; rather, it facilitated the establishment of the market with the concomitant monetarization of economic action and exchange. This is a much neglected aspect, as the state's function is predominantly viewed as consisting only of regulating the problems emerging in the course of societal differentiation.

5. Boli-Bennett (1981) has documented the rapid expansion of the institution of citizenship in his cross-national study of the definition of constitutional rights, 1870–1970.

6. Friedman (1981) has shown that the institutionalization of social rights follows the same logic as the social construction of civil and political rights.

7. The fact that individuals are attributed formally equal positions in the political structure does not preclude their actual political power being unequal.

8. Although the authors cited below differ to a great extent in their basic concepts and theoretical approaches to modern society, the individualization of membership in society is a common denominator. Marx ([1867] 1972) emphasizes the

role of the capitalist mode of production in weakening traditional authority relations (serfdom, bondage) and breaking up traditional relations of provision and care. Tönnies ([1887] 1979) conceives of societal individualization as a principle of social organization that he calls "Gesellschaft," that is, the juxtaposition of independent persons, which contrasts to the principle of "Gemeinschaft" found in traditional societies. Durkheim ([1893] 1964) stresses the expanding social division of labor and the attendant development of market-dependent social relations. Individuals thus are socially integrated through contractual relations. This process gradually replaces the structure of "mechanic solidarity," which attaches the individual to the domestic milieu and tradition by the structure of "organic solidarity." Elias ([1939] 1978) refers to the same social transformation as the civilizing process through which the individual actor is constituted. For Luckmann (1975), the segmentation of the institutional order in modern society—the quasi-autonomous spheres of the economy and polity—has modified the relationship of the individual to the social order. In the interstices of the segmented institutions, a "private-social" sphere could develop in which the individual experiences a sense of "freedom" and autonomy. Berger et al. (1973) and Berger and Luckmann (1979) analyze the same process in terms of the relationship between social mobility and personal identity. They maintain that personal identity in the individualized society is no longer intrusively ascribed; rather it has to be elaborated as an individual accomplishment.

9. According to Hobsbawm and Ranger (1985, p. 265), the loosening of social ties and affiliations weakened "the older devices by which social subordination had largely been maintained: relatively autonomous collectivities or cooperations under the ruler, but controlling their own members[;] pyramids of authority linked to higher authorities at their apexes[;] and stratified social hierarchies in which each stratum recognized its place."

10. The expansion of the welfare state seems to have slowed down or even halted recently (for a discussion of the structural limits of the welfare state, see Sachse, 1986). Moreover, the rapid growth over the last fifteen years of "self-help" movements in different spheres of life (e.g., health [Gross, 1982; Badura & von Ferber, 1983; von Ferber, 1985] and economy [Berger, 1984; Kreutz et al., 1984]) may be regarded as a kind of counterreaction to state intervention in formerly private domains of life.

11. One could hypothesize that, at a given point in time, a high degree of correspondence is conducive to social stability, whereas a low degree of matching furthers social change. Bourdieu (1980a, 1984a), especially, has devoted much of his theoretical work to this question, maintaining that objective social "di-visions" help constitute the individual's "vision" of the social reality. And the symbolic imposition of structural divisions (i.e., symbolic violence) may ultimately produce objective social differences.

12. Elias ([1939] 1978) has analyzed the process by which the individual is constituted as a social actor. He concludes that the "I," the individual in the literal

sense of the word, only becomes a unit of action in a highly mobile society based on the principle of social division of labor.

13. Although the cultural system contains elaborate theories of the ontology and the status of society in relation to external entities (God, Nature), I focus on the collective account of the relationship between individual and society since this is most relevant to my research. For a description of all other aspects, see Meyer et al. (1981).

14. Marcel Mauss ([1938] 1975) was one of the first social scientists to analyze the history of the concepts of the person and the "I." He maintains that the notion of the individual as a psychological being is a very recent idea.

15. The different branches of psychology represent scientific accounts of the individual as a person. Bellah et al. (1985) show how the language of individualism is the dominant mode of expression in American everyday life, and how the individualistic philosophy is reiterated in the language of therapists.

16. An often-neglected function of the educational system is to socialize individuals as citizens and to turn them into modern individuals (cf. Meyer, 1986b; Boli-Bennett et al., 1985; Lenhardt, 1985; Somerville, 1982; Bendix, 1964; Marshall, 1964; Janowitz, 1980).

17. The extent to which individuals are integrated into the structure of the institutionalized life course depends partly on social group membership. Meyer (1986b) argues that in the development of modern society, social groups are gradually subsumed into this structure through the concession of political rights and inclusion in the market.

18. The standardization of the life course in modern society is partly predicated on the increase in average life expectancy since the seventeenth century. Von Imhof (1981) has shown that this increase resulted mainly from a drastic drop in premature mortality. The concentration of death at later ages makes life events less contingent and, vice versa, more predictable—a prerequisite for any kind of standardization (Kohli, 1983; Brose, 1985b).

19. There is ample evidence that the significance of chronological age increases with the development of modern society. This is a peculiar aspect of Western modernization because this society relies more on achieved than on ascribed characteristics for regulating access to and distribution of material and symbolic goods. Brose (1985b) argues that age is a means for establishing continuity that counterbalances the contingency resulting from permanent social changes within modern society.

20. Ariès (1962), for instance, illustrates the shift from highly age-heterogeneous to highly age-homogeneous school classes in the course of the seventeenth, eighteenth, and nineteenth centuries.

21. The speed at which legal definitions couched in terms of chronological age spread and the range of behavioral domains that they transform into state-defined rights and obligations vary considerably across Western nations. A social history of age-related legislation in different nations would be a prerequisite for assessing

national differences in the significance of the state for regulating the individual life course.

22. Widmer (1983) presents an interesting analysis of the relationship between the two forms of age classification in modern society: age according to stages in the life cycle (i.e., age groups) and chronological age in terms of calendar years. He delineates the social situations in which one classification scheme is given priority over the other, and he assesses their respective contributions to the imposition of social order.

23. For a discussion of regularities as a result of practices or of explicit norms and their relationship, see Bourdieu (1985a).

24. For a detailed account of the increasing destandardization of the family cycle, see Chapter 2, "Diversification of Family Life."

25. This standardization is based on the organization of the educational and occupational system according to vocational and professional categories (cf. Beck et al., 1980; Brater & Beck, 1982).

26. State recognition of a particular set of skills and knowledge as the basis of an occupational role is the most important aspect of the professionalization of work. For a detailed discussion see Sarfatti-Larson (1977).

27. Mertens and Kaiser (1978) and Brater and Beck (1982) point out that the more the labor market is state-regulated, the higher seem to be the frictions and tensions between the supply of a certain kind of labor and the respective demand for it. In such a labor market, the over- and underproduction of specific types of professional qualifications is very likely.

28. Analyzing the dual structure of the "public man" and the "private man" over the last two hundred years, Sennett (1977) maintains that the notion of subjectivity has been decoupled from the social life and relegated to the psychological dimension—a process he calls the "tyranny of intimacy."

29. The social construction of age-appropriate tasks and behaviors is always subject to struggles between different social groups having an interest in defining these properties. Struggles between age groups—the generation gap—concern the definition and distribution of age-appropriate practices and, as such, the access to and the exclusion from power. In these struggles, older age groups tend to use strategies that define the younger age groups as irresponsible and immature, thus restricting and delaying the following generation's access to power. Conversely, younger age groups make use of strategies defining the older age group's knowledge and competencies as obsolete. They attempt to illegitimize the older generation's possession of power positions (cf. Chamboredon, 1983). The current employment policy is a good example of the competition between age groups over the distribution of age-appropriate attributes to define the legitimate access to scarce occupational positions (cf. Enial, 1985).

30. Neugarten et al. (1965) have devoted much of their work to the study of age norms. They furnished proof of the existence of very subtle age norms concerning wide ranges of everyday behavior, such as leisure activities, language, dressing,

drinking, gestures, facial expressions, and certain psychological attributes, which are supported by a differentiated system of sanctions in case of violation. From these lifestyle-related age norms, Neugarten and Hagestad (1976) distinguish age norms relating to the timing of life events (see the discussion in this chapter, "State Regulation of the Life Course").

31. Hoffmann-Nowotny (1987, p. 52) advances a similiar argument by maintaining that in bureaucratic institutions and in the corresponding cultural account incorporating universalistic values and norms, "people are generally comprehended as representatives of social categories, and not as individuals."

32. For a critique of subjectivist tendencies in biographical research, see Bourdieu (1986b) and Buchmann and Gurny (1984).

33. In this sense, the institutionalized life course represents an objective classification system regulating the individual's progression through social time and space.

34. There are societies in which the social order rests solely on the incorporated system of classification. The reproduction of these types of societies thus relies exclusively on direct social interaction, a much more time-consuming and precarious mode of social reproduction than that provided by partial reliance on institutionalized categories.

35. In Bourdieu's (1977b, p. 82–83) own words, the habitus is "the strategy generating principle enabling agents to cope with unforeseen and everchanging situations . . . , a system of lasting, transposable dispositions which, integrating past experiences, functions at every moment as a matrix of perceptions, appreciations, and action and makes possible the achievement of infinitely diversified tasks, thanks to the analogical transfer of schemes permitting the solution of similarly shaped problems."

36. This includes both the acquisition of resources and their "social closure," that is, the monopolization of the access to the desired resources (for a discussion of this aspect in Bourdieu's theory, see Honneth, 1984).

37. Swidler (1986) points out that most social theories adhere to the underlying assumption that individuals organize their actions one at a time, trying, each time, to maximize a given outcome with the best possible means. Such an assumption can be found in Parsons's (1951) action theory as well as in Weber's ([1922] 1968) conception of rational action orientation. Both theories claim that every "unit act" (Swidler, 1986) is a rational calculation of ends and means in order to maximize the chances of achieving a highly valued outcome. These conceptualizations prove to be of only limited value for explaining empirical findings regarding the rational status of action. Swidler advocates, therefore, a conceptualization of action that is very similar to Bourdieu's approach. Focusing on the idea that culture is a "tool kit" of symbols, habits, and skills, Swidler suggests that individuals make use of this cultural equipment for constructing lines of action, that is, strategies of action. The rationality of such strategies thus is related to the cultural "tools" individuals have at their disposal and handle with ease. Individuals prefer and value highly strategies of action for which their cultural equipment is well suited, because "one

can hardly pursue success in a world where the accepted skills, style, and informal know-how are unfamiliar" (Swidler, 1986, p. 275).

38. For instance, the logic of the gift, the religious activities of the priest, the mundane activities of the aristocrat.

39. For a research strategy analyzing such deviations in terms of status inconsistency, see Bornschier and Heintz (1977).

40. On the other hand, the convertibility of educational certificates into occupational positions and income must be objectively guaranteed to some degree in order for educational investments to be sensible.

41. We are dealing here, of course, with the subjective apprehension of structural opportunities.

42. For similar ideas, see Kohli (1981a), who conceives of the biographical orientation as a problem of action and as a structural problem.

For a trenchant critique of life course approaches that do not take into account the linkages between the subjective and the structural context, see Bourdieu (1986b).

## Chapter 2

1. For example, Neugarten and Hagestad (1976, p. 45) note that "political youth movements have appeared when unusually large cohorts of young people are present in society."

2. In the remainder of this chapter, the discussion draws on literature referring to the United States, France, Germany, and Switzerland; the focus is on general trends in these social institutions without regard to specific countries. All aspects of change do not occur with the same intensity, nor at the same time or speed, in these countries. Yet the literature suggests that, since the late 1960s, changes of some importance did occur in each of these countries.

3. This presumes that the affected individuals do not perceive the diminishing value of specific educational certificates. If they do, these individuals could conceivably switch to an educational track with exchange relations that have remained stable. The chances of realizing such options, however, depend strongly on the available resources and competencies.

4. Classifying occupations on the basis of the type of knowledge they incorporate, Geser's (1981) approach would be most useful for analyzing development patterns of professional qualifications and their social determinants in detail.

5. This varies by (industrialized) country. Individuals in the United States, for example, have always had a greater propensity to change occupations (cf. Treiman, 1985) than workers in European industrialized countries.

6. Studies of workers in temporary jobs illustrate the impact of highly unstable work careers on individual orientations and strategies of action. According to Brose (1982, 1985a), temporary workers tend to postpone decisions. The fact that temporary work turns out to be permanent, although most of these individuals initially conceived of it as a provisional arrangement, reflects the tendency toward "bio-

graphical undecidedness." Temporary work is a means for controlling the irreversibility of life situations through the limitation of commitment. This attitude affects the definition of the private life: There is a preference for defining personal relationships as open-ended.

7. Some authors (cf. Offe, 1982) conclude that under these conditions work can no longer be regarded as the key concept for describing advanced capitalist society or as the central value in individuals' lives. For a critique of this position, see Beckenbach (1984).

8. For a review and critique of different positions, see Beckenbach (1984); for the best-known position in the German language area, see Kern and Schumann (1984a, 1984b).

9. The emergence of new professions is partially attributable to the decline of core industries and the concomitant loss of workplaces; to the overproduction of educational certificates and the corresponding lack of equivalent occupational opportunities; and to the restructuring of work tasks brought about by the implementation of new technologies. For my purposes, the details of this development are less important than its impact on how professional trajectories are structured and how biographical strategies are chosen.

10. For the concept of the perception of structural chances, see Heintz et al. (1978).

11. The literature suggests that these changes do not occur with the same intensity, nor at exactly the same time, in different European countries and the United States (for the United States, see Cherlin, 1983; Collins, 1985; Rodgers & Thornton, 1985; for France, see Audirac, 1982; Les Ages de la vie, 1982–1983; Roussel, 1978, 1980a, 1980b; Gokalp, 1981; Fouquet & Morin, 1984; for an international review, see Eekelaar & Katz, 1980; for a detailed review of trends in Western European countries, see Hoffmann-Nowotny, 1987).

12. Analyzing trends in marriage, divorce, and remarriage since the end of the nineteenth century, Cherlin (1983) points out that the current changes generally fit the overall demographic pattern since the end of the century, although they are somewhat accelerated. The widespread belief that radical demographic changes have occurred in the family cycle over the last twenty years is mostly based on a comparison of the 1950s and 1970s, not an analysis of long-term development. Cherlin concludes that the trends in the 1970s are more representative of the family cycle in this century than are those of the 1950s. Nevertheless, we may speak of current changes in the family cycle, since the respective rates of change increase or decrease much more rapidly. The development of the divorce rate in France since 1885 supports this interpretation (cf. Boigeol et al., 1984).

13. For a theoretical model of the relationship between social change and changes in the family system, see Hoffmann-Nowotny (1980b).

14. Cherlin (1978) reports a sharp decline in the proportion of women who planned to be housewives, especially among women with higher education. This decline occurred between 1969 and 1975.

15. The burdens of the gradual individualization of the female life course should

not be underestimated. As Hochschild (1986) puts it, "Women are trying to squeeze themselves into jobs and careers originally designated for men who had someone else to care for their children, and they are doing so with precious few social supports outside the home and with husbands who do not yet share chores within it." Ehrenreich (1983, p. 176) makes the same argument by saying that women are able to enter the labor market on an equal footing with men only on the condition that a variety of social supports are provided: above all, high-quality child care.

16. Ehrenreich (1983, p. 104) quotes Caroline Bird's observation that "the number of ill-paid, dead-end 'women's jobs' grew so much faster [in the seventies] than better paid 'men's work' that by 1976 only 40% of the jobs in the country paid enough to support a family."

17. According to a 1985 study on divorce in California, conducted by Leonore Weitzman, women and children are, one year after divorce, 73 percent poorer; men, on the contrary, are 42 percent richer than before (see the *San Francisco Chronicle*, Feb. 16, 1986).

18. Sociological studies of time (cf. Rammstedt, 1975; Ullrich, 1981; Brose, 1982; for a review, see Bergmann, 1983; Elias, 1985) stress the distinction between social and subjective time structures. Social time can be conceived of as socially defined forms of time orientation encompassing (institutional) regulations and (culturally defined) expectations of the temporal structure of life (Brose, 1984). In industrial society, examples are the regulation of the work day and of the work time, the institutionalization of retirement age, age typifications, and the cultural orientation toward the future. Subjective time is the individual perception and experience of time that results in specific, individual time structures. Individual time develops within the frame set by social time; nonetheless, it varies according to social attributes (social class, sex, age) and specific life circumstances.

19. The term "new information and communication technologies" is used to cover an ensemble of technologies based on microelectronics, including developments in data-processing and office technology, as well as in telecommunications.

20. Taking the peculiarities of service work into account, especially the relatively high level of uncertainty with regard to the work load (e.g., emergency services, sales), Engfer (1983) regards time flexibility as the major means for further rationalization of the service sector.

21. The tendency to dissolve the standard work day affects not only the actual distribution but also the normative regulation of working hours. Until quite recently, the state and labor unions have been the most important actors regulating the location, duration, and distribution of work time. Both state and union policy favored its standardization and homogenization. Deviations from the standard work day therefore bring about a shift in the relevant actors who regulate working hours, from the state and the labor unions to the individual company (cf. Offe et al., 1983; Negt, 1984).

22. For convenience, I use the term "individualization of working hours" for describing the increasing flexibility of work time patterns.

23. To designate the process of shifting paid labor to private work, I use the term "substitution of labor."

24. Sweet (1983) shows that part-time work among teenagers is Australia's fastest growing employment category. Sales and service categories were the sectors of the economy where most of the new part-time jobs were created. Sweet draws the conclusion "that there is a significant tendency for the first experience of work after leaving school to be a part-time job" (p. 24). This altered structural situation is likely to have a profound impact on the (biographical) significance of work.

Pialoux's (1979) study on temporary work among youths in France shows that a discontinuous work career is likely to become a "normal" element in the lives of these youths.

25. I deliberately do not address the problem of how different social groups intervene in the process of redefining the cultural imagery of given life stages. It is important to note, however, that this redefinition is the end product of a struggle among different groups in society—especially between those in charge of the production of symbolic representations. It is a struggle for the imposition of the legitimate worldview. In this respect, shifts in the cultural meaning system are not direct outcomes of structural changes. Rather, structural transformations redistribute the social positions of different social groups and thus affect the setting within which the struggle for the production of the legitimate worldview takes place (cf. Lenoir [1985a, 1985b] for an analysis of the shifts in the social representation of the family). Yet this is only one aspect of the process: New languages, new models, new symbols have to find their "customers"—the public for which the new imagery provides a more satisfactory answer to everyday life problems (cf. Lefaucheur [1982] for an analysis of the diffusion and adoption of new family models by the new middle class).

26. In the third mode of coping, the typesetters try to uphold the collectively defined standards concerning the social relationships among workers, the forms of solidarity as well as the moral considerations with regard to the rejection of individualistic striving for professional success. The renunciation of individual career attempts is based on the assessment that the individual's advancement is, under the capitalist mode of production, only realized to the collective disadvantage. In other words, individual career achievements will bring negative effects for the rest of the workers. This attempt to impose the traditional cultural account of work on the changed objective work situation is a form of resistance against the further rationalization and individualization of social life.

27. This interpretation is analogous to one made by Boli-Bennett (1981) in his study of the development of the individual's political and economic rights and obligations over the last hundred years. He found that the scope of psychology widens and the emphasis on socialization increases with the gradual individualization of action and exchange.

28. Swidler's (1986) argument, that the culture of individualism represents less a value directed to particular ends and more a way of organizing action, supports this line of reasoning.

29. See especially Hirschman (1982; 1986, Chapter 3) for an incisive analysis of the social determinants of public involvements.

30. Mayer and Müller's (1986) examples illustrate this logic clearly. For instance, the decision to build a new house might be more dependent on the availability of housing subsidies than on the personally felt needs or wishes of being a homeowner. Similarly, public loans or grants for higher education might trigger the decision to continue one's studies; education as a personal goal might be of less importance.

31. There is a consensus within the scientific community over the definition of modernity; the same does not hold for the notion of postmodernity. This suggests that this concept designates less a distinct trend in time than an attitude of mind appearing in times of social crises, as Eco (1984) maintains (cf. Vester, 1985).

32. As Wuthnow et al. (1985, p. 238) point out, Habermas's conception "remains largely an approach rather than a substantive theory or precise guide to empirical investigation." It provides more of a perspective than a guide for investigation.

33. For Lasch (1983), the individual's growing reliance on professional experts has contributed to the "culture of narcissism" in contemporary society, that is, the narcissistic preoccupation of the individual with the self, because professional dominance replicates the condition of childhood in which the child is totally dependent on the adult world.

34. For a similar argument, see Baudrillard (1973). He maintains that advanced industrial societies rely more and more on the code, that is, the symbolic definition of reality, to reproduce their own structure.

35. In a critical review of postmodern theory, especially discussing the work of Foucault and Derrida, Wolin (1984, p. 26) maintains that one of the underlying assumptions of this intellectual trend is "to be freed of the burdens of a 'centered' subjectivity, of responsible, autonomous individuality, and a kindred celebration of the 'end of history' which is conceived of as merely a 'drag' on the activities of the new decentered, amorphous, libidinal self."

36. Gross (1985) has coined the term "tinker-mentality" to describe the postmodern consciousness with its affinity to eclecticism, which is reflected in the attitude of "anything goes." As Lyotard (1984, p. 76) states, "Eclecticism is the degree zero of contemporary general culture: one listens to reggae, watches a Western, eats McDonald's food for lunch and local cuisine for dinner, wears Paris perfume in Tokyo and 'retro' in Hong Kong; knowledge is a matter of TV games."

37. For an excellent critique of the "groundless relativism" of postmodern theory, especially in Derrida's theory of deconstruction, see Asher (1984).

38. This may seem a radical interpretation of postmodern intellectual culture. Vester (1985) points out that the postmodern code, with its emphasis on transformability and openness, makes possible subversive readings of the dominant code (e.g., the language of individualism). Thus, postmodern ideology may carry within it the seeds of the deconstruction of this ideology.

39. Whether individuals in fact make use of the potentially increased freedom

of action depends on the individual awareness of action opportunities, which varies, of course, with social class position and education.

## Chapter 3

1. Somerville (1982) describes this late-nineteenth-century process as the standardization of childhood, which aimed at providing a "proper childhood to every citizen" (p. 193) and at "shaping all children more closely to the ideal of childhood" (p. 195). Boli-Bennett and Meyer (1978) document the close relationship between the progressive differentiation of childhood and the growing authority of the state by analyzing the rules regarding children in national constitutions over the last century.

2. For data on the introduction of compulsory schooling in Europe and the United States, see Ramirez and Boli-Bennett (1981) and Meyer and Rubinson (1975).

3. See Platt (1969); Bremner (1970–1974, part two) for a comprehensive documentary history of this period (1866–1932) for the United States; Gillis (1974); and von Trotha (1982).

4. Hogan (1978) interprets this as evidence of normative prescriptions in the ordering of events in the transition to adulthood. Marini (1984a, 1984b) rightly criticizes this interpretation. Regularities in the transition to adulthood are less the expression of explicit norms and are more the result of individual strategies for coping with educational, occupational, and family requirements. At the aggregate level, these produce the (observed) regularities.

5. For more detail about this differentiation, see especially Bourdieu (1984c).

6. Coleman's book, *The Adolescent Society* (1961), was most influential in spreading the idea that youth as a social group adheres to common values, goals, and behaviors (what he called "peer culture"). Empirical evidence did not support the global cultural differentiation of youth from the dominant society, however. Various forms and styles of juvenile cultural expressions have always coexisted, displaying some common elements. In this respect, Murdock and McCron (1979) assume that every juvenile subculture consists of specific linkages between class consciousness and generational consciousness. It would be very interesting to know at what times juvenile subcultural expressions are dominated by class consciousness and, vice versa, at what times the element of generational consciousness predominates. Empirical evidence suggests that a few rather clear-cut juvenile subcultures existed in the late 1950s and early 1960s. In the 1970s and 1980s, however, a proliferation of juvenile cultural expressions occurred, producing a highly differentiated juvenile environment (cf. Scanagatta, 1985).

## Chapter 4

1. This diagram is based on ideas developed by Riley (1986).

2. Data provided by Norton (1974) show that in the 1930s the median age of white husbands at birth of first child was 24.5 years and approximately 33.0 years at birth of last child. Knowing that the great majority of 1980 senior cohort mem-

bers were born in 1962, we can calculate the probable span of father's age at birth of these children.

## Chapter 5

1. To be precise, I should always refer to "white persons of the 1960 and the 1980 cohort." For convenience, however, throughout the text I shorten this to "the 1960 and 1980 senior cohort."

2. The big shift in the proportion of individuals planning a teaching career reflects the normal cycle of teacher recruitment.

3. To a lesser degree, well-educated women perceive the opportunity for going into semiprofessional work, especially nursing (about 8 percent).

4. Unfortunately, the 1980 cohort data only differentiate between professions in the strict sense of the term (physicians, dentists, lawyers, college professors, etc.) and a larger category encompassing professional work that I label semiprofessional.

5. This result reemphasizes the problem that occupations "are amorphous entities within which there is frequently stratification by sex" (Baron & Bielby, 1985, p. 235). Within the same occupation, women occupy lower-level positions and positions offering little career advancement.

6. In both studies, respondents were asked to indicate the age at which they expect to marry. I recoded this information into expected calendar year of marriage (based on respondent's birth year) in order to control for the variation in respondents' ages at the time they completed high school. Expected time of marriage thus refers to the number of years after high school graduation—the event the two cohorts have in common. For clarity of the figure, I indicate the age of expected marriage based on the calendar years in which most 1960 and 1980 senior cohort members were born (i.e., 1942 or 1962).

7. Although this result is based on expectations, it corresponds with trends in family sizes found in most highly industrialized countries (cf. Hoffmann-Nowotny, 1987).

8. For a detailed discussion of this process, see Chapter 2, "Social Dynamics between Rationalization and Individualization."

9. The socioeconomic position variable is a composite of parents' social standing across five categories: father's occupation, family income, father's and mother's education, and specific household possessions. Both studies use the same categories and very similar computations, so the two composites are fairly comparable. For the present and several forthcoming analyses, the socioeconomic status (SES) index was subdivided into quartiles.

10. Strong sex differences in biographical orientations in the 1960 cohort (discussed in the last section of this chapter) prompted the inclusion of a breakdown by sex in these analyses.

11. Examining educational expectations of eighteen-year-old men and women by father's educational status in the Federal Republic of Germany in 1962 and 1983, Allerbeck (1985; Allerbeck & Hoag, 1985) found that women from well-educated families in 1962 were discriminated against in higher education compared

to their male counterparts. By contrast, daughters of fathers with lower educational status had slightly higher educational opportunities than comparable men. My data for the United States at approximately the same time (i.e., 1960) do not confirm this pattern. In the early 1960s, educational status expectations increased with the socioeconomic and cultural standing of the family for both white men and women. These cross-national differences may indicate different parental strategies in ensuring the social position of their sons and daughters. Interestingly, Allerbeck (1985; Allerbeck & Hoag, 1985) reports for 1983 the same patterns of educational expectations in the Federal Republic of Germany that I have found for the United States in the 1980s: Women of all social origins have caught up with men or have surpassed them. This cross-national assimilation in schooling expectations may be the result of the pervasive influence of education on the structuring of the life course in advanced industrial society.

12. For more evidence on the impact of the trend toward accelerated individualization of the female life course, see Beck-Gernsheim (1983, 1986), Kohli (1986), and Meyer (1986b).

13. Due to limitations of the Project TALENT data, I could not include respondents' labor-force status (i.e., whether the respondent held a full-time job in the fourth year after high school) in the analysis.

14. This figure includes all male respondents. Among these, about 25 percent had no idea what to do about military service.

15. I cannot reconstruct the military status of the 1960 respondents for the ideal year 1964 because the 1971 follow-up does not provide information on the timing of military service. For this we must rely on the 1965 follow-up which, as mentioned before, is hampered by a poor response rate (51.7 percent).

16. Hornstein (1985) presents a similar argument. He maintains that the social organization of youth two decades ago was closely tied to the family's social background. Participation in the life stage youth was more or less confined to youth from well-to-do and well-educated families.

17. Ideally, I would define a group mean difference of .50 and above as a "social barrier." As the difference between the low-medium and high-medium quartile for the 1960 cohort men almost reaches this level and none of the 1980 cohort group differences do so, I interpret the male transition to adulthood in the 1960s as marked by social barriers.

## Chapter 6

1. *Statistical Abstract of the United States* 1986, Table 250.

2. This underestimation is likely to be greater in the 1980 senior cohort because of the increasing proportion of master's degrees and doctorates conferred in the 1980s. In 1960, 17.6 percent of all college degrees conferred were master's degrees and doctorates, compared to 24.9 percent in 1980 (*Statistical Abstract of the United States* 1986, Table 272).

3. This educational category includes community college students in vocational and college-transfer programs and dropouts from regular four-year colleges.

4. A chi-square test shows statistically significant differences in the distribution of educational attainment in the 1960 and 1980 senior cohorts (63.6; df = 3; p = .0000). The same is true of the two groups of fathers as reported earlier (see Table 4.3).

5. To further support this interpretation I compare college enrollment rates of white eighteen- to twenty-four-year-old persons based on decennial census data (i.e., including the entire cohort and not only the noninstitutional civilian population as in the Current Population Survey [C.P.S.]) between 1960 and 1984: 1960, 15.2 percent; 1970, 25.7 percent; 1980, 25.0 percent; 1984, 26.9 percent (*Statistical Abstract of the United States* 1986, Tables 28 and 250; *Statistical Abstract of the United States* 1978, Table 29).

College attendance rates based on the C.P.S. are considerably higher. The figures for the same age group are 34.8 percent in 1970 and 41.1 percent in 1980 (National Center for Educational Statistics, *The Conditions of Education*, 1982).

Still another way of calculating college attendance rates is the ratio of high school graduates enrolled in college. This method produces the following figures: 1960, 24.2 percent; 1970, 33.2 percent; 1975, 32.4 percent; 1980, 32.0 percent; 1984, 33.7 percent (*Statistical Abstract of the United States* 1986, Table 250).

6. Pincus (1980) reports higher enrollment rates for nonwhite students in these institutions than for white students.

7. The unemployment rates among persons with terminal high school diplomas help illustrate the different employment prospects in the 1960s and 1980s. Although the following percentages are based on white persons of all ages, they indicate increased vulnerability to unemployment among persons with no post-secondary education compared to those with college education.

| | Unemployment Rate (%) | | | | |
| --- | --- | --- | --- | --- | --- |
| | 1965 | 1970 | 1975 | 1980 | 1985 |
| High school diploma | 3.7 | 3.6 | 8.4 | 5.9 | 7.0 |
| College, one to three years | — | 3.7 | 6.6 | 4.4 | 4.2 |
| College, four years and more | — | 1.5 | 2.8 | 1.9 | 2.3 |

*Source: Statistical Abstract of the United States* 1986, Table 686.

8. Community college enrollments show that in 1960 only 16 percent of all students in higher education were enrolled in these institutions. By 1978, this figure had grown to 36 percent (Pincus, 1980).

9. Pincus (1980) cites several studies showing that the proportions of community college students enrolled in vocational programs increased from around 10 percent in the mid-1960s to over half of all students in the mid-1970s.

10. To be precise, I should relate my statement to women attending the senior high school year, because approximately 25 percent of the corresponding age cohort leave school earlier.

11. To further support this interpretation I compare college enrollment rates of white eighteen- to twenty-four-year-old men and women based on decennial census

data (i.e., including the entire cohort and not only the noninstitutional civilian population as in the C.P.S. between 1960 and 1984.

The elevated proportion of male college enrollment in 1970 seems to reflect young men's evasion of military service, especially since no equivalent rise and drop occurs for women (cf. Hamilton & Wright, 1975).

| | College Enrollment | | | |
| --- | --- | --- | --- | --- |
| | 1960 (%) | 1970 (%) | 1980 (%) | 1984 (%) |
| White men | 18.8 | 30.6 | 25.2 | 27.9 |
| White women | 11.7 | 21.0 | 24.7 | 26.0 |

*Source: Statistical Abstract of the United States* 1986, Tables 28 and 250; 1978, Table 29.

12. A lucid recent discussion of these questions is offered in Robinson and Garnier (1985). A detailed review of various education theories may be found in Lenhardt (1985).

13. For similar arguments, see Meyer (1977) and Collins (1979).

14. I am not able to empirically test these hypotheses in terms of social class membership because the information provided by the two data sets does not allow construction of an indicator of social class that would be defensible in theoretical terms. For this reason, I apply a more modest test, using socioeconomic position and father's educational status as indicators of the family's social standing.

15. I would expect, for example, larger values of group mean differences in lower SES quartiles (floor effects) and smaller group mean differences in higher SES quartiles (ceiling effects). My hypothesis is strengthened by the fact that the reverse is true: smaller values in the two lower SES quartiles, and higher values in the two upper quartiles (low, .22; medium-low, .26; medium-high, .45; high, .34).

16. The trend is the optimal linear fit of a given distribution of values. It is calculated in such a way that the sum of the squared residuals, that is, the difference between the actual and the estimated values, is minimized.

## Chapter 7

1. For a discussion of the two basic types of data describing work histories, that is, continuous event histories and events at selected points in time, see Treiman (1985).

2. For a short review see Treiman (1985); for a detailed study of the development of women's participation in the labor force over the last 150 years, see Bergmann (1986).

3. Those who join the armed forces are an exception. The 1960 census found 11.6 percent of twenty- to twenty-one-year-old men in the armed forces; the 1970 census reports 14.3 percent (cited after Hamilton & Wright, 1975).

4. In the United States, 28 percent of the sixteen- to nineteen-year-old students and 32 percent of the twenty- to twenty-four-year-old students were employed in

1953. In 1980, corresponding percentages had risen to 36 and 51, indicating the increasing importance of student employment (Hills & Reubens, 1983, p. 277).

5. Part-time employment (i.e., less than thirty-five hours per week) for sixteen- to nineteen-year-old persons of all races has risen since 1965. The figures presented below are not controlled for completion of school.

|  | 1965 | 1970 | 1975 | 1980 | 1985 |
|---|---|---|---|---|---|
| Part-time work as percentage of total employment | 40.7 | 47.0 | 46.4 | 47.7 | 50.2 |

*Source: Statistical Abstract of the United States* 1986, Table 665; 1984, Table 677.

The increase in part-time work is not entirely attributable to shifts in the job structure. It is partly due to increases in school retention rates for this age group, especially among the nineteen-year-olds.

For Australia, Sweet (1983) shows that part-time work among teenagers is the fastest growing employment category. Most of these jobs are in the sales and service industry.

6. For a detailed description, see Chapter 2, "Rationalization of Lifetime: The Impact of New Information Technologies."

7. The lack of continuous work histories in the Project TALENT data precludes reconstructing employment status in the fourth year after high school graduation.

8. National unemployment rates for sixteen- to twenty-four-year-olds not enrolled in school for 1974–1977 address the latter assumption. They show that high school graduates had an unemployment rate of 11.3 percent (see Pincus, 1980). For 1980 respondents, the unemployment rates by level of education and sex in 1984 are listed in the table; Project TALENT does not provide enough information to calculate the unemployment rate by level of education in 1964.

|  | Unemployment Rate | | | |
|---|---|---|---|---|
|  | High School Graduate (%) | Noncollegiate Education (%) | Some College Education (%) | Four-Year College (%) |
| Men | 4.4 | 5.4 | 3.6 | .6 |
| Women | 4.4 | 2.0 | 4.1 | 1.1 |

9. I find the same relationship using data from the follow-up eleven years later: 43.2 percent of college-educated women are full-time employed; 33.3 percent of women with some college or noncollegiate education have full-time jobs; and only 21.1 percent of women with no postsecondary education have full-time jobs.

10. The lower proportion of full-time employment among four-year college–educated women is not an exception; most are still in school.

11. Comparison with total age-specific rates of female labor-force participation since 1960 clearly shows the upward trend. Although the figures are not directly comparable (they include all races and persons with less than a high school di-

ploma), we may roughly equate the eighteen- to nineteen-year-old group to the figures for the first year after high school graduation, and the twenty- to twenty-four-year-olds to the figures for the fourth/fifth year after completing secondary education. The slower rate of change in the youngest age group reflects the increasing school retention rate over this period.

| | Women in Labor Force | | | | | |
|---|---|---|---|---|---|---|
| | 1960 (%) | 1965 (%) | 1970 (%) | 1975 (%) | 1980 (%) | 1984 (%) |
| 18–19 years old | 50.9 | 49.3 | 53.5 | 58.1 | 61.9 | 61.8 |
| 20–24 years old | 46.1 | 49.9 | 57.7 | 64.1 | 68.9 | 70.4 |
| 25–34 years old | 36.0 | 38.5 | 45.0 | 54.9 | 65.5 | 69.8 |

*Source: Statistical Abstract of the United States* 1982/1983, Table 626; 1986, Table 660.

It is worth noting that female labor-force participation in 1960 steadily declines with increasing age. This pattern slowly dissolves so that in later decades, we observe increasing or at least stable rates as women grow older. This suggests that women are less willing in the 1980s to leave the labor force for childrearing.

12. The results are reinforced by the age-specific rates of labor-force participation of married women (including all races) between 1960 and 1985 presented here. Participation rates are defined as percentage of married civilian noninstitutional women in the labor force. For all age groups, we observe rapid increases after 1965. Moreover, participation rates by age are U-shaped until 1975; in the 1980s we find linear trends. This suggests the slow dissolution of the "double-peak" pattern of female labor-force participation.

| | Married Women in Labor Force | | | | | |
|---|---|---|---|---|---|---|
| | 1960 (%) | 1965 (%) | 1970 (%) | 1975 (%) | 1980 (%) | 1985 (%) |
| 20–24 years old | 30.0 | 35.6 | 47.4 | 57.3 | 60.5 | 64.9 |
| 25–34 years old | 27.7 | 32.1 | 39.3 | 48.3 | 59.3 | 65.6 |
| 35–44 years old | 36.2 | 40.6 | 47.2 | 51.9 | 62.5 | 68.1 |

*Source: Statistical Abstract of the United States* 1986, Table 673.

13. Examining employment status for the 1980 senior cohort men and women in the fourth year after high school graduation by year of completing school, I find in each year (i.e., 1980, 1981, 1982) about 15 percent employed part-time. These figures confirm that part-time employment in the 1980s constitutes a regular work status.

14. Hornstein (1985) reports similar trends for the Federal Republic of Germany; particularly since the early 1970s, status linkages between education and occupation have become precarious.

15. Citing the Carnegie Commission, Pincus (1980) concludes that high school graduates have the qualifications for at least 80 percent of the jobs that now exist.

16. These findings are based on a national sample of full-time employed residents of the United States eighteen years old and over.

17. Women's jobs in both cohorts show, on average, a slightly higher prestige than men's jobs. This finding is consistent with the higher prestige of expected occupational positions that I found among women at these educational levels (see Chapter 5, "Continuity and Change in Status Expectations and Anticipated Timing of Life Events"). According to Sewell et al. (1980, p. 579), the relatively higher levels of status can be explained by the kinds of occupations women typically enter: "Women with educational levels between 12 and 15 years usually take first jobs in lower-white-collar occupations (clerical and sales jobs)." In the highly sex-segregated lower strata of the occupational structure, typical women's jobs (unlike men's) rate a bit higher in prestige because they are "clean jobs" and require typically female qualities and attributes. Men with the same levels of education tend to enter blue-collar jobs.

18. In order to homogenize the category "some college education," I included only respondents with two or three years of college education.

19. The mean of occupational status expectations is 43.0 for women employed full time who anticipate no postsecondary education, whereas it is 44.7 for those expecting some noncollegiate postsecondary or some college education.

20. This trend is less marked for 1960 cohort women employed full time.

21. The corresponding means for 1960 cohort full-time employed women are 53.2 in the category "four-year college degree" and 56.5 in the category "advanced college degree."

22. Among men, there is no need to control the analysis for employment status because most work full time.

23. Shifts in the distribution of employed civilians of all races twenty-five years and over in professional/technical and related occupations by educational attainment and sex between 1970 and 1981 bolster the validity of my interpretation.

|  | Educational Attainment[a] | | | | | | | | |
|  | 4 Years of High School | | | 1–3 Years of College | | | 4 Years of College and More | | |
| Professional/Technical Occupations | 1970 (%) | 1975 (%) | 1980 (%) | 1970 (%) | 1975 (%) | 1980 (%) | 1970 (%) | 1975 (%) | 1980 (%) |
|---|---|---|---|---|---|---|---|---|---|
| Men | 16.3 | 13.2 | 12.2 | 17.2 | 15.7 | 15.3 | 60.5 | 68.5 | 70.7 |
| Women | 19.7 | 17.9 | 15.9 | 19.1 | 17.1 | 20.5 | 54.2 | 62.3 | 61.4 |

*Source: Statistical Abstract of the United States* 1982/1983, Table 649.
[a] Distribution of persons with less than four years of high school not shown, so both male and female figures do not add up to 100 percent.

Although labor market devaluation of educational status affects newcomers to the labor force to a greater extent than experienced workers (cf. Burris, 1983), the proportion of men with educational attainments below college degree level decreases in this occupational category, while the proportion of those with college degrees increases. These shifts indicate that men without college degrees have less access to professional/technical occupations. We observe the same trends for women, except that the proportion of women with one to three years of college increases in 1980. This suggests shifts in the direction of more paraprofessional and semiprofessional jobs, which are filled particularly by women.

24. Elementary teaching and, more recently, secondary teaching are good examples of this process. It is accompanied by deteriorating levels of pay, fringe benefits, working conditions, and so forth. Reviewing literature on sex segregation in the professional occupations, Sokoloff (1986, p. 15) maintains that a similiar process is to be observed now in academia. The explosion of women in college teaching over the last decade is predominantly in lower-status two-year colleges (i.e., community colleges).

25. Since I analyze income attainment in the two cohorts with the aim of estimating sex differences, annual earnings in dollars are not adjusted to inflation, but they are standardized (z-transformation). For comparative reasons, I standardize the occupational prestige scale, too.

26. Using longitudinal data, Sewell et al. (1980) show that this "status advantage" at the beginnning of women's work careers is counterbalanced by a lack of opportunity for upward mobility over the course of their work lives. Unlike men, women gain little occupational status during their occupational trajectory.

27. The unequal number of cases on which the 1960 and 1980 cohort analysis is based makes it difficult to deduce from the T-value and the corresponding level of significance the exact extent to which sex differences have increased or declined. This limitation applies especially to the category of high school graduates.

28. In order to homogenize the category "some college education," I again included only respondents with two or three years of college education.

29. The poor response rate in the 1965 follow-up survey and the low women's rate of full-time employment contribute to the small number of cases in the 1960 cohort analysis.

30. For a short review of the sex-segregated labor market and female educational opportunities, see Ostner (1984).

31. In this respect, Robinson and Garnier's (1985) critique of Bourdieu's empirical tests of the growing importance of educational credentials for the placement in the social hierarchy is correct. They maintain that, given that Bourdieu's tests are based solely on student samples, the positions students will occupy in their work lives are neglected.

32. I conduct this analysis only for men to ensure comparability. Using measures of the occupational status attainment from the eleven-year follow-up, I find less than 30.5 percent of women employed full time. These women represent a highly distorted group with regard to their educational status attainment.

33. Only the measures of association are displayed because I am interested mainly in changes in strength of relationship.

34. Studies of occupational career patterns (see Blossfeld, 1985) show, however, that the occupational entry point is decisive for the future work career. It greatly determines, for example, occupational mobility patterns.

35. Both elementary and secondary teaching have required a college degree since World War I (cf. Collins, 1979). Burris (1983, p. 458) draws the same conclusion that female college graduates "are more concentrated in fields like teaching, social work, and health professions where the standards of certification correspond more closely to the actual skill requirements of the occupation."

36. I include expectations of future occupational position (as reported in the fourth year after high school graduation) in the analysis for 1980 cohort respondents still in school (four-year college). For comparability, I also use the occupation that 1960 cohort respondents with a college degree expect to make their life work (as reported in the fifth year after high school graduation). I am aware that these data limitations lessen the validity of my analysis. Analysis of 1960 cohort respondents using the actual occupational position in the fifth year after high school graduation for all cases yielded results very similar to those reported in the text and tables, however. This indicates that occupational anticipation is a fairly good proxy of future position.

37. For a detailed discussion of this trend, see Chapter 6, "Access to Higher Education: Who Profits from the Educational Expansion?"

38. The relationship between the two indicators of family background was not conceived as causal, since family income could be composed of various sources of revenue (e.g., father's/mother's income, property).

39. For a detailed analysis of female labor-force participation, see the first section of this chapter.

40. The small number of selected cases for both men and women in the 1960 cohort results from the poor response rate to the 1965 survey (51.7 percent). As noted before, the 1971 follow-up does not provide information on continuous work histories that would allow me to reconstruct the occupational status for nonrespondents to the 1965 follow-up.

41. The higher proportion of explained variance (49 percent) compared to the other groups also supports this interpretation.

## Chapter 8

1. The few divorced or widowed respondents are included in the category "married" because I am interested in the timing of family formation.

2. In 1984, among twenty- to twenty-four-year-old persons of all races, 25.1 percent of the men and 43.1 percent of the women were or had been married (*Statistical Abstract of the United States* 1986, Table 45; percentage based on C.P.S.). Although 1980 senior cohort respondents are only approximately twenty-

two years old, the lower marriage rates indicate the greater likelihood of white men and women with at least a high school diploma to postpone marriage.

3. For a similar conclusion based on British data for the same time period, see Kiernan and Eldrige (1986).

4. I base this interpretation on the very low rate of marriage among male four-year college students in the 1980s and also infer it from the smaller proportion of married 1980 cohort respondents, using school attendance in the fourth year after high school graduation as the measure: 10.7 percent versus 18.6 percent.

5. It is possible that, if the 1980 cohort men were surveyed at a later point in time, the association between social standing and marital status would resume the same strength as among 1960 cohort men. This is a relatively minor objection, however, since my analysis compares two cohorts at a selected point in time, that is, four years after high school graduation. The question of interest is how social characteristics relate to the assumption of particular life course statuses at this point in time.

6. Hornstein (1985) also argues that the social organization of youth has lost its close connection to social standing and shows more finely graded (i.e., more individualized) patterns of inequality.

7. I base this interpretation also on the weak labor-force participation among married women in the 1960 cohort (see Chapter 7, "Male and Female Labor Force Participation Patterns").

8. This hypothesis is based on the characteristics of the modern life course outlined in Chapter 1.

9. This would be compatible with the interpretation that marriage in families of higher socioeconomic status is to a greater extent a selective process, since the reproduction of the (family) capital is more at stake than in families of modest socioeconomic background.

10. The objection that these findings are artifacts of different intervals between completion of school and the time at which parent status was surveyed is overcome by the downward trend of parenthood for respondents with no postsecondary education (42.6 percent versus 28.1 percent).

11. I am aware that the strength of this relationship might be overestimated in both cohorts, since early marriages are more closely linked to parent status than later ones. Assuming that the extent of overestimation has not changed between cohorts, this fact does not in itself affect the interpretation.

12. Recall that the "weaker" change in men's behavior is partly due to the fact that the proportion of men who are fathers in the fourth year after high school graduation is already quite small in 1960. The low starting level impedes further decrease.

13. This is best seen by comparing the ratio between 1960 and 1980 cohort women with a child in each SES quartile.

14. See the discussion of the characteristics of the modern life course presented in Chapter 1.

15. The variance explained by the model ($R^2$) is fairly good for women and

modest for men. I assume that the poor result for 1980 cohort men is due partly to the small proportion of respondents with a child, which minimizes the variation in the dependent variable.

16. Compare the figures presented in Table 8.1.

17. Because the log-linear analysis conducted for 1960 and 1980 cohort men and 1980 cohort women revealed no interaction effects, these results are omitted.

18. The slightly higher proportion of married college-educated women of lower social origin (29.2 percent) compared with corresponding higher status women (24.0 percent) does not contradict this interpretation, as it is less marital status that precludes women from entering the labor force than the assumption of the role of mother.

19. See Chapter 9, "Outcomes of High School Educational Plans" for further support of this interpretation.

## Chapter 9

1. Separate analyses for men and women yielded similar results, so I present only the findings for entire cohorts.

2. I used the same method in Chapter 6, "Access to Higher Education: Who Profits from the Educatinal Expansion?"

3. See Chapter 6, "Access to Higher Education: Who Profits from the Educational Expansion?"

4. See also results on this topic presented in Chapter 8, "Timetables for Parenthood."

5. The same test applied to the 1980 cohort data by definition would exclude all respondents still in school in the fourth year after high school graduation. It would yield, therefore, an overestimated proportion of respondents who did not attain the expected occupational status due, for the most part, to college dropouts in the sample of selected respondents.

6. I use the scale developed by Flanagan et al. (1979) introduced in Chapter 5, "Continuity and Change in Status Expectations and Anticipated Timing of Life Events."

7. Respondents employed part-time and housewives are excluded. This deletes a large proportion of women, as approximately two-thirds were housewives eleven years after high school graduation (see Chapter 7, "Male and Female Labor-Force Participation Patterns").

8. Recall that type of occupational attainment is a relative indicator referring to the way in which occupational positions are related to the status expectations independent of the level (i.e., the absolute value) in the occupational status hierarchy.

# References

Adatto, Kiku, and Stephen Cole. 1981. "The Functions of Classical Theory in Contemporary Sociological Research: The Case of Max Weber." In *Knowledge and Society: Studies in the Sociology of Culture. Past and Present*, 3:137–162. Greenwich, Conn.: JAI Press.

Affichard, Joëlle. 1981. "Quels emplois après l'école: La valeur des titres scolaires depuis 1973." *Economie et statistique* 134 (June): 7–26.

Affichard, Joëlle, and Françoise Amal. 1984. "L'entrée des jeunes dans la vie active." In INSEE, *Données sociales*, 69–80. Paris: INSEE.

*Les Ages de la vie.* 1982–1983. Actes du Colloque, VIIe Colloque national de démographie. Travaux et documents, Cahiers 96 et 102. Paris: INED.

Allerbeck, Klaus. 1985. "Arbeitswerte im Wandel." *Mitteilungen aus der Arbeitsmarkt- und Berufsforschung* 18 (no.2): 209–216.

Allerbeck, Klaus, and Wendy Hoag. 1985. *Jugend ohne Zukunft?* Munich: Piper.

Amos, Jacques. 1985. "Valeur scolaire et stratification socio-profesionelle." *Revue suisse de sociologie* 11 (no.2): 253–264.

Apel, Heinz, ed. 1984. *Keine Arbeit—keine Zukunft? Die Bildungs- und Beschäftigungsperspektive der geburtenstarken Jahrgänge.* Frankfurt: Diesterweg.

Ariès, Philippe. 1962. *Centuries of Childhood.* New York: Random House.

———. 1983. "Les Classes d'âge dans les sociétés modernes occidentales." In *Les Ages de la vie.* Actes du Colloque, VIIe Colloque national de démographie. Travaux et documents, cahier 102. Paris: INED.

Asher, Kenneth. 1984. "Deconstruction's Use and Abuse of Nietzsche." *New German Critique* 22:169–178.

Audirac, P. A. 1982. "Cohabitation et marriage: Qui vit avec qui?" *Economie et statistique* 145 (June): 41–59.

Baacke, Dieter. 1972. *Jugend und Subkultur.* Munich: Juventa.

Badura, Bernhard, and Christian von Ferber, eds. 1983. *Laienpotential, Patientenaktivierung und Gesundheitsselbsthilfe.* Munich: Oldenburg.

Baethge, Martin. 1985. "Individualisierung als Hoffnung und Verhängnis: Aporien und Paradoxien in spätbürgerlichen Gesellschaften oder: die Bedrohung von Subjektivität." *Soziale Welt* 36:299–312.

Baethge, Martin, Frank Gerlach, and Jürgen Müller. 1980. "Zu den Veränderungen des Ueberganges Jugendlicher aus der Schule in Arbeit und Beruf in den siebziger Jahren." *WSI Mitteilungen* 11:660–667.

Baethge, Martin, Harald Schomburg, and Ulrich Voskamp. 1983. *Jugend in der Krise: Krise der aktuellen Jugendforschung.* Frankfurt: Campus.

Baltes, Paul B., and Orville G. Brim, Jr., eds. 1980. *Life-Span Development and Behavior.* Vol. 3. New York: Academic Press.

Bahrdt, Hans P. 1975. "Erzählte Lebensgeschichte von Arbeitern." In Martin Osterland, ed., *Arbeitssituation, Lebenslage und Konfliktpotential,* 9–37. Frankfurt: Europäische Verlagsanstalt.

Barnhouse-Walters, Pamela. 1984. "Occupational and Labor Market Effects on Secondary and Postsecondary Educational Expansion in the United States: 1922 to 1979." *American Sociological Review* 49: 659–671.

Baron, James N., and William T. Bielby. 1985. "Organizational Barriers to Gender Equality: Sex Segregation of Jobs and Opportunities." In Alice S. Rossi, ed., *Gender and the Life Course,* 233–251. New York: Aldine.

Baudrillard, Jean. 1973. *Le Miroir de la production ou l'illusion critique du matérialisms historique.* Paris: Castermann–poche.

Beck, Ulrich. 1983. "Jenseits von Stand und Klasse? Gesellschaftliche Individualisierungsprozess und die Entstehung neuer sozialer Formationen und Identitäten." *Soziale Welt,* Sonderband 2: Reinhard Kreckel, ed., *Soziale Ungleichheiten,* 35–74.

———. 1985. "Von der Vergänglichkeit der Industriegesellschaft." In Thomas Schmid, ed., *Das pfeifende Schwein,* 85–114. Berlin: Wagenbach.

Beck, Ulrich, Michael Brater, and Hans-Jürgen Daheim. 1980. *Soziologie der Arbeit und der Berufe.* Reinbek, West Germany: Rowohlt.

Beckenbach, Niels. 1984. "Zukunft der Arbeit und Beschäftigungskrise: Zu den gesellschaftlichen Rahmenbedingungen der Neuen Techniken." *Prokla* 55: 22–40.

Beck-Gernsheim, Elisabeth. 1982. "Familie im Modernisierungsprozess: Zum historisch neuen Spannungsverhältnis zwischen Elternschaft und eigener Lebensgeschichte." In Karl Martin Bolte and Erhard Treutner, eds., *Subjektorientierte Arbeits– und Berufssoziologie,* 270–292. Frankfurt: Campus.

———. 1983. "Vom 'Dasein für andere' zum Anspruch auf ein 'eigenes Stück Leben': Individualisierungsprozesse im weiblichen Lebenszusammenhang." *Soziale Welt* 34: 307–340.

———. 1986. "Von der Liebe zur Beziehung? Veränderungen im Verhältnis von Mann und Frau in der individualisierten Gesellschaft." *Soziale Welt,* Sonderband 4: Johannes Berger, ed., *Die Moderne: Kontinuitäten und Zäsuren,* 209–234.

Bell, Daniel. 1973. *The Coming of Postindustrial Society.* New York: Basic Books.

————. 1976. *The Cultural Contradictions of Capitalism*. New York: Basic Books.

Bellah, Robert N., Richard Madsen, William M. Sullivan, Ann Swidler, and Stephen M. Tipton. 1985. *Habits of the Heart: Individualism and Commitment in American Life*. Berkeley: University of California Press.

Bendix, Reinhart. 1964. *Nation-Building and Citizenship*. New York: Wiley.

Berger, Johannes. 1984. "Alternativen zum Arbeitsmarkt." *Mitteilungen aus der Arbeitsmarkt- und Berufsforschung* 17 (no.1): 63–72.

————. 1985. "An den Grenzen der Lohnarbeit: Ist der gesellschaftliche Fortschritt an Beschäftigungsverhältnisse gebunden?" In Thomas Schmid, ed., *Das pfeifende Schwein*, 33–48. Berlin: Wagenbach.

Berger, Peter, Brigitte Berger, and Hansfried Kellner. 1973. *The Homeless Mind*. Harmondsworth, England: Penguin Books.

Berger, Peter, and Thomas Luckmann. 1979. "Social Mobility and Personal Identity." In H. Aschoff, M. von Cronach, and Wolf Lepenies, eds., *Human Ecology: Claims and Limits of a New Discipline*. Cambridge.

Bergmann, Barbara R. 1986. *The Economic Emergence of Women*. New York: Basic Books.

Bergmann, Werner. 1983. "Das Problem der Zeit in der Soziologie: Ein Literaturüberblick zum Stand der 'zeitsoziologischen' Theorie und Forschung." *Kölner Zeitschrift für Soziologie und Sozialpsychologie* 35:462–504.

Best, Fred. 1980. *Flexible Life Scheduling: Breaking the Education-Work-Retirement Lockstep*. New York: Praeger.

Bielby, William, T. 1981. "Models of Status Attainment." In Donald J. Treiman and Robert V. Robinson, eds., *Research in Social Stratification and Mobility*, 1: 3–26. Greenwich, Conn.: JAI.

Bilden, Helga, and Angelika Diezinger. 1984. "Individualisierte Jugendbiographie? Zur Diskrepanz von Anforderungen, Ansprüchen und Möglichkeiten. *Zeitschrift für Pädagogik* 30 (no.2): 191–207.

Bird, Caroline. 1979. *The Two-Paycheck Marriage*. New York: Wade Rawson Publications.

Blau, Peter M., and Otis D. Duncan. 1967. *The American Occupational Structure*. New York: Wiley.

Blossfeld, Peter. 1983. "Höherqualifizierung und Verdrängung: Konsequenzen der Bildungsexpansion in den siebziger Jahren." In Max Haller and Walter Müller, eds., *Beschäftigungssystem im gesellschaftlichen Wandel*, 184–240. Frankfurt: Campus.

————. 1985. "Berufseintritt und Berufsverlauf: Eine Kohortenanalyse über die Bedeutung des ersten Berufes in der Erwerbsbiographie." *Mitteilungen aus der Arbeitsmarkt- und Berufsforschung* 18 (no.2): 177–197.

Boigeol, Anne, Jacques Commaille, and Brigitte Muñoz-Perez. 1984. "Le divorce." In INSEE, *Données sociales*, 428–446. Paris: INSEE.

Boli-Bennett, John. 1981. "Human Rights or State Expansion?" In Ved P. Nanda,

James R. Scarritt, and George W. Shepherd, eds., *Global Human Rights: Public Policies, Comparative Measures, and NGO Strategies*, 173–193. Boulder, Colo.: Westview Press.

Boli-Bennett, John, and John W. Meyer. 1978. "The Ideology of Childhood and the State: Rules Distinguishing Children in National Constitutions, 1870–1970." *American Sociological Review* 43:797–812.

Boli-Bennett, John, Francisco O. Ramirez, and John W. Meyer. 1985. "Explaining the Origins and Expansion of Mass Education." *Comparative Educational Review* 29 (no.2): 145–170.

Bonss, Wolfgang, and Rolf G. Heinze. 1984. *Arbeitslosigkeit in der Arbeitsgesellschaft*. Frankfurt: Campus.

Bonss, Wolfgang, and Barbara Riedmüller. 1982. "Ausgrenzung von Arbeitskraft und Psychiatrisierung: Zum sozialpolitischen Funktionswandel der Psychiatriereform." In Joachim Matthes, ed., *Krise der Arbeitsgesellschaft?*, 622–640. Frankfurt: Campus.

Bornschier, Volker, and Peter Heintz. 1977. "Statusinkonsistenz und Schichtung: Eine Erweiterung der Statusinkonsistenztheorie." *Zeitschrift für Soziologie* 6:29–48.

Bourdieu, Pierre. 1975. "Avenir de classe et causalité du probable." *Revue française de sociologie* 15: 9–42.

———. 1977a. "Cultural Reproduction and Social Reproduction." In J. Karabel and A. H. Halsey eds., *Power and Ideology in Education*, 487–511. New York: Oxford University Press.

———. 1977b. *Outline of a Theory of Practice*. Cambridge: Cambridge University Press.

———. 1977c. "La production de la croyance: Contribution à une économie des biens symboliques." *Actes de la recherche en sciences sociales* 13:3–43.

———. 1978. "Classement, déclassement et reclassement." *Actes de la recherche en sciences sociales* 24:2–22.

———. 1980a. "Le mort saisit le vif: Les relations entre l'histoire réifiée et l'histoire incorporée." *Actes de la recherche en sciences sociales* 32/33:3–14.

———. 1980b. *Le sens pratique*. Paris: Editions de Minuit.

———. 1980c. "Les trois états du capital culturel." *Actes de la recherche en sciences sociales* 30:3–6.

———. 1982. "Les rites comme actes d'institution." *Actes de la recherche en sciences sociales* 43:58–63.

———. 1983. "Oekonomisches, kulturelles und soziales Kapital." *Soziale Welt*, Sonderband 2: Reinhard Kreckel, ed., *Soziale Ungleichheiten*, 183–198.

———. 1984a. *Distinction: A Social Critique of the Judgement of Taste*. Cambridge: Harvard University Press.

———. 1984b. "Espace social et genèse des classes." *Actes de la recherche en sciences sociales* 52/53:3–14.

———. 1984c. "La 'jeunesse' n'est qu'un mot." In *Questions de sociologie*, 143–154. Paris: Editions de Minuit.

————. 1984d. "Réponses aux économistes." *Economies et sociétés* 19 (no.10): 23–32. (Reprint in Pierre Bourdieu. 1987. *Choses dites*. 124–131. Paris: Editions de Minuit.)

————. 1985a. "De la règle aux stratégies." *Revue Terrain* 4:93–100. (Reprint in Pierre Bourdieu. 1987. *Choses dites*, 75–93. Paris: Les Editions de Minuit.)

————. 1985b. *Homo academicus*. Paris: Les Editions de Minuit.

————. 1986a. "Habitus, code et codification." *Actes de la recherche en sciences sociales*, 64 40–44. (Reprint in Pierre Bourdieu. 1987. *Choses dites*, 94–105. Paris: Les Editions de Minuit.)

————. 1986b. "L'illusion biographique." *Actes de la recherche en sciences sociales* 62/63:69–72.

Bourdieu, Pierre, and Luc Boltanski. 1975. "Le Titre et le poste: Rapport entre le système de production et le système de reproduction." *Actes de la recherche en sciences sociales* 2:95–108.

————. 1978. "Changes in Social Structure and Changes in the Demand for Education." In Salvador Giner and Margaret S. Archer, eds., *Contemporary Europe: Structural Change and Cultural Patterns*, 197–227. London: Routledge & Kegan Paul.

Bourdieu, Pierre, and Jean-Claude Passeron. 1977. *Reproduction in Education, Society, and Culture*. London: Sage.

Bowles, Samuel, and Herbert Gintis. 1977. *Schooling in Capitalist America*. New York: Basic.

Brater, Michael, and Ulrich Beck. 1982. "Berufe als Organisationsformen menschlichen Arbeitsvermögens." In Wolfgang Littek, Werner Rammert, and Günther Wachtler, eds., *Einführung in die Arbeits- und Industriesoziologie*, 60–84. Frankfurt: Campus.

Bremner, Robert H. 1970–1974. *Children and Youth in America: A Documentary History*. 5 vols. Vol. 1: *Part 1, 1600–1665*; vols. 2,3: *Part 2, 1866–1932*; vols. 4,5: *Part 3, 1933–1973*. Cambridge: Harvard University Press.

Brinkmann, Christian. 1982. "Arbeitslosigkeit und berufliche Ausgliederung älterer und leistungsgeminderter Arbeitnehmer." In Knuth Dose, Ulrich Jürgens, and Harald Russig, eds., *Aeltere Arbeitnehmer zwischen Unternehmensinteressen und Sozialpolitik*, 139–156. Frankfurt: Campus.

Brock, Ditmar, and Hans-Rolf Vetter. 1984. "Biographische Erosionsprozesse als Folge technologisch-sozialer Umbrüche: Das Beispiel der Einführung neuer Techniken in der Druckindustrie." In Ditmar Brock, Christine Preis, Claus J. Tully, and Hans-Rolf Vetter, eds., *Arbeit und Reproduktion*, 205–244. Munich: Deutsches Jugendinstitut.

Brose, Hanns-Georg. 1982. "Die Vermittlung von sozialen und biographischen Zeitstrukturen." *Kölner Zeitschrift für Soziologie und Sozialpsychologie*, Sonderheft 24: *Materialien zur Industriesoziologie*, 385–407.

————. 1984. "Arbeit auf Zeit: Biographie auf Zeit?" In Martin Kohli and Günther Robert, eds., *Biographie und soziale Wirklichkeit*, 192–216. Stuttgart: Metzler.

————. 1985a. "Die Bedeutung der Zeitdimension für die Analyse des Verhältnisses von Arbeit und Persönlichkeit." in Ernst-H. Hoff, Lothar Lappe, and Wolfgang Lempert, eds., *Arbeitsbiographie und Persönlichkeitsentwicklung*, 142–153. Bern: Huber.

————. 1985b. "Die Modernisierung der Zeit und die Zeit nach der Moderne." in Burkart Lutz, ed., *Soziologie und gesellschaftliche Entwicklung*, 537–542. Verhandlungen des 22. Soziologentages in Dortmund 1984. Frankfurt: Campus.

Buchmann, Marlis. 1983. *Koformität und Abweichung im Jugendalter*. Diessenhofen, Switzerland: Rüegger.

————. 1984. "Wandel des jugendlichen Vergesellschaftungsprozesses? Zum Stand der heutigen Jugendsoziologie?" *Schweizerische Zeitschrift für Soziologie* 10:267–285.

Buchmann, Marlis, and Ruth Gurny. 1984. "Wenn Subjektivität zu Subjektivismus wird . . . "*Kölner Zeitschrift für Soziologie und Sozialpsychologie* 36: 3773–782.

Buchmann, Marlis, and Michel Vuille. 1985. "La Jeunesse dans toutes ses marges." *Revue suisse de sociologie* 11 (no.2): 157–182.

Buck, Bernhard. 1985. "Berufe und neue Technologien: Ueber den Bedeutungsverlust berufsförmig organisierter Arbeit und Konsequenzen für die Berufsbildung." *Soziale Welt* 36: 83–105.

Burris, Val. 1983. "The Social and Political Consequences of Overeducation." *American Sociological Review* 48: 453–467.

Carroll, Peter N. 1982. *It Seemed Like Nothing Happened*. New York: Holt, Rinehart, & Winston.

Chamboredon, Jean-Claude. 1983. "Adolescence et post-adolescence: La 'juvénisation.' " In Anne-Marie Alleon, Odile Morvan, and Serge Lebovici, eds., *Adolescence terminée, adolescence interminable*, 13–28. Colloque nationale sur la post-adolescence. Paris.

Cherlin, Andrew. 1978. "Postponing Marriage: The Influence of Schooling, Working, and Work Plans for Young Women." Paper presented at the annual meeting of the American Sociological Association, San Francisco. (Cited in Tittle, 1981.)

————. 1983. "The Trends: Marriage, Divorce, Remarriage." In Arlene S. Skolnick and Jerome H. Skolnick, eds., *Family in Transition*, 4th edition, 128–137. Boston: Little, Brown & Company.

Clarke, John et al. 1979. *Jugendkultur als Widerstand: Milieus, Ritual, Provokationen*. Frankfurt: Syndikat.

Clausen, John A. 1972. "The Life Course of Individuals." In Mathilda W. Riley, Marilyn Johnson, and Anne Foner, eds., *Aging and Society*. Vol. 3. *A Sociology of Age Stratification*, 457–514. New York: Russell Sage.

————. 1981. "Men's Occupational Careers in the Middle Years." In Dorothy Eichhorn, Paul H. Mussen, John A. Clausen, Norma Haan, and Marjorie P. Honzik, eds., *Present and Past in Middle Life*, 321–351. New York: Academic Press.

————. 1986. *The Life Course: A Sociological Perspective*. Englewood Cliffs, N.J.: Prentice Hall.

Coleman, John. 1961. *The Adolescent Society*. New York: Free Press.

Collins, Randall. 1971. "Functional and Conflict Theories of Educational Stratification." *American Sociological Review* 36:1002–1019.

————. 1979. *The Credential Society*. New York: Academic Press.

————. 1985. *Sociology of Marriage and the Family: Gender, Love, and Property*. Chicago: Nelson-Hall.

————. 1986. *Weberian Sociological Theory*. Cambridge: Cambridge University Press.

Conrad, Christoph, and Hans-Joachim Kondratowitz, eds. 1983. *Gerontologie und Sozialgeschichte: Wege zu einer historischen Betrachtung des Alterns*. Berlin: Deutsches Zentrum für Altersfragen.

Deleuze, Gilles, and Félix Guattari. 1983. *Anti-Oedipus: Capitalism and Schizophrenia*. Minneapolis: University of Minnesota Press.

Demos, John, and Sarane Spence Boocock, eds. 1978. *Turning Points: Historical and Sociological Essays on the Family*. *American Journal of Sociology* 84, supplement.

Demos, John, and Virginia Demos. 1969. "Adolescence in Historical Perspective." *Journal of Marriage and the Family* 31 (no.4): 632–638.

Derrida, Jacques. 1982. "The Ends of Men." In *Margins of Philosophy*. Chicago: University of Chicago Press.

Döbert, Rainer. 1985. "Formale Rationalität als Kern der Weberschen Modernisierungstheorie." In Burkart Lutz, ed., *Soziologie und gesellschaftliche Entwicklung*, 523–529. Verhandlungen des 22. Soziologentages in Dortmund 1984. Frankfurt: Campus.

Durkheim, Emile. [1893] 1964. *De la division du travail social*. Reprint. Paris: Presse Universitaire de France.

Eagleton, Terry. 1985. "Capitalism, Modernism and Postmodernism." *New Left Review* 152:60–73.

Eco, Umberto. 1984. "Postmodernismus, Ironie und Vergnügen." In *Nachschrift zum "Namen der Rose"*, 76–82. Munich and Vienna: Hanser.

Eekelaar, John M., and Sanford N. Katz. 1980. *Marriage and Cohabitation in Contemporary Societies: Areas of Legal, Social, and Ethical Change*. Toronto: Bilterworths.

Ehrenreich, Barbara. 1983. *In the Heart of Men: American Dreams and the Flight from Commitment*. Garden City, N.Y.: Anchor.

Eichhorn, Dorothy H., Paul H. Mussen, John A. Clausen, Norma Haan, and Marjorie P. Honzik, eds. 1981. *Present and Past in Middle Life*. New York: Academic Press.

Eisenstadt, Shmuel N. 1956. *From Generation to Generation*. New York: Free Press.

Elder, Glen H., Jr. 1974. *Children of the Great Depression*. Chicago: University of Chicago Press.

———. 1975. "Age Differentiation and the Life Course." *Annual Review of Sociology* 1:165–190.

———. 1978. "Approaches to Social Change and the Family." *American Journal of Sociology* 84, supplement: John Demos and Sarane Spence Boocock, eds., *Turning Points: Historical and Sociological Essays on the Family*, 1–38.

———. ed. 1985. *Life Course Dynamics*. Ithaca: Cornell University Press.

Elias, Norbert. [1939] 1978. *The Civilizing Process: The Development of Manners*. Reprint. New York: Urizen Books.

———. 1985. "An Essay on Time." In Simonetta Taboni, ed., *Tempo e società*, 79–118. Milan: Angelli.

Elkind, David. 1979. *The Child and Society*. New York: Oxford University Press.

Engfer, Uwe. 1983. "Arbeitszeitflexibilisierung als Rationalisierungsstrategie im Dienstleistungssektor." In Claus Offe, Karl Hinrichs, and Helmut Wiesenthal, eds., *Arbeitszeitpolitik: Formen und Folgen einer Neuverteilung der Arbeitszeit*. 2d edition, 106–115. Frankfurt: Campus.

Enial, Michel. 1985. "Le début de la jeunesse comme catégorie sociale . . . marginale!" *Revue suisse de sociologie* 11 (no.2): 183–190.

Featherman, David L., and Annemette Sorensen. 1983. "Societal Transformation in Norway and Change in the Life Course Transition into Adulthood." *Acta Sociologica* 26 (no.2): 105–126.

von Ferber, Christian. 1985. "Mobilisierung der Laien: Deprofessionalisierung der Hilfen: Ein Verlust an gesellschaftlicher Rationalität? In Burkart Lutz, ed., *Soziologie und gesellschaftliche Entwicklung*, 497–508. Verhandlungen des 22. Soziologentages in Dortmund 1984. Frankfurt: Campus.

Flanagan, John C., M. F. Shaycoft, J. M. Richards, and J. G. Claudy. 1979. "Talent Career Codes." In Lauress L. Wise, Donald H. McLaughlin, and Lauri Steel, eds., *The Project TALENT Data Bank Handbook*, F2-F8. Palo Alto: American Institutes for Research.

Flora, Peter, and Arnold J. Heidenheimer, eds. 1981. *The Development of Welfare States in Europe and America*. New Brunswick: Transaction.

Folger, John K., and Charles B. Nam. 1964. "Trends in Education in Relation to the Occupational Structure." *Sociology of Education* 38:19–33.

Foucault, Michel. 1970. *The Order of Things: An Archeology of the Human Sciences*. New York: Random House.

Fouquet, Annie, and Anne-Catherine Morin. 1984. "Mariages, naissances, familles." In INSEE, *Données sociales*, 408–424. Paris: INSEE.

Friedman, Kathi V. 1981. *Legitimation of Social Rights and the Western Welfare State: A Weberian Perspective*. Chapel Hill: University of North Carolina Press.

Fuchs, Werner. 1983. "Jugendliche Statuspassage oder individualisierte Jugendbiographie." *Soziale Welt* 34:341–371.

Galland, Olivier. 1984a. "Précarité et entrée dans la vie." *Revue française de sociologie* 25:49–66.

———. 1984b. "La prolongation de la jeunesse: Vers un nouvel âge de la vie?"

*Contradictions* 40/41:7–16: *Jeunesse et société*. Actes de Colloque de Lille.

———. 1985a. "Formes et transformations de l'entrée dans la vie adulte." *Sociologie de travail* 37 (no.1): 32–52.

———. 1985b. *Les jeunes*. Paris: Edition la Découverte.

Garnham, Nicholas, and Raymond Williams. 1980. "Pierre Bourdieu and the Sociology of Culture: An Introduction." *Media, Culture, and Society* 2:209–223.

Gélis, Jacques. 1986. "L'Individualisation de l'enfant." In Philippe Ariès and Georges Duby, eds., *Histoire de la vie privée*. Vol. 3, *De la Renaissance aux lumières*, 311–330, edited by Roger Chartier. Paris: Seuil.

Gerson, Kathleen. 1985. *Hard Choices: How Women Decide about Work, Career, and Motherhood*. Berkeley: University of California Press.

Geser, Hans. 1981. "Eine funktional-morphologische Theorie der Berufsqualifikationen." *Schweizerische Zeitschrift für Soziologie* 7:399–434.

Gillis, John. 1974. *Youth and History: Tradition and Change in European Age Relations*. New York: Academic Press.

Gokalp, Catherine. 1981. *Quand vient l'âge des choix?* Cahier 95. Paris: INED.

Graebner, William. 1980. *A History of Retirement*. New Haven: Yale University Press.

Gross, Peter. 1982. "Der Wohlfahrtsstaat und die Bedeutung der Selbsthilfebewegung." *Soziale Welt* 33:26–47.

———. 1985. "Bastelmentalität: Ein 'postmoderner' Schwebezustand?" In Thomas Schmid, ed., *Das pfeifende Schwein*, 63–84. Berlin: Wagenbach.

Gurny, Ruth, Paul Cassée, Hans-Peter Hauser, and Andreas Meyer. 1984. *Karrieren und Sackgassen*. Diessenhofen, Switzerland: Rüegger.

Habermas, Jürgen. 1979. *Communication and the Evolution of Society*. Chapter 5, "Legitimation Problems in the Modern State." Boston: Beacon.

———. 1981. "Die Moderne: Ein unvollendetes Projekt. In *Kleine politische Schriften*, 444–464. Frankfurt: Suhrkamp.

———. 1983. *The Theory of Communicative Action*. 2 vols. Boston: Beacon.

———. 1984. "Modernity versus Postmodernity." *New German Critique* 22:3–14.

———. 1985. "Neoconservative Culture Criticism in the United States and West Germany: An Intellectual Movement in Two Political Cultures." In Richard Bernstein, ed., *Habermas and Modernity*, 78–94. Cambridge: Polity Press.

Hagestad, Gunhild O., and Bernice L. Neugarten. 1985. "Age and the Life Course." In Robert H. Binstock and Ethel Shanas, eds., *Handbook of Aging and the Social Sciences*, 2d edition, 35–61. New York: Van Nostrand Reinhold.

Hamilton, Richard, and James Wright. 1975. "Coming of Age: A Comparison of the United States and the Federal Republic of Germany. *Zeitschrift für Soziologie* 4:335–349.

Hareven, Tamara K. 1977. "Family Time and Historical Time." In Alice S. Rossi, Jerome Kegan, and Tamara K. Hareven, eds., *The Family*, 57–70. New York: Norton.

———— K. 1983. "American Families in Transition: Historical Perspective on Change." In Arlene S. Skolnick and Jerome H. Skolnick, eds., *Family in Transition*, 4th edition, 73–91. Boston: Little, Brown & Company.

———— K. 1986. "Historical Changes in the Social Construction of the Life Course." *Human Development* 29: Martin Kohli and John W. Meyer, eds., *Social Structure and Social Construction of Life Stages*, 171–177.

Heintz, Peter, ed. 1972. *A Macrosociological Theory of Societal Systems*. Vol. 1, *Theory of Societal Systems, and Structural and Anomic Tensions*. Bern: Huber.

Heintz, Peter, Thomas Held, Hans-Joachim Hoffmann-Nowotny, and René Levy. 1978. "Strukturelle Bedingungen von sozialen Vorurteilen." In Anitra Karsten, ed., *Vorurteil*, 321–350. Darmstadt: Wissenschaftliche Buchgesellschaft.

Heinze, Rolf G., Karl Hinrichs, H.-Willy Hohn, and Thomas Olk. 1981. "Armut und Arbeitsmarkt: Zum Zusammenhang von Klassenlagen und Verarmungsrisiko im Sozialstaat." *Zeitschrift für Soziologie* 10:219–243.

————. 1984. *Der Arbeitsschock: Die Erwerbsgesellschaft in der Krise*. Cologne: Diederichs.

Held, Thomas. 1986. "Institutionalization and De-Institutionalization of the Life Course." *Human Development* 29: Martin Kohli and John W. Meyer, eds., *Social Structure and Social Construction of Life Stages*, 157–162.

Hengst, Heinz. 1981. "Tendenzen der Liquidierung von Kindheit." In Heinz Hengst, Michael Köhler, Barbara Riedmüller, and Manfred Max Wambach, eds., *Kindheit als Fiktion*, 11–72. Frankfurt: Suhrkamp.

Hills, Stephen M., and Beatrice G. Reubens. 1983. "Youth Employment in the United States." In Beatrice G. Reubens, ed., *Youth at Work: An International Survey*, 269–318. Totowa, N.J.: Rowman & Allanheld.

Hirschman, Albert O. 1982. *Shifting Involvements: Private Interest and Public Action*. Oxford: Robertson.

————. 1986. *Vers une économie politique élargie*. Paris: Editions de Minuit.

Hobsbawm, Eric, and Terence Ranger, eds. 1985. *The Invention of Tradition*. Cambridge: Cambridge University Press.

Hochschild, Arlie. 1986. "The Totaled Woman?" *New York Times Book Review*, May 11, 17.

Hodgson, Godfrey. 1976. *In Our Time: America from World War II to Nixon*. London: Macmillan.

————. 1986. "How the Rebels Seized the Palace." *New York Times Book Review*, October 5, 7.

Hoffmann, Ute. 1982. "Informationstechniken und die neue Oekonomie der Lebenszeit." In Karl Martin Bolte and Erhard Treutner, eds., *Subjektorientierte Arbeits- und Berufssoziologie*, 141–168. Frankfurt: Campus.

Hoffmann-Nowotny, Hans-Joachim. 1980a. "Auf dem Weg zur autistischen Gesellschaft." In Sabine Rupp, Karl Schwarz, and Max Wingen, eds., *Eheschliessung und Familienbildung heute*, 161–180. Wiesbaden: Selbstverlag der Deutschen Gesellschaft für Bevölkerungswissenschaft.

————. 1980b. "Ein theoretisches Modell gesellschaftlichen und familialen Wandels." In Guido Hischier, René Levy, and Werner Obrecht, eds., *Weltgesellschaft und Sozialstruktur*, 483–502. Diessenhofen, Switzerland: Rüegger.

————. 1987. "The Future of the Family." Paper presented at the European Population Conference, Jyväskylä, Finland, June 11–16.

Hoffmann-Nowotny, Hans-Joachim, François Höpflinger, Franz Kühne, Christiane Ryffel, and Denise Erni. 1984. *Planspiel Familie*. Diessenhofen, Switzerland: Rüegger.

Hogan, Dennis P. 1978. "The Variable Order of Events in the Life Course." *American Sociological Review* 43: 573–586.

————. 1980. "The Transition to Adulthood as a Career Contingency." *American Sociological Review* 45:261–276.

————. 1981. *Transitions and Social Change: The Early Lives of American Men*. New York: Academic Press.

————. 1982. "Subgroup Variations in Early Life Transitions." In Mathilda W. Riley, Ronald P. Abeles, and Michael Teitelbaum, eds., *Aging from Birth to Death*. Vol. 2, *Sociotemporal Perspectives*, 87–103. AAAS Selected Symposium 79. Boulder, Colo.: Westview Press.

————. 1985. "The Demography of Life-Span Transitions: Temporal and Gender Comparisons." In Alice S. Rossi, ed., *Gender and the Life Course*, 65–78. New York: Aldine.

Hogan, Dennis P., and Nan Marie Astone. 1986. "The Transition to Adulthood." *Annual Review of Sociology* 12:109–130.

Honneth, Axel. 1984. "Die zerissene Welt der symbolischen Formen: Zum kultursoziologischen Werk Pierre Bourdieus." *Kölner Zeitschrift für Soziologie und Sozialpsychologie* 36:147–164.

Hornstein, Walter. 1985. "Jugend 1985: Strukturwandel, neues Selbstverständnis und neue Problemlagen." *Mitteilungen aus der Arbeitsmarkt- und Berufsforschung* 18 (no.2): 157–166.

Huet, Maryse, and Bernard Monnier. 1984. "Le Chômage." In INSEE, *Données sociales*, 56–68. Paris: INSEE.

von Imhof, Arthur E. 1981. *Die gewonnenen Jahre*. Munich: Beck.

————. 1985. "Die verlängerte Lebenszeit: Auswirkungen auf unser Zusammenleben." *Saeculum* 36 (no.1): 46–69.

Jameson, Frederic. 1984. "Postmodernism, or the Cultural Logic of Late Capitalism." *New Left Review* 146:53–92.

Janowitz, Morris. 1980. "Observations on the Sociology of Citizenship: Obligations and Rights." *Social Forces* 59:1–24.

Jugendwerk der Deutschen Shell, ed. 1982. *Lebensentwürfe, Alltagskulturen, Zukunftsbilder*. Opladen, West Germany: Leske & Budrich.

Keniston, Kenneth. 1968. *The Young Radicals: Notes on Committed Youth*. New York: Harcourt, Brace, & World.

————. 1971. "Prologue: Youth as a Stage of Life." In *Youth and Dissent: The*

*Rise of a New Opposition*, 3–21. New York: Harcourt, Brace, Jovanovich.

Kern, Horst, and Michael Schumann. 1982. "Arbeit und Sozialcharakter: Alte und neue Konturen." In Joachim Matthes, ed., *Krise der Arbeitsgesellschaft?* 353–365. Frankfurt: Campus.

——. 1984a. *Das Ende der Arbeitsteilung: Rationalisierung in der industriellen Produktion.* Munich: Beck.

——. 1984b. "Neue Produktionskonzepte haben Chancen: Erfahrungen und erste Befunde der Folgestudie zu 'Industriearbeit und Arbeiterbewusstsein.' " *Soziale Welt* 35:146–158.

Kett, Joseph F. 1971. "Adolescence and Youth in Nineteenth Century America." *Journal of Interdisciplinary History* 2 (no.2): 283–298.

Kiernan, Kathleen E., and Sandra M. Eldrige. 1986. "Age at Marriage: Inter and Intra Cohort Variation." *British Journal of Sociology* 38 (no.1): 44–65.

Kloas, Peter-Werner, Gertrud Kühnlein, and Angela Paul-Kohlhoff. 1985. "Auswirkungen der Verwertungskrise von Berufsausbildung auf die Zukunftsorientierung Jugendlicher." In Ernst-H. Hoff, Lothar Lappe, and Wolfgang Lempert, eds., *Arbeitsbiographie und Persönlichkeitsentwicklung*, 154–164. Bern: Huber.

Kohli, Martin, ed. 1978. *Soziologie des Lebenslaufs.* Darmstadt: Luchterhand.

——. 1981a. "Biographische Organisation als Handlungs- und Strukturproblem." In Joachim Matthes, ed., *Biographie in handlungswissenschaftlicher Perspektive*, 157–168. Nürnberg: Nürnberger Forschungsvereinigung.

——. 1981b. "Zur biographischen Selbst- und Fremdthematisierung." In Joachim Matthes, ed., *Lebenswelt und soziale Probleme*, 501–520. Frankfurt: Campus.

——. 1983. "Thesen zur Geschichte des Lebenslaufes als sozialer Institution." In Christoph Conrad and Hans-Joachim Kondratowitz, eds., *Gerontologie und Sozialgeschichte: Wege zu einer historischen Betrachtung des Alterns*, 133–147. Berlin: Deutsches Zentrum für Altersfragen.

——. 1985a. "Die Institutionalisierung des Lebenslaufes." *Kölner Zeitschrift für Soziologie und Sozialpsychologie* 37:1–29.

——. 1985b. "The World We Forgot: A Historical Review of the Life Course." In Victor W. Marshall, ed., *Later Life: The Social Psychology of Aging*, 271–303. Beverly Hills: Sage.

——. 1986. "Gesellschaftszeit und Lebenszeit: Der Lebenslauf im Strukturwandel der Moderne." *Soziale Welt*, Sonderband 4: Johannes Berger, ed., *Die Moderne: Kontinuitäten und Zäsuren*, 183–208.

Kohli, Martin, and Günther Robert, eds. 1984. *Biographie und soziale Wirklichkeit.* Stuttgart: Metzler.

Kohli, Martin, and John W. Meyer. 1986. "Social Structure and the Construction of Life Stages." *Human Development* 29: Kohli and Meyer, eds., *Social Structure and Social Construction of Life Stages*, 145–149.

König, Gerhard, and Wilhelm Schumm. 1985. "Interessenorientierung, Arbeitserfahrung und Berufsverlauf." In Ernst-H. Hoff, Lothar Lappe, and Wolfgang

Lempert, eds., *Arbeitsbiographie und Persönlichkeitsentwicklung*, 165–178. Bern: Huber.

Kreutz, Henrik, Gerhard Fröhlich, and Dieter Maly. 1985. *Eine Alternative zur Industriegesellschaft? Alternative Projekte in der Bewährungsprobe des Alltags.* Nürnberg: Institut der Arbeitsmarkt- und Berufsforschung der Bundesanstalt für Arbeit.

Lappe, Lothar. 1985. "Berufsverlaufsmuster und Reproduktionsinteressen junger Facharbeiter." In Ernst-H. Hoff, Lothar Lappe, and Wolfgang Lempert, eds., *Arbeitsbiographie und Persönlichkeitsentwicklung*, 179–199. Bern: Huber.

Lasch, Christopher. 1983. *The Culture of Narcissism.* New York: Warner Books.

Lefaucheur, Nadine. 1982. "De la diffusion (et) des (nouveaux) modèles familiaux et sexuels." *Recherches économiques et sociales*, n. s. 2: 1–60.

Lenhardt, Gero, ed. 1979. *Der hilflose Sozialstaat: Jugendarbeitslosigkeit und Sozialpolitik.* Frankfurt: Suhrkamp.

———. 1984. *Schule und bürokratische Rationalität.* Frankfurt: Suhrkamp.

———. 1985. "From Contract to Status: The Educational System in Weber's Theory of Bureaucratic Rationalization." Paper presented at the international conference on Max Weber and Problems of the Contemporary World, Jablona/ Warsaw.

Lenoir, Remi. 1979. "L'Invention du 'troisième âge' et la constitution du champ des agents de gestion de la vieillesse." *Actes de la recherche en sciences sociales* 26/27: 79–82.

———. 1985a. "L'Effondrement des bases sociales du familialisme." *Actes de la recherche en sciences sociales* 57/58: 69–88.

———. 1985b. "Transformations du familialisme et reconversions morales." *Actes de la recherche en sciences sociales* 59: 3–48.

Lenski, Gerhard E. 1954. "Status Crystallization: A Non-Vertical Dimension of Social Status." *American Sociological Review* 19: 405–413.

Lerner, Richard. 1984. *On the Nature of Human Plasticity.* Cambridge: Cambridge University Press.

Leupold, Andrea. 1983. "Liebe und Partnerschaft: Formen der Codierung von Ehen." *Zeitschrift für Soziologie* 4: 297–327.

Levy, René. 1977. *Der Lebenslauf als Statusbiographie.* Stuttgart: Enke.

Ley, Katharina. 1984. "Von der Normal- zur Wahlbiographie?" In Martin Kohli and Günther Robert, eds., *Biographie und soziale Wirklichkeit*, 239–260. Stuttgart: Metzler.

Luckmann, Thomas. 1975. "On the Rationality of Institutions in Modern Life." *European Journal of Sociology* 1: 3–15.

Lüscher, Kurt. 1985. "Moderne familiale Lebensformen als Herausforderung der Soziologie." In Burkart Lutz, ed., *Soziologie und gesellschaftliche Entwicklung*, 110–127. Verhandlungen des 22. Soziologentages in Dortmund 1984. Frankfurt: Campus.

Lutz, Burkart. 1983. "Bildungsexpansion und Tertiarisierungsprozess: Eine histoisch-soziologische Skizze." *Soziale Welt*, Sonderband 2: Reinhard Kreckel, ed., *Soziale Ungleichheiten*, 221–248.

Lyotard, Jean-François. 1984. *The Postmodern Condition: A Report on Knowledge*. Minneapolis: University of Minnesota Press.

Mannheim, Karl. [1928] 1978. "Das Problem der Generationen." Reprint. In Martin Kohli, ed., *Soziologie des Lebenslaufs*, 38–53. Darmstadt: Luchterhand.

Marini, Margaret. 1978. "The Transition to Adulthood: Sex Differences in Educational Attainment and Age at Marriage." *American Sociological Review* 43:483–507.

———. 1984a. "Age and Sequencing Norms in the Transition to Adulthood." *Social Forces* 63:229–244.

———. 1984b. "The Order of Events in the Transition to Adulthood." *Sociology of Education* 57:63–84.

———. 1984c. "Women's Educational Attainment and the Timing of Entry into Parenthood." *American Sociological Review* 49:491–511.

Marshall, Thomas H. 1964. *Class, Citizenship, and Social Development*. Chicago: University of Chicago Press.

Marx, Karl. [1867] 1972. *Das Kapital*. Vol. 1, *Kritik der politischen Oekonomie*. Reprint. *Marx-Engels Werke*, vol. 23. Berlin: Dietz.

Matthes, Joachim, ed. 1982. *Krise der Arbeitsgesellschaft?* Frankfurt: Campus.

de Mause, Lloyd, ed. 1974. *The History of Childhood*. New York: Psychohistory Press.

Mauss, Marcel. [1938] 1975. *Soziologie und Anthropologie II. Siebenter Teil: Eine Kategorie des menschlichen Geistes: Der Begriff der Person und des "Ich"*. Edited by Wolf Lepenies and Hans Henning Ritter. Munich and Vienna: Hanser.

Mayer, Karl-Ulrich. 1981. "Gesellschaftlicher Wandel und soziale Struktur des Lebenslaufes." In Joachim Matthes, ed., *Lebenswelt und soziale Probleme*, 492–501. Frankfurt: Campus.

———. 1986. "Structural Constraints on the Life Course." *Human Development* 29: Martin Kohli and John W. Meyer, eds., *Social Structure and Social Construction of Life Stages*, 163–170.

Mayer, Karl-Ulrich, and Walter Müller. 1986. "The State and the Structure of the Life Course." In Aage Sorensen, L. Sherrod, and F. Weinert, eds., *Human Development and the Life Course: Multidisciplinary Perspectives*, 217–245. Hillsdale, N.J.: Erlbaum.

Mertens, Dieter. 1984. "Das Qualifikationsparadox: Bildung und Beschäftigung bei kritischer Arbeitsmarktperspektive." *Zeitschrift für Pädagogik* 30 (no.4): 439–455.

Mertens, Dieter, and Manfred Kaiser, eds. 1978. *Berufliche Flexibilitätsforschung in der Diskussion*. 3 vols. Nürnberg: Institut der Arbeitsmarkt- und Berufsforschung der Bundesanstalt für Arbeit.

Meyer, John W. 1977. "The Effects of Education as an Institution." *American Journal of Sociology* 83 (no.1): 55–77.

————. 1986a. "Myths of Socialization and of Personality." In Thomas Heller, Morton Sosna, and David Wellberry, eds., *Reconstructing Individualism*, 212–225. Stanford: Stanford University Press.

————. 1986b. "Self and the Life Course: Institutionalization and Its Effects." In Aage Sorensen, L. Sherrod, and F. Weinert, eds., *Human Development and the Life Course: Multidisciplinary Perspectives*, 199–216. Hillsdale, N.J.: Erlbaum.

Meyer, John W., John Boli-Bennett, and George M. Thomas. 1981. "Rationalization and Ontology in the Evolving World System." Paper presented at the Pacific Sociological Association Meeting, Portland, Oregon.

Meyer, John W., and Richard Rubinson. 1975. "Education and Political Development." *Review of Research in Education* 3 (no.2): 134–162.

Meyer, Sibylle, and Eva Schulze. 1983. "Nichteheliche Lebensgemeinschafte: Alternativen zur Ehe? Eine internationale Datenübersicht." *Kölner Zeitschrift für Soziologie und Sozialpsychologie* 35:735–754.

Modell, John, Frank Furstenberg, Jr., and Theodor Hershberg. 1976. "Social Change and Transitions to Adulthood in Historical Perspective." *Journal of Family History* 1 (no.1): 7–32.

Modell, John, Frank Furstenberg, Jr., and Douglas Strong. 1978. "The Timing of Marriage in the Transition to Adulthood: Continuity and Change." *American Journal of Sociology* 84, supplement: John Demos and Sarane Spence Boocock, eds., *Turning Points: Historical and Sociological Essays on the Family*, 120–150.

Müller, Walter. 1978. "Der Lebenslauf von Geburtskohorten." In Martin Kohli, ed., *Soziologie des Lebenslaufs*, 54–77. Darmstadt: Luchterhand.

————. 1983. "Frauenerwerbstätigkeit im Lebenslauf." In Walter Müller, Angelika Wilms, and Johann Handl, eds., *Strukturwandel der Frauenarbeit 1880–1980*, 55–106. Frankfurt: Campus.

Murdock, G., and R. McCron. 1979. "Klassenbewusstsein und Generationsbewusstsein." In John Clarke, ed., *Jugendkultur als Widerstand: Milieus, Ritual, Provokationen*, 15–38. Frankfurt: Syndikat.

Negt, Oskar. 1984. *Lebendige Zeit, enteignete Zeit: Politische und kulturelle Dimensionen des Kampfes um die Arbeitszeit*. Frankfurt: Canmpus.

Neugarten, Bernice L. 1968. *Middle Age and Aging*. Chicago: University of Chicago Press.

Neugarten, Bernice L., and Gunhild O. Hagestad. 1976. "Aging and the Life Course." In Robert H. Binstock and Ethel Shanas, eds., *Handbook of Aging and the Social Sciences*, 35–55. New York: Van Nostrand Reinhold.

Neugarten, Bernice L., Joan W. Moore, and John C. Lowe. 1965. "Age Norms, Age Constraints, and Adult Socialization." *American Journal of Sociology* 70:710–717.

Norton, Arthur J. 1974. "The Family Cycle Updated: Components and Uses." In Robert F. Winch and Graham B. Spanier, eds., *Selected Studies in the Marriage and the Family*, 162–170. New York: Holt, Rinehart, & Winston.

Oeuvrard, Françoise. 1984. "Le système éducatif." In INSEE, *Données sociales*, 470–482. Paris: INSEE.

Offe, Claus. 1982. "Arbeit als Schlüsselkategorie?" In Joachim Matthes, ed., *Krise der Arbeitsgesellschaft?* 38–65. Frankfurt: Campus.

———. 1984. *Arbeitsgesellschaft: Strukturprobleme und Zukunftsperspektiven.* Frankfurt: Campus.

Offe, Claus, Karl Hinrichs, and Helmut Wiesenthal, eds. 1983. *Arbeitszeitpolitik: Formen und Folgen einer Neuverteilung der Arbeitszeit.* 2d edition. Frankfurt: Campus.

Oakley, A. 1974. *The Sociology of Housework.* London: Robertson.

von Onna, Ben. 1976. *Jugend und Vergesellschaftung: Eine Auseinandersetzung mit der Jugendsoziologie.* Frankfurt: Aspekte.

Ostner, Ilona. 1984. "Arbeitsmarktsegmentation und Bildungsschancen von Frauen." *Zeitschrift für Pädagogik* 30 (no.4): 471–486.

———. 1986. "Die Entdeckung der Mädchen: Neue Perspektiven für die Jugendsoziologie." *Kölner Zeitschrift für Soziologie und Sozialpsychologie* 38: 352–371.

Ostner, Ilona, and Angelika Wilms. 1982. "Strukturelle Veränderungen der Frauenarbeit in Beruf und Familie." In Joachim Matthes, ed., *Krise der Arbeitsgesellschaft?* Frankfurt: Campus.

Parsons, Talcott. 1951. *The Social System.* New York: Free Press.

Pearce, Diana. 1978. "The Feminization of Poverty: Women, Work, and Welfare." *Urban and Social Change Review*, (February). (Cited in Ehrenreich, 1983)

Perrenoud, Philippe. 1985. "Scolarisation et sens des savoirs: De l'obsession d'instruire la jeunesse pour son bien." *Revue suisse de sociologie* 11 (no.2): 213–226.

Pialoux, Michel. 1979. "Jeunes sans avénir et travail intérimaire." *Actes de la recherche en sciences sociales* 26/27: 19–47.

Pincus, Fred L. 1980. "The False Promises of Community Colleges: Class Conflict and Vocational Education." *Harvard Educational Review* 50 (no.3): 332–361.

Platt, Anthony M. 1969. *The Child Savers: The Invention of Delinquency.* Chicago: University of Chicago Press.

Postman, Neil. 1982. *The Disappearance of Childhood.* London: Allen.

Power, Colin. 1983. "Research Approaches and Methods." In Don Anderson and Cath Blakers, eds., *Youth, Transition, & Social Research*, 115–129. Canberra: Australian National University Press.

Projektgruppe Automation und Qualifikation. 1983. *Zerreissproben: Automation im Arbeiterleben.* Empirische Untersuchungen, Teil 4, Argument-Sonderband 79, Berlin.

Ramirez, Francisco O., and John Boli-Bennett. 1981. "Global Patterns of Educational Institutionalization." In Philip Altbach, Robert Arnove, and Gail Kelly, eds., *Comparative Education*, 15–38. New York: Macmillan.

Rammstedt, Ottheim. 1975. "Alltagsbewusstsein von Zeit." *Kölner Zeitschrift für Soziologie und Sozialpsychologie* 27: 47–63.

Riedmüller, Barbara. 1981. "Hilfe, Schutz und Kontrolle: Zur Verrechtlichung der Kindheit." In Heinz Hengst, Michael Köhler, Barbara Riedmüller, and Manfred Max Wambach, eds., *Kindheit als Fiktion*, 131–190. Frankfurt: Suhrkamp.

Riley, Mathilda W. 1976. "Age Strata in Social Systems." In Robert H. Binstock and Ethel Shanas, eds., *Handbook of Aging and the Social Sciences*, 189–217. New York: Van Nostrand Reinhold.

———. 1982. "Aging and Social Change." In Mathilda W. Riley, Ronald P. Abeles, and Michael Teitelbaum, eds., *Aging from Birth to Death*. Vol. 2, *Sociotemporal Perspectives*, 11–26. AAAS Selected Symposium 79. Boulder, Colo.: Westview Press.

———. 1986. "The Dynamics of Life Stages: Roles, People, and Age." *Human Development* 29: Martin Kohli and John W. Meyer, eds., *Social Structure and Social Construction of Life Stages*, 150–156.

———. 1987. "On the Significance of Age in Sociology." *American Sociological Review* 52:1–14.

Riley, Mathilda W., Marilyn Johnson, and Anne Foner. 1972. *Aging and Society*. Vol. 3, *A Sociology of Age Stratification*. New York: Russell Sage.

Robinson, Robert V., and Maurice A. Garnier. 1985. "Class Reproduction among Men and Women in France: Reproduction Theory on Its Home Ground." *American Journal of Sociology* 91 (no.2): 250–280.

Rodgers, W. L., and A. Thornton. 1985. "Changing Patterns of First Marriage in the United States." *Demography* 22 (no.2): 265–279.

Rodriguez, Orlando. 1978. "Occupational Shifts and Educational Upgrading in the American Labor Force between 1950 and 1970." *Sociology of Education* 51:55–67.

Rosenmayr, Leopold, ed. 1978. *Die menschlichen Lebensalter: Kontinuität und Krisen*. Munich: Piper.

———. 1985. "Wege zum Ich vor bedrohter Zukunft: Jugend im Spiegel multidisziplinärer Forschung und Theorie." *Soziale Welt* 36:274–298.

Roussel, Louis. 1978. "La Cohabitation juvénile en France." *Population* 1:21–39.

———. 1980a. "Changements démographiques et nouveaux modèles familiaux." *Colloque nationale sur la démographie française*. Paris: INED.

———. 1980b. "Mariages et divorces: Contribution à une analyse systématique des modèles matrimoniaux." *Population* 6:1025–1040.

Ryder, Norman B. 1965. "The Cohort as a Concept in the Study of Social Change." *American Sociological Review* 30:843–861.

Sachse, Christoph. 1986. "Verrechtlichung und Sozialisation: Ueber Grenzen des Wohlfahrtsstaates." *Leviathan* 14:528–545.

Sarfatti-Larson, M. 1977. *The Rise of Professionalism*. Berkeley: University of California Press.

Scanagatta, Silvio. 1985. "Jeunes Italiens dans les grandes villes du Nord: Transformations culturelles dans les années 80." *Revue suisse de sociologie* 11 (no.2): 359–372.

Schluchter, Wolfgang. 1981. *The Rise of Western Rationalism*. Berkeley: University of California Press.

Schmid, Thomas, ed. 1985. *Das Ende der starren Zeit: Vorschläge zur flexiblen Arbeitszeit*. Berlin: Wagenbach.

Sennett, Richard. 1977. *The Fall of Public Man*. Cambridge: Cambridge University Press.

Sewell, William H., Robert M. Hauser, and Wendy C. Wolf. 1980. "Sex, Schooling and Occupational Success." *American Journal of Sociology* 86 (no.3): 551–583.

Skolnick, Arlene S., and Jerome H. Skolnick, eds. 1983. *Family in Transition*, 4th edition. Boston: Little, Brown & Company.

Smelser, Neil J. 1980a. "Issues in the Study of Work and Love in Adulthood." In Neil J. Smelser and Erik H. Erikson, eds., *Themes of Work and Love in Adulthood*, 1–26. London: Grant McIntyre.

————. 1980b. "Vicissitudes of Work and Love in Anglo-American Society." In Neil J. Smelser and Erik H. Erikson, eds., *Themes of Work and Love in Adulthood*, 105–119. London: Grant McIntyre.

Smelser, Neil J., and Erik H. Erikson, eds. 1980. *Themes of Work and Love in Adulthood*. London: Grant McIntyre.

Smelser, Neil J., and Sydney Halpern. 1978. "The Historical Triangulation of Family, Economy, and Education." *American Journal of Sociology* 84, supplement: John Demos and Sarane Spence Boocock, eds., *Turning Points: Historical and Sociological Essays on the Family*, 288–315.

Sokoloff, Natalie J. 1986. "A Review of the Aggregate Sex and Race Segregation Literature: A Profile of the General Labor Force and the Professions." Unpublished manuscript.

Somerville, John C. 1982. *The Rise and Fall of Childhood*. London: Sage.

*Statistical Abstract of the United States*. 1978 (99th edition); 1982/1983 (103th edition); 1986 (106th edition). Washington, D.C.: U.S. Bureau of the Census.

Staudt, Erich. 1984. "Wachsende Freiräume in der Gestaltung von Arbeitsorganisationen." *Mitteilungen aus der Arbeitsmarkt- und Berufsforschung* 17 (no 1): 94–104.

Sweet, Richard. 1983. "Changing Patterns of Work and Education." In Don Anderson and Cath Blakers, eds., *Youth, Transition, & Social Research*, 18–38. Canberra: Australian National University Press.

Swidler, Ann. 1980. "Love and Adulthood in American Culture." In Neil J. Smelser and Erik H. Erikson, eds., *Themes of Work and Love in Adulthood*, 120–147. London: Grant McIntyre.

————. 1986. "Culture in Action: Symbols and Strategies." *American Sociological Review* 51:273–286.

Templeton, K., Jr., ed. 1979. *The Politization of Society*. Indianapolis: Liberty.

Thomas, George M., and John W. Meyer. 1984. "The Expansion of the State." *Annual Review of Sociology* 10:461–482.

Tittle, Carol K. 1981. *Careers and Family: Sex Roles and Adolescent Life Plans.* Beverly Hills: Sage.

Tönnies, Ferdinand. [1887] 1979. *Gemeinschaft und Gesellschaft: Grundbegriffe der reinen Soziologie.* Reprint. Darmstadt: Wissenschaftliche Buchgesellschaft.

Touraine, Alain. 1978. *La Voix et le regard.* Paris: Seuil.

Treiman, Donald J. 1977. *Occupational Prestige in Comparative Perspective.* New York: Academic Press.

————. 1984. "The Work Histories of Women and Men: What We Know and What We Need to Find Out." In Alice S. Rossi, ed., *Gender and the Life Course*, 213–231. New York: Aldine.

Treiman, Donald J., and Heidi I. Hartman, eds. 1981. *Women, Work, and Wages: Equal Pay for Jobs of Equal Value.* Washington, D.C.: National Academy Press.

von Trotha, Trutz. 1982. "Zur Entstehung von Jugend." *Kölner Zeitschrift für Soziologie und Sozialpsychologie* 34:254–277.

Tully, Claus J., and Peter Wahler. 1983. "Ausbildung als Lebenslage: Das Ausbildungsverhältnis als Fokus jugendspezifischer Problemlagen." *Soziale Welt* 34:372–397.

————. 1985. "Jugend und Ausbildung: Von der Statuspassage zur Uebergangsbiographie mit 'open end.'" *Schweizerische Zeitschrift für Soziologie* 11:191–212.

Uhlenberg, Peter. 1974. "Cohort Variations in Family Life Cycle Experiences of U.S. Females." *Journal of Marriage and the Family* 36 (no.2): 284–292.

Ullrich, Otto. 1981. "Industrialisierung der Zeit und soziale Kontrolle." In Bodo von Greiff, ed. *Das Orwellsche Jahrzehnt und die Zukunft der Wissenschaft: Hochschultage der Freien Universität Berlin*, 110–116. Wiesbaden: Westdeutscher Verlag.

Vester, Heinz-Günther. 1985. "Modernismus und Postmodernismus: Intellektuelle Spielereien?" *Soziale Welt* 36:3–27.

Wacker, Ali. 1982. "Psychologische Aspekte der Arbeitslosigkeit älterer Arbeitnehmer und ihre Ausgliederung aus dem Arbeitsprozess." In Knuth Dose, Ulrich Jürgens, and Harald Russig, eds., *Aeltere Arbeitnehmer zwischen Unternehmensinteressen und Sozialpolitik*, 157–183. Frankfurt: Campus.

Weber, Max. [1922] 1968. *Economy and Society.* Edited by Günther Roth and Klaus Wittich. New York: Bedminster Press.

Widmer, Jean. 1983. "Remarques sur les classements d'âge." *Revue suisse de sociologie* 9:337–363.

Winsborough, Halliman. 1979. "Changes in the Transition to Adulthood." In Mathilda W. Riley, ed., *Aging from Birth to Death: Interdisciplinary Perspective*, 137–152. Boulder, Colo.: Westview Press.

Wise, Lauress L., Donald H. McLaughlin, and Lauri Steel, eds. 1979. *The Project TALENT Data Bank Handbook.* Palo Alto: American Institutes for Research.

Wolf, Hartmut, Klaus Hurrelmann, and Bernd Rosewitz. 1985. "Biographische

Konsequenzen von Schulerfolg und Schulversagen." *Schweizerische Zeitschrift für Soziologie* 11:241–252.

Wolf, Jürgen, Martin Kohli, and Joachim Rosenow. 1985. "Die Veränderung beruflicher Erwartungen: Biographische Analysen." in Ernst-H. Hoff, Lothar Lappe, and Wolfgang Lempert, eds., *Arbeitsbiographie und Persönlichkeitsentwicklung*, 128–141. Bern: Huber.

Wolfe, Alain. 1981. *America's Impasse*. New York: Pantheon Books.

Wolin, Richard. 1984. "Modernism versus Postmodernism." *Telos* 62:9–29.

Wuthnow, Robert, James D. Hunter, Albert Bergesen, and Edith Kurzweil. 1985. *Cultural Analysis: The Work of Peter L. Berger, Mary Douglas, Michel Foucault, and Jürgen Habermas*. London: Routledge & Kegan Paul.

# Name Index

Adatto, Kiku, 19
Affichard, Joëlle, 46, 49
Allerbeck, Klaus, 102
Amal, Françoise, 49
Amos, Jacques, 46
Apel, Heinz, 49
Ariès, Phillipe, 25, 80, 81, 83
Astone, Nan Marie, 82

Baacke, Dieter, 83
Baethge, Martin, 48, 49, 85, 86, 111
Bahrdt, Hans P., 41
Baltes, Paul B., 67
Barnhouse-Walters, Pamela, 46, 47, 101, 111, 117, 119
Beck, Ulrich, 18, 48, 52, 56, 63, 69, 70
Beckenbach, Niels, 49
Beck-Gernsheim, Elisabeth, 18, 53, 68
Bell, Daniel, 22, 73, 74
Bellah, Robert N., 71
Bendix, Reinhart, 20
Berger, Johannes, 57
Best, Fred, 68
Bielby, William T., 122
Bilden, Helga, 111
Bird, Caroline, 141
Blau, Peter M., 122
Blossfeld, Peter, 46
Boigeol, Anne, 53
Boli-Bennett, John, 21, 30, 46, 117
Boltanski, Luc, 28, 123
Bonss, Wolfgang, 48, 49

Boocock, Sarane Spence, 27
Bourdieu, Pierre, 28, 30, 32, 33, 34, 35, 36, 39, 40, 46, 62, 110, 123, 156, 170
Brater, Michael, 62
Brim, Orville G., 67
Brinkmann, Christian, 49
Brock, Dimar, 49, 50, 64–66
Brose, Hanns-Georg, 41, 49, 57, 77
Buchmann, Marlis, 24, 83, 84, 111
Buck, Bernhard, 49
Burris, Val, 46, 136, 137

Carroll, Peter N., 94
Chamboredon, Jean-Claude, 84
Clarke, John, 83
Clausen, John A., 26
Cole, Stephen, 19
Collins, Randall, 19, 28, 46, 47, 81, 117, 135, 137
Conrad, Christoph, 25

Deleuze, Gilles, 74
Demos, John, 25, 27
Demos, Virginia, 25
Derrida, Jacques, 74
Diezinger, Angelika, 111
Döbert, Rainer, 19
Duncan, Otis D., 122

Eagleton, Terry, 75
Ehrenreich, Barbara, 54
Eichhorn, Dorothy H., 49

Eisenstadt, Shmuel N., 83
Elder, Glen H., Jr., 24, 26, 95
Elkind, David, 85
Erikson, Erik H., 59

Featherman, David L., 81, 82, 111
Flanagan, John C., 101, 145
Flora, Peter, 21
Folger, John K., 136
Foucault, Michel, 74
Fuchs, Werner, 86, 111

Galland, Olivier, 85, 131
Garnham, Nicholas, 33, 36
Garnier, Maurice A., 123, 152
Gélis, Jacques, 79
Gerson, Kathleen, 55
Gillis, John, 25, 81, 84
Graebner, William, 25
Guattari, Félix, 74
Gurny, Ruth, 85

Habermas, Jürgen, 19, 22, 72, 73, 75
Hagestad, Gunhild, 24, 25, 26, 27, 189
Halpern, Sydney, 24
Hamilton, Richard, 104, 131
Hareven, Tamara K., 26, 27, 52
Heidenheimer, Arnold J., 21
Heintz, Peter, 38
Heinze, Rolf G., 48, 49, 56
Held, Thomas, 52, 53, 55, 62, 69, 85
Hengst, Heinz, 80, 85, 86
Hills, Stephen M., 49, 81, 131
Hobsbawm, Eric, 21
Hodgson, Godfrey, 93, 95, 97
Hoffmann, Ute, 56, 58
Hoffmann-Nowotny, Hans-Joachim, 52, 53,
    55, 69, 106
Hogan, Dennis P., 81, 82, 111, 131
Hornstein, Walter, 84
Huet, Maryse, 49

Imhof, Arthur E. von, 27

Jameson, Frederic, 74
Jugendwerk der Deutschen Shell, 84

Kaiser, Manfred, 50, 56
Keniston, Kenneth, 25, 84
Kern, Horst, 63
Kett, Joseph F., 25
Kohli, Martin, 17, 23, 24, 27, 42, 52, 68, 69
Kondratowitz, Hans-Joachim, 25
König, Gerhard, 42

Lappe, Lothar, 31, 49
Lefaucheur, Nadine, 53, 55
Lenhardt, Gero, 19, 21, 22, 28, 30, 41, 46,
    49
Lenoir, Remi, 25
Lenski, Gerhard E., 25
Lerner, Richard, 67
Leupold, Andrea, 53, 61
Levy, René, 17
Ley, Katharina, 53
Locke, John, 79
Lüscher, Kurt, 52
Lutz, Burkart, 46
Lyotard, Jean-François, 74, 75

Marini, Margaret, 27, 82, 156, 164
Marshall, Thomas H., 20
Matthes, Joachim, 48
Mause, Lloyd de, 80
Mayer, Karl-Ulrich, 16, 17, 21, 24, 28, 39,
    41
Mertens, Dieter, 46, 50, 56, 63
Meyer, John W., 17, 19, 20, 21, 23, 24, 30,
    41, 67, 68, 70, 75
Meyer, Sibylle, 52
Modell, John, 27, 81, 111
Monnier, Bernard, 49
Müller, Walter, 16, 17, 21, 24, 28, 41, 48,
    49

Nam, Charles B., 136
Negt, Oskar, 50, 56
Neugarten, Bernice L., 24, 25, 26, 27, 189

Oeuvrard, Françoise, 46
Offe, Claus, 48
Onna, Ben von, 83, 84
Ostner, Ilona, 57, 59, 102, 104, 156

Passeron, Jean-Claude, 123
Pearce, Diana, 54
Perrenoud, Philippe, 46
Pialoux, Michel, 131
Pincus, Fred L., 104, 118, 121, 136, 137, 143
Platt, Anthony M., 25, 81
Postman, Neil, 85

Ranger, Terence, 21
Reubens, Beatrice G., 49, 81, 131
Riedmüller, Barbara, 49, 86
Riley, Mathilda, 24, 44
Robert, Günther, 42
Robinson, Robert V., 123, 152
Rodriguez, Orlando, 136
Rosenmayr, Leopold, 27, 86
Rousseau, Jean-Jacques, 79

Sachse, Christoph, 86
Schmid, Thomas, 56
Schulze, Eva, 52
Schumann, Michael, 63
Schumm, Wilhelm, 42
Sewell, William H., 141
Skolnick, Arlene S., 53
Skolnick, Jerome H., 53
Smelser, Neil J., 24, 25, 59

Somerville, John C., 21, 25
Sorensen, Annemette, 81, 82, 111
Staudt, Erich, 56
Sweet, Richard, 131
Swidler, Ann, 59, 60, 77, 78

Thomas, George M., 20, 21, 23
Touraine, Alain, 71
Treiman, Donald J., 105, 131, 143
Trotha, Trutz von, 85
Tully, Claus J., 46, 84

Uhlenberg, Peter, 27

Vetter, Hans-Rolf, 49, 50, 64–66
Vuille, Michel, 83

Wacker, Ali, 49
Wahler, Peter, 46, 84
Weber, Max, 18, 19, 22, 69, 71
Williams, Raymond, 33, 36
Wilms, Angelika, 57, 59
Winsborough, Halliman, 81, 111, 131
Wolf, Hartmut, 40, 48
Wolf, Jürgen, 42
Wolfe, Alain, 94
Wright, James, 104, 131

# Subject Index

Action
  scope of, 53, 70–71
  strategy of, 31, 35
Action orientation, typology of, 18
Action without actors, 31
Adulthood
  cultural imagery of, 59
  transition to
    diversification of, 111, 155–56, 161
    extension of, 110–11
    individualization of, 147
    partial destandardization of, 83
    standardization of, 82
    status passage, 83, 111
    time-use approach, 82
Affinity, structural, 18, 33
Age
  annalistic, 91
  chronological, 24–25, 91
  social, 25, 91
Age-grading, 24–27, 81
Age norm, 25, 26, 37
Age status, 29, 38–39
Age typification, 25
Alienation, 72
Anticommunism, 94
Automation, 49

Birthrate, 52
Breadwinner ethic, 54, 175

Capital
  convertibility of, 34
  cultural, 34, 123, 126, 148
    incorporated, 34
    objectified, 34
  economic, 34, 38, 148
  educational, 53, 55
  rate of conversion, 38, 40, 137, 139, 180
  structure of, 35
  volume of, 35
Career
  off-track, 38
  on-track, 38
Career, occupational
  calculability/predictability of, 48, 49, 50
  discontinuity of, 50, 68
  flexibility of, 50, 62, 68
Certification (title), professional, 24, 27,
    30, 39
Child, individualization of, 79
Child ghetto, 80
Childhood, 25
  disappearance of, 85
  institutionalization of, 80
  pedagogical, 80
  standardization of, 80
Child labor, regulation of, 80
Children, expected number of
  by cohort, 106–7
  by sex, 106
Citizenship, 19, 20
  civil rights, 20

245

Citizenship (*continued*)
  political rights, 20
  social rights, 20
Class barrier, 97, 108, 109
Classification, principles of
  explicit (law), 32
  implicit (habitus), 32
Class struggle, 34
Cohabitation, 55, 154
Cold War, 94
Collectivity, sociocultural, 69, 108
College dropout, 174–75
Community college
  liberal arts curriculum, 139
  terminal vocational program, 121, 139
Consciousness
  collective, 45
  political, 94
Contract
  annual work time, 56
  free, 28
Craft, 63
Credentials (certificate), educational, 24,
    27, 30, 39, 46
  ambivalent meaning of, 48
  devaluation of, 47, 126, 135–41
  inflation of, 47, 135
  investment in, 135
  objective relevance of, 172
  subjective relevance of, 172, 174
  symbolic significance of, 123
Culture
  layman's, 72
  professional, 72
    reappropriation of, 73

Destiny, collective, 36, 41, 76, 170
Divorce rate, 52

Ecology movement, 94
Education, formal
  compulsory, 79–80
  enrollment in
    primary, 117
    secondary, 117
    tertiary, 117, 118
  expansion of, 47, 101, 117–18, 174

and flexibility of tracking, 119
  ideological function of, 122–23
  individual investment in, 47
  mobility through, 122, 124, 156, 173
  reproductive function of, 122, 123, 124, 173
Education-work-retirement lockstep, 68
Employment, strategy of, 132, 138
Employment rate, 56
Employment status, 131
  full time, 131–32, 135
  part time, 131–32, 135
Ethnomethodology, 32
Ethos, professional, 63
Event history, 82
Experience, structural individualization of, 77

Family
  demographic change in, 52–53, 62
  female dependence on, 53, 62
  functional importance of, 53, 62
  new models of, 53, 55
  traditional (bourgeois) model of, 53, 69
Family cycle, standardization of, 27
Family dependency, new form of, 85
Family enterprise, 53
Family orientation, extent of, 163–66
Family wage system, principle of, 54
Flextime, 56
Floor and ceiling effects, 125, 174
Functionalism, 32
Future, disposition toward, 36

Gratification, deferred, 61
Great Depression, 95
Great Society, 94

Habitus, 32–33
  postmodern, 75
Hedonism, 74
History, end of, 74
Home economy, monetarization of, 68
Homework, new, 56, 57
Homology, 34

Identity
  collective, 41
  flexible, 61

multidimensional, 77
personal, 29
public, 29
self-centered, 77
social, 29–31, 39
stable, 60, 61
Immediacy, emphasis on, 78
Imposition, symbolic, 30
Individualism, ideology of, 23, 67–68
and equality of individuals, 23
reconstruction of, 73, 75
and socialization, 24
and theory of personality, 23
Innovation, cycle of technological, 49, 68
Integration, subcultural, 108
Investment, strategy of, 34–35

Job performance, 144, 145
Job sharing, 56
Job skill level, 137
Junior college, 120

Labor
marketability of, 50
social division of, gender-based, 163
Labor-force participation
"double-peak" pattern of, 131, 135
by educational and marital status, 132–35
by educational status, 131–32
by sex, 131–35
timing of, 131
Labor market, sex segregation in, 54,
179–80
Life course
chronology of, 24, 56
cultural representation of, 16, 29, 31,
44, 59
gender-based assimilation of, 150, 157,
166
individualization of female, 53, 68, 157,
160
institutionalization of, 15, 17–18
partial destandardization of, 68–69,
76–78
private, 17, 26, 29, 69, 105, 163, 166, 169
public, 26, 28, 39, 69, 105, 163, 166–67,
169

segmentation of, 28
standardization of, 18
status/role configuration, 17, 25
actual, 16, 37–39
institutionalized, 16, 37–39
Life expectancy, 27
Life stage status, 110
Lifestyle enclave, 71
Life world, 72–73
Living standard, 54
Love ideology
current shift in, 61–62
dominant, 59–60

Majority, age of, 84
Man, end of, 74
McCarthyism, 94
Marriage
expected timing of
by cohort, 105
by sex, 106
by social class, 108–9
market, 55, 169, 175
rate, 52
Miniature adult, 79
Mobility, social, 21
aspiration toward, 177
downward, 126, 172, 176
unachieved, 177
upward, 37, 169, 172, 176
Modernity, 72–73
Monetarization of, 19
Movement, new social, 71, 94

Narcissism, culture of, 72, 74
National state, 19
Nest, empty, 52
New Frontier, 94
Norm, subcultural
timing of marriage, 158
timing of parenthood, 164

Occupation, educational upgrading of,
137–38
On-the-job training, 143, 144
Opportunity, structural, 172
overestimation of, 77, 170, 176, 178

Opportunity (*continued*)
  underestimation of, 51, 77, 170, 176, 178
  visibility of, 172, 176
Orientation (perspective), biographical, 16,
      39–42, 76–78, 100–110
  flexibility of, 66
  long-term, 49
  short-term, 50, 51
  status-related, 100
  time-related, 100
Orphanage, 80

Parent, single, 52, 54, 55
Parenthood, expected timing of
  by cohort, 106
  by sex, 107
Parent status
  by cohort, 159
  by educational status, 160
  by sex, 159–61
  by social class, 161–62
Phenomenology, 32
Plasticity, human, 67
Postadolescence, 84
Postmodernity, 72, 74–75
Postponement
  of marriage, 54, 155
  of parenthood, 160, 161
Poverty, feminization of, 54
Poverty line, 54
Practice, 34
  age-appropriate, 29
  probabilistic logic of, 36, 109, 170
Pressure group, 46
Prestige, occupational, 105
Principle, meritocratic, 23, 27, 123–24
Printing industry, 64–66
Procreation, role of, 161
Prophecy, self-fulfilling, 172
Protest, antinuclear, 94
Pseudo-youth subculture, 85
Psychology, life-span, 67

Qualification, professional
  devaluation of, 49
  half-life, 49

temporal validity of, 49
  updating of, 50, 67, 68

Racial unrest, 94
Random subjectivity, 75
Rank tension, 37
Rationalization, 18–19, 67–68, 74
  of (entire) lifetime, 56, 57–58
  of the economy, 19, 68
  of the polity, 19–20
Remarriage, divorce rate of, 52
Reproduction, social, 32, 33, 34, 172, 178
  direct, 123, 147–51
  female strategy of, 55
  indirect, 123, 147–52
Retirement, 28, 30

School as warehouse, 47, 102, 119
Self, private, 29
Self-blame, 77
Sex ratio, 44
  feminization of, 55
Socialization, 53, 95–96, 100, 170
  lifelong, 45
  theory of, 67
Social Security, 21, 28
Society
  bureaucratization of, 22
  individualization of, 21, 68–69
  politization of, 21
  postindustrial, 72, 73–74, 84
Stand, 71
Standard work day, 57
State
  expansion of, 22
  labor-market regulation of, 28, 46
  welfare, 21, 53
Status, marital
  by cohort, 153
  by educational status, 155
  by sex, 154
  by social class, 156–59
Status attainment, educational
  by father's education, 126
    trend of, 127–28
  parental, 96

by sex, 121
by social class, 124–26
  trend of, 127–28
Status attainment, occupational, 145,
  147–52
  dependency on educational credential,
    145, 147
  parental, 97–98, 145
  by sex and educational status, 141
  types of
    overachiever, 176
    realizer, 176
    underachiever, 176
Status expectation, educational
  by cohort, 101
  cooling out of, 121, 173
  by sex, 101–2
  by social class, 108–10
Status expectation, occupational
  by cohort, 102
  by sex, 103–5
  by social class, 108–10
Status inconsistency, 25
Status/role configuration
  incomplete, 38
  nonequilibrated, 38
Structural blame, 77
Structuralism, 32
Structure, occupational
  entry point in, 31
  feminization of lower, 141
  polarization of, 51
  professionalization of, 27, 46–47, 62
  sex segregation in, 104
Student protest, 94
Suburban nouvelle pauvre, 54
Symbolic interactionism, 32

Technology, new
  of information and communication, 56
  of microelectronics, 49
Theorist, postmodern, 74–75
Third age, 25

Time
  economical utilization of, 56, 58
  social, 55
  sovereignty over, 58
  subjective, 55
  synchronization between work and non-
    work, 58, 66
Timetable, social, 26, 40, 44, 100
  family life, 27
Typesetting technology, computer-
    controlled, 64
  and downgrading of workplaces, 66
  and upgrading of workplaces, 66

Unemployment rate, 136
  by age, 49
  by occupational status, 49
  through recession, 48
  by sex, 49
  structural, 48

Vietnam War, 94
Virtue of necessity, 35

Women's liberation, 94
Work, temporary, 56
Work day, individualization of, 57
Work ideology
  current shift in, 65
  of professional attachment, 65
  of professional detachment, 66
  traditional (centered on skilled labor),
    63–64
World War II, 93

Years, formative, 95
Youth, 25
  end of, 85
  individualization of, 87
  long-term, 83
  short-term, 82
  standardization of, 81
Youthfulness, value of, 85